DEMOSTHENES
VII

LCL 374

DEMOSTHENES

FUNERAL SPEECH
EROTIC ESSAY
LX–LXI

EXORDIA AND LETTERS

WITH AN ENGLISH TRANSLATION BY

NORMAN W. DeWITT

AND

NORMAN J. DeWITT

HARVARD UNIVERSITY PRESS

CAMBRIDGE, MASSACHUSETTS

LONDON, ENGLAND

First published 1949
Reprinted 1962, 1986, 2000

LOEB CLASSICAL LIBRARY® is a registered trademark
of the President and Fellows of Harvard College

ISBN 0-674-99412-4

Printed in Great Britain by St Edmundsbury Press Ltd,
Bury St Edmunds, Suffolk, on acid-free paper.
Bound by Hunter & Foulis Ltd, Edinburgh, Scotland.

CONTENTS

PREFACE

THE Public and Private Orations of Demosthenes have appeared in the preceding six volumes. They represent the deliberative and forensic styles respectively. The third category recognized by the ancients, epideictic oratory, is represented in this volume by the *Funeral Speech* and the *Erotic Essay*. Such compositions were not designed to persuade the hearers but to delight them and confirm them in sentiments already endorsed by habit and tradition. The *Erotic Essay* is usually called a speech, but is supposed to have been read from a written copy to a small select group.

The *Prooemia* or *Exordia* are closely related to the Public Orations. They comprise fifty-six paragraphs intended for use as introductions to speeches before the Council or Assembly. Of the six *Letters* five are addressed to the Council and Assembly and contain matters of public interest ; they also belong, therefore, with the Public Orations. It must be added that the authenticity of all items contained in this volume has been suspected.

The late Professor A. T. Murray had made a first draft of his version of the *Funeral Speech* before relinquishing his work ; this has been used with profit. His practice has been followed in adopting the text of Blass with some reservations.

N. W. D.
N. J. D.

BIBLIOGRAPHY

The editions of *Demosthenes* in the Teubner and Oxford series.

Arnold Schaefer, *Demosthenes und seine Zeit*, Leipzig, 1858.

F. Blass, *Die attische Beredsamkeit*, ed. 2, Leipzig, 1893.

S. H. Butcher, *Demosthenes*, London, 1881.

A. W. Pickard-Cambridge, *Demosthenes*, New York and London, 1914.

C. R. Kennedy, *The Orations of Demosthenes*, translated with notes, etc., five vols. in Bohn's Classical Library.

S. Preuss, *Index Demosthenicus*, Leipzig, 1895.

———

A. Boeckh, *The Public Economy of Athens*, translated by Lewis, London, 1842 ; ed. 2, translated by Lamb, Boston, 1857.

K. F. Hermann, *Lehrbuch der griechischen Rechtsalterthümer*, ed. 3, revised by Thalheim, Freiburg, 1884.

G. F. Schömann, *Antiquities of Greece*, translated by Hardy and Mann, London, 1890.

Gardner and Jevons, *Manual of Greek Antiquities*, New York, 1895.

Gustav Gilbert, *The Constitutional Antiquities of Sparta and Athens*, translated by Brooks and Nicklin, London and New York, 1895.

H. Rackham, *Aristotle, The Athenian Constitution*, Loeb Classical Library, London, 1935.

L. Whibley, *Companion to Greek Studies*, Cambridge, 1931.

Meier und Schömann, *Der attische Process*, revised by Lipsius, Berlin, 1883–1887.

Lipsius, *Das attische Recht*, 1905–1912.

viii

THE ORATIONS OF DEMOSTHENES

The numbers of the Orations are those used in Blass's text and generally followed by editors.

THE ORATIONS OF DEMOSTHENES

THE ORATIONS OF DEMOSTHENES

THE FUNERAL SPEECH

INTRODUCTION

THE custom of bestowing in a public sepulchre the remains of those who had died in battle was sanctioned by law in Athens. The concluding part of the ceremonies, described by Thucydides ii. 34, was a funeral oration. For such occasions a lofty platform was erected near the tomb in the Cerameicus, most picturesque of Athenian suburbs. The populace approached in procession, citizen and alien, male and female. The speaker, chosen by the people for his distinction in public life, followed a conventional line of thought, suggested by circumstance and confirmed by custom. Among the topics that seem to have recurred more often were the birth of the Athenian race from the soil of Attica, the legendary and historical exploits of the ancestors, especially the victories of Marathon and Salamis, the superiority of Athenian education and training, and the advantages of the Athenian form of government. Lastly, the State declared its gratitude for the self-sacrifice of the fallen and offered its consolation and protection to the surviving children and parents. The speaker dismissed the assemblage.

In the esteem of modern readers the grandest of extant Athenian funeral speeches is that of Pericles as recorded by Thucydides ii. 35-46. In ancient times, however, the preference seems to have been

3

given to the specimen preserved in the *Menexenus* of
Plato, delivered by Socrates though ascribed to
Aspasia. From Cicero's *Orator* 151 we learn that
this speech was read in public annually in Athens.
It seems to have enjoyed a popularity comparable to
that of Lincoln's Gettysburg Speech in the United
States.

Dionysius of Halicarnassus, who lived under
Augustus Caesar, treats briefly of funeral speeches in
his *Art of Rhetoric* vi. 1-4. Besides that of Pericles he
knew specimens by Lysias, Hypereides, Demosthenes
and Naucrates respectively. The last is known only
by this reference. Under the name of Lysias there
is one still extant. Of the speech by Hypereides a
fortunate chance brought to light in an Egyptian
papyrus in 1856 sufficient to fill nine pages of a Teubner text. From Stobaeus a substantial paragraph
was already known. The last edition of these frag-
ments by Blass appeared in 1894 ; they were more
attractively edited by F. G. Kenyon in 1906.

As for the example ascribed by our manuscripts to
Demosthenes, both ancient and modern critics deny
its authenticity. Blass quotes Dionysius as judging
it " commonplace, thin and amateurish." He cites
similarities to the *Menexenus*, to the *Panegyricus* of
Isocrates and to the speech of Hypereides. Upon
close examination, however, these parallels are quite
unimpressive, even in the aggregate. All occasional
speeches develop numerous commonplaces.

From the oration *On the Crown* 285 (320) we learn
that Demosthenes was chosen to pronounce the
eulogy over those who fell at Chaeronea in 338 B.C.
The extant speech fits this occasion. It was not an
enviable task to be asked to praise the fallen after

THE FUNERAL SPEECH

such a disastrous defeat nor one to inspire a master-piece. Moreover, the epideictic style, which the ceremony required, was alien to the combative nature of Demosthenes. The modern reader, therefore, will do well to suspend judgement, at least until after a careful and sympathetic reading.

Short shrift is accorded the oration by Blass, iii. pp. 404-406. There is a commentary in Dindorf's *Demosthenes* vii. pp. 1393-1412. Mention is lacking in Jebb's *Attic Orators*.

ΔΗΜΟΣΘΕΝΟΥΣ

LX

ΕΠΙΤΑΦΙΟΣ

Ἐπειδὴ τοὺς ἐν τῷδε τῷ τάφῳ κειμένους, ἄνδρας ἀγαθοὺς ἐν τῷ πολέμῳ γεγονότας, ἔδοξε τῇ πόλει δημοσίᾳ θάπτειν καὶ προσέταξεν ἐμοὶ τὸν νομιζό-[1389] μενον λόγον εἰπεῖν ἐπ' αὐτοῖς, ἐσκόπουν μὲν εὐθὺς ὅπως τοῦ προσήκοντος ἐπαίνου τεύξονται, ἐξετάζων δὲ καὶ σκοπῶν ἀξίως εἰπεῖν τῶν τετελευτηκότων ἕν τι τῶν ἀδυνάτων εὕρισκον ὄν. οἳ γὰρ τὴν ὑπάρχουσαν πᾶσιν ἔμφυτον τοῦ ζῆν ὑπερεῖδον ἐπιθυμίαν, καὶ τελευτῆσαι καλῶς μᾶλλον ἠβουλήθησαν ἢ ζῶντες τὴν Ἑλλάδ' ἰδεῖν ἀτυχοῦσαν, πῶς οὐκ ἀνυπέρβλητον παντὶ λόγῳ τὴν αὑτῶν ἀρετὴν καταλελοίπασιν; ὁμοίως μέντοι διαλεχθῆναι τοῖς πρότερόν ποτ' εἰρηκόσιν ἐνθάδ' εἶναί μοι δοκεῖ.

2 Ὡς μὲν οὖν ἡ πόλις σπουδάζει περὶ τοὺς ἐν τῷ πολέμῳ τελευτῶντας ἔκ τε τῶν ἄλλων ἔστιν

---

[a] In this genre ὦ ἄνδρες Ἀθηναῖοι is unusable because aliens

6

DEMOSTHENES

LX

THE FUNERAL SPEECH [a]

AFTER the State decreed that those who repose in this
tomb, having acquitted themselves as brave men in
the war, should have a state-funeral, and appointed
me to the duty of delivering over them the customary
speech, I began straightway to study how they might
receive their due tribute of praise ; but as I studied
and searched my mind the conclusion forced itself
upon me that to speak as these dead deserve was one
of those things that cannot be done.   For, since they
scorned the love of life that is inborn in all men and
chose rather to die nobly than to live and look upon
Greece in misfortune, how can they have failed to
leave behind them a record of valour surpassing all
power of words to express ?   Nevertheless I propose
to treat the theme in the same vein as those who
have previously spoken in this place from time to
time.

That the State seriously concerns itself with those 2
who die in battle it is possible to infer both from these

and women were present ; there was no salutation for mixed
audiences.

ἰδεῖν καὶ μάλιστ' ἐκ τοῦδε τοῦ νόμου καθ' ὃν
αἱρεῖται τὸν ἐροῦντ' ἐπὶ ταῖς δημοσίαις ταφαῖς·
εἰδυῖα γὰρ παρὰ τοῖς ἀγαθοῖς ἀνδράσιν τὰς μὲν
τῶν χρημάτων κτήσεις καὶ τῶν κατὰ τὸν βίον
ἡδονῶν ἀπολαύσεις ὑπερεωραμένας, τῆς δ' ἀρετῆς
καὶ τῶν ἐπαίνων πᾶσαν τὴν ἐπιθυμίαν οὖσαν, ἐξ
ὧν ταῦτ' ἂν αὐτοῖς μάλιστα γένοιτο λόγων, τούτοις ᾠήθησαν δεῖν αὐτοὺς τιμᾶν, ἵν' ἣν ζῶντες
ἐκτήσαντ' εὐδοξίαν, αὕτη καὶ τετελευτηκόσιν αὐ-
3 τοῖς ἀποδοθείη. εἰ μὲν οὖν τὴν ἀνδρείαν μόνον
αὐτοῖς τῶν εἰς ἀρετὴν ἀνηκόντων ὑπάρχουσαν
ἑώρων, ταύτην ἂν ἐπαινέσας ἀπηλλαττόμην τῶν
λόγων· ἐπειδὴ δὲ καὶ γεγενῆσθαι καλῶς καὶ πε-
παιδεῦσθαι σωφρόνως καὶ βεβιωκέναι φιλοτίμως
συμβέβηκεν αὐτοῖς, ἐξ ὧν εἰκότως ἦσαν σπουδαῖοι,
αἰσχυνοίμην ἂν εἴ τι τούτων φανείην παραλιπών.
ἄρξομαι δ' ἀπὸ τῆς τοῦ γένους αὐτῶν ἀρχῆς.

4   Ἡ γὰρ εὐγένεια τῶνδε τῶν ἀνδρῶν ἐκ πλείστου
χρόνου παρὰ πᾶσιν ἀνθρώποις ἀνωμολόγηται. οὐ
[1390] γὰρ μόνον εἰς πατέρ' αὐτοῖς καὶ τῶν ἄνω προγόνων κατ' ἄνδρ' ἀνενεγκεῖν ἑκάστῳ τὴν φύσιν
ἔστιν, ἀλλ' εἰς ὅλην κοινῇ τὴν ὑπάρχουσαν πα-
τρίδα, ἧς αὐτόχθονες ὁμολογοῦνται εἶναι. μόνοι
γὰρ πάντων ἀνθρώπων, ἐξ ἧσπερ ἔφυσαν, ταύτην
ᾤκησαν καὶ τοῖς ἐξ αὐτῶν παρέδωκαν, ὥστε δικαίως ἄν τις ὑπολάβοι, τοὺς μὲν ἐπήλυδας ἐλθόντας
εἰς τὰς πόλεις καὶ τούτων πολίτας προσαγορευο-

ᵃ A commonplace of funeral speeches : Thucyd. ii. 42. 4.
ᵇ Blass censures the author for not following in the sequel
a threefold division of his theme, which is here implied and
may be found in Plato, *Menex.* 237 A–B : nobility of birth,
upbringing and education, and exploits. These topics are
8

rites in general and, in particular, from this law in accordance with which it chooses the speaker at our state-funerals. For knowing that among good men the acquisition of wealth and the enjoyment of the pleasures that go with living are scorned,[a] and that their whole desire is for virtue and words of praise, the citizens were of the opinion that we ought to honour them with such eulogies as would most certainly secure them in death the glory they had won while living. Now, if it were my view that, of those **3** qualities that constitute virtue, courage alone was their possession, I might praise this and be done with the speaking, but since it fell to their lot also to have been nobly born and strictly brought up and to have lived with lofty ideals, because of all which they had every reason to be good men, I should be ashamed if I were found to have passed over any of these topics.[b] I shall begin from the origin of their race.[c]

The nobility of birth of these men has been acknow- **4** ledged from time immemorial by all mankind. For it is possible for them and for each one of their remote ancestors man by man to trace back their being, not only to a physical father, but also to this land of theirs as a whole, a common possession, of which they are acknowledged to be the indigenous children.[d] For alone of all mankind they settled the very land from which they were born and handed it down to their descendants, so that justly one may assume that those who came as migrants into their cities and are denominated citizens of the same are comparable

treated, but not consecutively. Peculiar to this speech is the passage on the ten tribes, §§ 27-32.

  [c] Blass compares Isocrates, *Helen* 16 τὴν μὲν οὖν ἀρχὴν τοῦ λόγου ποιήσομαι τοιαύτην τοῦ γένους αὐτῆς.

  [d] This topic appears in the *Menex.* 237 B–C.

9

μένους ὁμοίους εἶναι τοῖς εἰσποιητοῖς τῶν παίδων,
τούτους δὲ γνησίους γόνῳ τῆς πατρίδος πολίτας
5 εἶναι. δοκεῖ δέ μοι καὶ τὸ τοὺς καρποὺς οἷς ζῶσιν
ἄνθρωποι παρ' ἡμῖν πρώτοις φανῆναι, χωρὶς τοῦ
μέγιστον εὐεργέτημ' εἰς πάντας γενέσθαι, ὁμολο-
γούμενον σημεῖον ὑπάρχειν τοῦ μητέρα τὴν χώραν
εἶναι τῶν ἡμετέρων προγόνων. πάντα γὰρ τὰ
τίκτονθ' ἅμα καὶ τροφὴν τοῖς γιγνομένοις ἀπ' αὐτῆς
τῆς φύσεως φέρει· ὅπερ ἥδ' ἡ χώρα πεποίηκε.
6 Τὰ μὲν οὖν εἰς γένος ἀνήκοντα τοιαῦτα δι' αἰῶνος
ὑπάρχει τοῖς τῶνδε τῶν ἀνδρῶν προγόνοις. τὰ δ'
εἰς ἀνδρείαν καὶ τὴν ἄλλην ἀρετὴν πάντα μὲν κατ-
οκνῶ λέγειν, φυλαττόμενος μὴ μῆκος ἄκαιρον ἐγ-
γένηται τῷ λόγῳ· ἃ δὲ καὶ τοῖς εἰδόσι χρήσιμ'
ἀναμνησθῆναι καὶ τοῖς ἀπείροις κάλλιστ' ἀκοῦσαι,
καὶ ζῆλον ἔχει πολὺν καὶ μῆκος λόγων ἄλυπον,
7 ταῦτ' ἐπὶ κεφαλαίων εἰπεῖν πειράσομαι. οἱ γὰρ
τῆς κατὰ τὸν παρόντα χρόνον γενεᾶς πρόγονοι καὶ
πατέρες καὶ τούτων ἐπάνω τὰς προσηγορίας ἔχοντες αἷς ὑπὸ τῶν ἐν γένει γνωρίζονται, ἠδίκησαν
μὲν οὐδένα πώποτ' οὔθ' Ἕλλην' οὔτε βάρβαρον,
ἀλλ' ὑπῆρχεν αὐτοῖς πρὸς ἅπασι τοῖς ἄλλοις καλοῖς
[1391] κἀγαθοῖς καὶ δικαιοτάτοις εἶναι, ἀμυνόμενοι δὲ
8 πολλὰ καὶ λαμπρὰ διεπράξαντο. καὶ γὰρ τὸν
Ἀμαζόνων στρατὸν ἐλθόντ' ἐκράτησαν οὕτως ὥστ'

---

[a] This topic appears in Hyper. *Epitaph.* 7.

[b] According to tradition the olive was created by the
goddess Athena, while the culture of grain, especially wheat
and barley, was established by Demeter, whose mysteries
were celebrated at Eleusis close to Athens.

[c] Or, " by a law of nature herself."

to adopted children; but these men are citizens of their native land by right of legitimate birth.[a] In 5 my view also the fact that the fruits of the earth by which men live were first manifest among us,[b] even apart from their being a superlative boon to all men, constitutes an acknowledged proof that this land is the mother of our ancestors. For all things that bring forth young produce at the same time nutriment out of the organism itself[c] for those that are born. This very thing has been done by this land.[d]

Such is the pride of birth that belongs to the 6 ancestors of these men throughout the ages. As for courage and the other elements of virtue, I shrink from rehearsing the whole story, being on my guard for fear an untimely length shall attach to my speech,[e] but such facts as it is worth while even for those who are familiar with them to recall to mind and most profitable for the inexperienced to hear,[f] events of great power to inspire and calling for no tedious length of speech, these I shall endeavour to rehearse in summary fashion.[g] For the ancestors of this 7 present generation, both their fathers and those who bore the names of these men in time past, by which they are recognized by those of our race, never at any time wronged any man, whether Greek or barbarian, but it was their pride, in addition to all their other good qualities, to be true gentlemen and supremely just, and in defending themselves they accomplished a long list of noble deeds. They so 8 prevailed over the invading host of the Amazons as to

[d] This topic is treated in more detail in *Menex.* 237 E— 238 B.

[e] Another commonplace: Hyper. 4 expresses a similar fear.   [f] Thucyd. ii. 36. 4 may be compared.

[g] Hyper. 5 ἐπὶ κεφαλαίου.

11

ἔξω Φάσιδος ἐκβαλεῖν, καὶ τὸν Εὐμόλπου καὶ[1]
πολλῶν ἄλλων στόλον οὐ μόνον ἐκ τῆς οἰκείας,
ἀλλὰ καὶ ἐκ τῆς τῶν ἄλλων Ἑλλήνων χώρας ἐξ-
ήλασαν, οὓς οἱ πρὸ ἡμῶν οἰκοῦντες πρὸς ἑσπέραν
πάντες οὔθ᾽ ὑπέμειναν οὔτ᾽ ἐδυνήθησαν κωλῦσαι.
καὶ μὴν καὶ τῶν Ἡρακλέους παίδων, ὃς τοὺς
ἄλλους ἔσῳζε, σωτῆρες ὠνομάσθησαν, ἡνίκ᾽ ἦλθον
εἰς τήνδε τὴν γῆν ἱκέται, φεύγοντες Εὐρυσθέα.
καὶ πρὸς πᾶσι τούτοις καὶ πολλοῖς ἄλλοις καὶ
καλοῖς ἔργοις, τὰ τῶν κατοιχομένων νόμιμ᾽ οὐ
περιεῖδον ὑβριζόμενα ὅτε τοὺς ἕπτ᾽ ἐπὶ Θήβας
θάπτειν ἐκώλυε Κρέων.

9 Τῶν μὲν οὖν εἰς μύθους ἀνενηνεγμένων ἔργων
πολλὰ παραλιπὼν τούτων ἐπεμνήσθην ὧν οὕτως
ἕκαστον εὐσχήμονας καὶ πολλοὺς ἔχει λόγους, ὥστε
καὶ τοὺς ἐμμέτρους καὶ τοὺς τῶν ἀδομένων ποιητὰς
καὶ πολλοὺς τῶν συγγραφέων ὑποθέσεις τἀκείνων
ἔργα τῆς αὑτῶν μουσικῆς πεποιῆσθαι· ἃ δὲ τῇ μὲν
ἀξίᾳ τῶν ἔργων οὐδέν ἐστι τούτων ἐλάττω, τῷ δ᾽
ὑπογυιότερ᾽ εἶναι τοῖς χρόνοις οὔπω μεμυθολόγη-
ται οὐδ᾽ εἰς τὴν ἡρωϊκὴν ἐπανῆκται τάξιν, ταῦτ᾽
10 ἤδη λέξω. ἐκεῖνοι τὸν ἐξ ἁπάσης τῆς Ἀσίας
στόλον ἐλθόντα μόνοι δὶς ἠμύναντο καὶ κατὰ γῆν

---

[1] Blass added Θρᾳκῶν καὶ from Isocr. iv. 68.

[a] The female warriors known as Amazons were repelled
by Theseus. The Phasis River in Colchis, now the Rion,
was the legendary boundary between Europe and Asia.

expel them beyond the Phasis, and the host of Eumolpus and of many another foeman they drove not only out of their own land but also from the lands of all the other Greeks—invaders whom all those dwelling on our front to the westward neither withstood nor possessed the power to halt.[a] Moreover, they were styled the saviours of the sons of Heracles, who himself was the saviour of the rest of mankind, when they arrived in this land as suppliants, fleeing before Eurystheus. In addition to all these and many other noble deeds they refused to suffer the lawful rites of the departed to be treated with despite when Creon forbade the burial of " the seven against Thebes." [b]

Now, omitting mention of many exploits that are 9 classed as myths, I have recalled to mind the above-mentioned, each of which affords so many charming themes that our writers of poetry, whether recited or sung,[c] and many historians, have made the deeds of those men the subjects of their respective arts ; at the present time I shall mention the following deeds, which, though in point of merit they are no whit inferior to the former, still, through being closer in point of time, have not yet found their way into poetry or even been exalted to epic rank. Those men 10 single-handed twice repulsed by land and sea the

Eumolpus invaded Greece from Thrace but was halted by Erechtheus at Eleusis. The route to all parts of the mainland issued from Athens on the west side.

[b] This phrase became proverbial as the title of a drama by Aeschylus. Theseus, king of Athens, gave aid to the suppliant wives of the Argive heroes when Creon, king of Thebes, refused burial to their slain husbands : Euripides, *Suppliants*.

[c] The distinction is between epic and dramatic poetry, which was recited, and odes such as those of Pindar, and dithyrambs, which were sung to musical accompaniment.

DEMOSTHENES

καὶ κατὰ θάλατταν, καὶ διὰ τῶν ἰδίων κινδύνων κοινῆς σωτηρίας πᾶσι τοῖς Ἕλλησιν αἴτιοι κατέστησαν. καὶ προείρηται μὲν ὃ μέλλω λέγειν ὑπ' [1392] ἄλλων πρότερον, δεῖ δὲ μηδὲ νῦν τοῦ δικαίου καὶ καλῶς ἔχοντος ἐπαίνου τοὺς ἄνδρας ἐκείνους στερηθῆναι· τοσούτῳ γὰρ ἀμείνους τῶν ἐπὶ Τροίαν στρατευσαμένων νομίζοιντ' ἂν εἰκότως, ὅσον οἱ μὲν ἐξ ἁπάσης τῆς Ἑλλάδος ὄντες ἀριστεῖς δέκ' ἔτη τῆς Ἀσίας ἐν χωρίον πολιορκοῦντες μόλις 11 εἷλον, οὗτοι δὲ τὸν ἐκ πάσης τῆς ἠπείρου στόλον ἐλθόντα μόνοι, τἆλλα πάντα κατεστραμμένον, οὐ μόνον ἠμύναντο, ἀλλὰ καὶ τιμωρίαν ὑπὲρ ὧν τοὺς ἄλλους ἠδίκουν ἐπέθηκαν. ἔτι τοίνυν τὰς ἐν αὐτοῖς τοῖς Ἕλλησι πλεονεξίας κωλύοντες, πάντας ὅσους συνέβη γενέσθαι κινδύνους ὑπέμειναν, ὅπου τὸ δίκαιον εἴη τεταγμένον, ἐνταῦθα προσνέμοντες ἑαυτούς, ἕως εἰς τὴν νῦν ζῶσαν ἡλικίαν ὁ χρόνος προήγαγεν ἡμᾶς.

12 Μηδεὶς δ' ἡγείσθω με ἀποροῦντα, τί χρὴ περὶ τούτων εἰπεῖν ἑκάστου, ταῦτα τὰ πραχθέντ' ἀπηριθμηκέναι. εἰ γὰρ ἁπάντων ἀμηχανώτατος ἦν ὅ τι χρὴ λέγειν πορίσασθαι, ἡ 'κείνων ἀρετὴ δείκνυσιν αὐτὴ ἃ καὶ πρόχειρα καὶ ῥᾴδι' ἐπελθεῖν ἐστιν. ἀλλὰ προαιροῦμαι τῆς εὐγενείας καὶ τῶν παρὰ τοῖς προγόνοις μεγίστων μνησθείς, ὡς τάχιστα συνάψαι τὸν λόγον πρὸς τὰ τοῖσδε πεπραγμένα, ἵν', ὥσπερ τὰς φύσεις ἦσαν συγγενεῖς, οὕτω τοὺς ἐπαίνους ἐπ'

---

a King Darius of Persia was repulsed at Marathon, 490, and Xerxes at Salamis, 480 B.C. The Persian wars are discussed at length in the *Menex.* 239 D ff.

expedition assembled out of the whole of Asia,[a] and at their individual risks established themselves as the authors of the joint salvation of all the Greeks. And though what I shall say next has been said before by many another, still even at this date those dead must not be deprived of their just and excellent praise. For I say that with good reason those men might be judged so far superior to those who campaigned against Troy, that the latter, the foremost princes out of the whole of Greece, with difficulty captured a single stronghold of Asia after besieging it for ten years,[b] whereas those men single-handed not only repulsed 11 a host assembled from an entire continent, which had already subdued all other lands, but also inflicted punishment for the wrong done the rest of the Greeks. Furthermore, checking all acts of selfish aggrandisement among the Greeks themselves, assigning themselves to each station where justice was arrayed, they went on bearing the brunt of all dangers that chanced to arise until the lapse of time brings us to the generation now living.

Let no one think I have enumerated this list of 12 achievements because I am at a loss what to say about each of them ; for if I were the most helpless of all men in discovering what it becomes me to say, the sheer virtue of those dead reveals sentiments that lie to hand and are easy to rehearse. It is my intention, however, after calling to mind their noble birth and the magnificent things done by their ancestors, with all speed to link my speech with the deeds of these dead, to the end that, just as they were akin in the flesh, so I may make the words of praise spoken

[b] Blass notes this sentiment in Isocr. *Panegyr.* 83. It is found also in Hyper. 35.

αὐτῶν κοινοὺς ποιήσωμαι, ὑπολαμβάνων ταῦτ' ἂν
εἶναι κεχαρισμένα κἀκείνοις καὶ μάλιστ' ἀμφοτέροις, εἰ τῆς ἀλλήλων ἀρετῆς μὴ μόνον τῇ φύσει
μετάσχοιεν, ἀλλὰ καὶ τοῖς ἐπαίνοις.

13 Ἀνάγκη δ' ἐν τῷ μεταξὺ διαλαβεῖν, καὶ πρὸ τοῦ
τὰ τοῖσδε πεπραγμένα τοῖς ἀνδράσι δηλοῦν, καὶ
τοὺς ἔξω τοῦ γένους πρὸς τὸν τάφον ἠκολουθη-
[1393] κότας πρὸς εὔνοιαν παρακαλέσαι. καὶ γὰρ εἰ μὲν
εἰς χρημάτων δαπάνην ἤ τιν' ἄλλην θεωρίαν ἱπ-
πικῶν ἢ γυμνικῶν ἄθλων ἐτάχθην κοσμῆσαι τὸν
τάφον, ὅσῳπερ ἂν προθυμότερον καὶ ἀφειδέστερον
ταῦτα παρεσκευασάμην, τοσούτῳ μᾶλλον ἂν προσ-
ήκοντ' ἔδοξα πεποιηκέναι· λόγῳ δ' ἐπαινέσαι τούσδε
τοὺς ἄνδρας αἱρεθείς, ἂν μὴ τοὺς ἀκούοντας
συμβουλομένους λάβω, φοβοῦμαι μὴ τῇ προθυμίᾳ
14 τοὐναντίον οὗ δεῖ ποιήσω. ὁ μὲν γὰρ πλοῦτος καὶ
τὸ τάχος καὶ ἡ ἰσχὺς καὶ ὅσ' ἄλλα τούτοις ὅμοια,
αὐτάρκεις ἔχει τὰς ὀνήσεις τοῖς κεκτημένοις, καὶ
κρατοῦσιν ἐν αὐτοῖς οἷς ἂν παρῇ, κἂν μηδεὶς τῶν
ἄλλων βούληται· ἡ δὲ τῶν λόγων πειθὼ τῆς τῶν
ἀκουόντων εὐνοίας προσδεῖται, καὶ μετὰ ταύτης
μέν, κἂν μετρίως ῥηθῇ, δόξαν ἤνεγκε καὶ χάριν
προσποιεῖ, ἄνευ δὲ ταύτης, κἂν ὑπερβάλῃ τῷ λέγειν
καλῶς, προσέστη τοῖς ἀκούουσιν.

15 Πολλὰ τοίνυν ἔχων εἰπεῖν ὧν οἵδε πράξαντες
δικαίως ἐπαινεθήσονται, ἐπειδὴ πρὸς αὐτοῖς εἰμι
τοῖς ἔργοις, ἀπορῶ τί πρῶτον εἴπω· προσιστάμενα
γὰρ πάντ' εἰς ἕνα καιρόν, δύσκριτον καθίστησί μοι

ᵃ The welcome extended to aliens at the public funerals is
mentioned in Thucyd. ii. 34. 4. Pericles recognizes their
presence, 36. 4.

ᵇ Blass compares XVIII. 277, but the parallel is not precise.

over them to apply to both alike. I assume that this would be gratifying not only to the ancestors but, best of all, to both them and these dead, if they should come to share one another's merit not only by virtue of birth but also by reason of our words of praise.

In the meantime it is necessary to interrupt my 13 discourse for a moment, before declaring the deeds of these men, to solicit the goodwill of those born outside this race who have accompanied us to the tomb.[a] For if I had been appointed to do honour to this burial through expenditure of money or by providing some different kind of a spectacle consisting of equestrian or gymnastic contests, the greater my zeal and the more lavish my expenditure in preparing such spectacles, the better I should have been thought to have done my duty. Having been chosen, however, to extol these men in a speech, unless I have the sympathy of my hearers, I fear that because of my eagerness I may effect the very opposite of what I ought. For wealth and speed of foot and strength 14 of body and all other such things have their rewards self-assured to their possessors, and in those fields they win who have the luck, even if not one of the others wishes their success. On the other hand, the persuasiveness of words depends upon the goodwill of the hearers, and with the help of this, even if the eloquence be moderate, it reaps glory and gains favour, but lacking this help, even if it be surpassingly good, it is thwarted by those who hear.[b]

Now to resume my theme : though many deeds of 15 these men are at hand because of which they will be justly eulogized, I am at a loss what to mention first when I come face to face with the facts. For thronging into my mind as they do, all at one and

17

τὴν αἵρεσιν αὐτῶν. οὐ μὴν ἀλλὰ πειράσομαι τὴν
αὐτὴν ποιήσασθαι τοῦ λόγου τάξιν ἥπερ ὑπῆρξε
16 τοῦ βίου τούτοις. οἶδε γὰρ ἐξ ἀρχῆς ἐν πᾶσι τοῖς
παιδεύμασιν ἦσαν ἐπιφανεῖς, τὰ πρέποντα καθ'
ἡλικίαν ἀσκοῦντες ἑκάστην, καὶ πᾶσιν ἀρέσκοντες
οἷς χρή, γονεῦσι, φίλοις, οἰκείοις. τοιγαροῦν ὥσπερ ἴχνη γνωρίζουσα νῦν ἡ τῶν οἰκείων αὐτοῖς καὶ
φίλων μνήμη πᾶσαν ὥραν ἐπὶ τούτους φέρεται τῷ
πόθῳ, πόλλ' ὑπομνήματα λαμβάνουσα ἐν οἷς συν-
17
[1394] ῄδει τούτοις ἀρίστοις οὖσιν. ἐπειδὴ δ' εἰς ἄνδρας
ἀφίκοντο, οὐ μόνον τοῖς πολίταις γνώριμον τὴν
αὐτῶν φύσιν, ἀλλὰ καὶ πᾶσιν ἀνθρώποις κατέστησαν. ἔστι γάρ, ἔστιν ἁπάσης ἀρετῆς ἀρχὴ μὲν
σύνεσις, πέρας δ' ἀνδρεία· καὶ τῇ μὲν δοκιμάζεται
τί πρακτέον ἐστί, τῇ δὲ σῴζεται. ἐν τούτοις δ'
18 ἀμφοτέροις οἶδε πολὺ διήνεγκαν. καὶ γὰρ εἴ τις
ἐφύετο κοινὸς πᾶσι κίνδυνος τοῖς Ἕλλησιν, οὗτοι
πρῶτοι προείδοντο, καὶ πολλάκις εἰς σωτηρίαν
ἅπαντας παρεκάλεσαν, ὅπερ γνώμης ἀπόδειξίς
ἐστιν εὖ φρονούσης· καὶ τῆς παρὰ τοῖς Ἕλλησιν
ἀγνοίας μεμειγμένης κακίᾳ, ὅτ' ἐνῆν ταῦτα κωλύειν
ἀσφαλῶς, τὰ μὲν οὐ προορώσης, τὰ δ' εἰρωνευο-
μένης, ὅμως, ἡνίχ' ὑπήκουσαν καὶ τὰ δέοντα ποιεῖν

---

[a] Kennedy cites Cicero, *Pro Sestio* xl. 86 " hoc sentire
prudentiae est, facere fortitudinis."
[b] By "slackness" is meant the acceptance of Macedonian
bribes, mentioned by Hyper. 10 ; Blass compares XVIII. 20,
where " folly " is used as a euphemism for "slackness."
[c] The attitude of the Greek states toward the aggressions
of Philip of Macedon may be compared to that of the small
democratic states of Europe toward Germany before the war
of 1939–1945. By his *Olynthiacs* and *Philippics* Demosthenes

18

the same time, it becomes difficult to make a choice among them. I shall endeavour, however, to maintain the same order of topics in my speech as marked the course of the lives of these men. From the 16 beginning these men were outstanding in all the activities that formed their schooling, engaging in the exercises that became each stage of life, causing gratification to all who had claim to it—parents, friends, kinsmen. Therefore, just as if recognizing footprints, the memory of those who were near and dear to them now turns to these men every hour in fond recollection, finding many a reminder of occasions when they knew in their hearts that these were lads of surpassing worth. Arrived at manhood they rendered their 17 innate nobility known, not only to their fellow-citizens, but to all men. For of all virtue, I say, and I repeat it, the beginning is understanding and the fulfilment is courage ; by the one it is judged what ought to be done and by the other this is carried to success.[a] In both these qualities these men were distinctly superior ; for if ever a danger affecting all the Greeks 18 was brewing, these were the first to foresee it, and time and again they challenged the rest to save the situation. This action is a demonstration of sound judgement joined with public spirit. Although, again, there was much folly among the Greeks, not unmixed with slackness,[b] a folly which failed to foresee some dangers and feigned not to see others at a time when it was possible to avert these misfortunes without sacrificing safety, nevertheless, when they did hearken and evinced willingness to do their duty,[c]

tried to arouse and unite them but with little success until the year 338 B.C., when he achieved his great diplomatic triumph in uniting Thebes with Athens, ancient rivals.

ἠθέλησαν, οὐκ ἐμνησικάκησαν, ἀλλὰ προστάντες
καὶ παρασχόντες ἅπαντα προθύμως, καὶ σώματα καὶ
χρήματα καὶ συμμάχους, εἰς πεῖραν ἦλθον ἀγῶνος,
εἰς ὃν οὐδὲ τῆς ψυχῆς ἐφείσαντο.

19 Ἐξ ἀνάγκης δὲ συμβαίνει, ὅταν μάχη γίγνηται,
τοῖς μὲν ἡττᾶσθαι, τοῖς δὲ νικᾶν· οὐκ ἂν ὀκνήσαιμι
δ' εἰπεῖν, ὅτι μοι δοκοῦσιν οἱ τελευτῶντες ἑκατέρων ἐν τάξει τῆς μὲν ἥττης οὐ μετέχειν, νικᾶν δ'
ὁμοίως ἀμφότεροι. τὸ μὲν γὰρ κρατεῖν ἐν τοῖς
ζῶσιν ὡς ἂν ὁ δαίμων παραδῷ κρίνεται· ὃ δ' εἰς
τοῦθ' ἕκαστον ἔδει παρασχέσθαι, πᾶς ὁ μένων ἐν
τάξει πεποίηκεν. εἰ δὲ θνητὸς ὢν τὴν εἱμαρμένην
ἔσχε, τῇ τύχῃ πέπονθε τὸ συμβαῖνον, οὐχὶ τὴν
20 ψυχὴν ἥττηται τῶν ἐναντίων. νομίζω τοίνυν καὶ
τοῦ τῆς χώρας ἡμῶν μὴ ἐπιβῆναι τοὺς πολεμίους,
[1395] πρὸς τῇ τῶν ἐναντίων ἀγνωμοσύνῃ τὴν τούτων
ἀρετὴν αἰτίαν γεγενῆσθαι· κατ' ἄνδρα γὰρ πεῖραν
εἰληφότες οἱ τότε συμμείξαντες ἐκεῖ οὐκ ἐβού-
λοντ' αὖθις εἰς ἀγῶνα καθίστασθαι τοῖς ἐκείνων
οἰκείοις, ὑπολαμβάνοντες ταῖς μὲν φύσεσιν ταῖς
ὁμοίαις ἀπαντήσεσθαι, τύχην δ' οὐκ εὔπορον εἶναι
τὴν ὁμοίαν λαβεῖν.

Δηλοῖ δ' οὐχ ἥκισθ' ὅτι ταῦθ' οὕτως ἔχει καὶ τὰ
τῆς γεγονυίας εἰρήνης· οὐ γὰρ ἔνεστ' εἰπεῖν οὔτ'
ἀληθεστέραν οὔτε καλλίω πρόφασιν, τοῦ τῆς τῶν
τετελευτηκότων ἀγασθέντ' ἀρετῆς τὸν τῶν ἐναν-

---

[a] The particular reference is to the battle of Chaeronea,
338 B.C., where the Greeks were defeated by Philip of Macedon.
[b] Blass notes this sentiment in XVIII. 208, and in Isocr.

these men did not bear a grudge but stepping forward and eagerly offering their all, bodies, money, and allies, they entered upon the ordeal of the contest, in which they were not sparing even of their lives.

Of necessity it happens, when a battle takes place,[a] 19 that the one side is beaten and the other victorious ; but I should not hesitate to assert that in my judgement the men who die at the post of duty on either side do not share the defeat but are both alike victors. For the mastery among the survivors is decided as the deity disposes, but that which each was in duty bound to contribute to this end, every man who has kept his post in battle has done. But if, as a mortal being, he meets his doom, what he has suffered is an incident caused by chance, but in spirit he remains unconquered by his opponents.[b] It is my judge- 20 ment, therefore, that we have to thank the valour of these men, along with the folly of our opponents, that our enemies did not set foot upon our land ; because, every man of them having had proof of their mettle, those who there engaged them on that occasion had no wish to confront in battle a second time the kinsmen of those men, suspecting that, although they would confront men of the same breed, they were not likely to find the fortune of battle so kind.

Not the least reason for believing that this was their state of mind is afforded by the peace that was made ; for it is impossible to cite a more plausible or more creditable reason than that the master of our opponents, astounded at the valour of these who

Panegyr. 92. It is subsidiary to the recognition of the supremacy of the deity, fate or fortune, XVIII. 192, 207, 208. To commemorate the valour of the fallen Thebans a monumental seated lion was erected facing in the direction of the enemy. It is still extant.

τίων κύριον, φίλον γενέσθαι τοῖς οἰκείοις βούλεσθαι
μᾶλλον ἢ πάλιν τὸν ὑπὲρ τῶν ὅλων κίνδυνον ἄρ-
21 ασθαι. οἶμαι δ' ἄν, εἴ τις αὐτοὺς τοὺς παραταξαμένους ἐρωτήσειε, πότερ' ἡγοῦνται ταῖς αὐτῶν
ἀρεταῖς ἢ τῇ παραδόξῳ καὶ χαλεπῇ τύχῃ κατωρ-
θωκέναι καὶ τῇ τοῦ προεστηκότος αὐτῶν ἐμπειρίᾳ
καὶ τόλμῃ, οὐδέν' οὔτ' ἀναίσχυντον οὔτε τολμηρὸν
οὕτως εἶναι ὄντιν' ἀντιποιήσεσθαι τῶν πεπραγμένων. ἀλλὰ μὴν ὑπὲρ ὧν ὁ πάντων κύριος δαίμων ὡς ἐβούλετ' ἔνειμεν τὸ τέλος, ἅπαντας
ἀφεῖσθαι κακίας ἀνάγκη τοὺς λοιπούς, ἀνθρώπους
γ' ὄντας· περὶ ὧν δ' ὁ τῶν ἐναντίων ἡγεμὼν
ὑπερῆρε τοὺς ἐπὶ τούτῳ ταχθέντας, οὐχὶ τοὺς πολλοὺς οὔτ' ἐκείνων οὔθ' ἡμῶν αἰτιάσαιτ' ἄν τις
22 εἰκότως. εἰ δ' ἄρ' ἔστι τις ἀνθρώπων ὅτῳ περὶ
τούτων ἐγκαλέσαι προσήκει, τοῖς ἐπὶ τούτῳ ταχ-
θεῖσι Θηβαίων, οὐχὶ τοῖς πολλοῖς οὔτ' ἐκείνων οὔθ'
[1396] ἡμῶν ἐγκαλέσειεν ἄν τις εἰκότως· οἳ δύναμιν λαβόντες ἔχουσαν θυμὸν ἀήττητον κἀπροφάσιστον καὶ
23 φιλοτιμίαν ἐφάμιλλον, οὐδενὶ τούτων ὀρθῶς ἐχρήσαντο. καὶ τὰ μὲν ἄλλ' ἔστι τούτων ὡς ἕκαστος
ἔχει γνώμης, οὕτως ὑπολαμβάνειν· ὃ δ' ἅπασιν
ὁμοίως τοῖς οὖσιν ἀνθρώποις γεγένηται φανερόν,
ὅτι ἡ πάσης τῆς Ἑλλάδος ἄρ' ἐλευθερία ἐν ταῖς
τῶνδε τῶν ἀνδρῶν ψυχαῖς διεσῴζετο· ἐπειδὴ γοῦν

---

[a] Philip exacted no vengeance after his victory; Attica
was not invaded. The Greek states retained the right of self-
government and became allies, not subjects, of the victor.
[b] Philip seems to have deceived the Athenians by a feigned

died, chose rather to be friendly toward their kinsmen than once more to assume the risk of all his
fortunes.[a] I believe also that if someone were to 21
ask those in the opposite ranks whether they thought
they had won by their own deeds of valour or by a
startling and cruel turn of fortune and by the skill
and daring of their own commander, not one of them
would be so shameless or audacious as to claim credit
for what happened. Furthermore, in contests of which
the deity, the master of all, has disposed the outcome
as it chose, it is necessary of course to acquit all others,
being but human, of the charge of showing weakness,
and where victory was won because the leader of our
opponents prevailed over those appointed to the command of our army, no one could justly locate the cause
in the rank and file of either the enemy or ourselves.
But if, after all, there is any human being who might 22
rightly lay a charge concerning the issue of that battle,
he would with good reason advance it against those of
the Thebans who were appointed to this command,[b]
nor could anyone rightly lay blame upon the rank
and file of either the Thebans or ourselves. Those
men, receiving command of a military force that
would neither brook defeat nor make excuse and had
an emulous zest for glory, made the right use of none
of these. As for the other questions touching this 23
campaign, each individual is at liberty to draw conclusions according to his judgement, but what has
become manifest to all living men alike is this—that
in effect, the freedom of the whole Greek world could
be preserved only with the lives of these men. At

retreat while throwing his strongest troops against the
Thebans. This stratagem broke the line and decided the
battle. The Theban general Theagenes and his colleagues
seem to have been no more to blame than the rest.

ἡ πεπρωμένη τούτους ἀνεῖλεν, οὐδεὶς ἀντέστη τῶν
λοιπῶν. καὶ φθόνος μὲν ἀπείη τοῦ λόγου, δοκεῖ
δέ μοί τις ἂν εἰπὼν ὡς ἡ τῶνδε τῶν ἀνδρῶν ἀρετὴ
24 τῆς Ἑλλάδος ἦν ψυχὴ τἀληθὲς εἰπεῖν· ἅμα γὰρ τά
τε τούτων πνεύματ' ἀπηλλάγη τῶν οἰκείων σω-
μάτων, καὶ τὸ τῆς Ἑλλάδος ἀξίωμ' ἀνῄρηται.
μεγάλην μὲν οὖν ἴσως ὑπερβολὴν δόξομεν λέγειν,
ῥητέον δ' ὅμως· ὥσπερ γάρ, εἴ τις ἐκ τοῦ καθ-
εστηκότος κόσμου τὸ φῶς ἐξέλοι, δυσχερὴς καὶ
χαλεπὸς πᾶς ὁ λειπόμενος βίος γένοιτ' ἄν, οὕτω
τῶνδε τῶν ἀνδρῶν ἀναιρεθέντων, ἐν σκότει καὶ
πολλῇ δυσκλείᾳ πᾶς ὁ πρὸ τοῦ ζῆλος τῶν Ἑλλήνων γέγονεν.
25 Διὰ πολλὰ δ' εἰκότως ὄντες τοιοῦτοι, διὰ τὴν
πολιτείαν οὐχ ἥκιστ' ἦσαν σπουδαῖοι. αἱ μὲν γὰρ
διὰ τῶν ὀλίγων δυναστεῖαι δέος μὲν ἐνεργάζονται
τοῖς πολίταις, αἰσχύνην δ' οὐ παριστᾶσιν· ἡνίκ' ἂν
οὖν ὁ ἀγὼν ἔλθῃ τοῦ πολέμου, πᾶς τις εὐχερῶς
ἑαυτὸν σώζει, συνειδὼς ὅτι, ἂν τοὺς κυρίους ἢ
δώροις ἢ δι' ἄλλης ἡστινοσοῦν ὁμιλίας ἐξαρέσηται,
κἂν τὰ δεινότατ' ἀσχημονήσῃ, μικρὸν ὄνειδος τὸ
26 λοιπὸν αὐτῷ καταστήσεται· αἱ δὲ δημοκρατίαι
πολλά τ' ἄλλα καὶ καλὰ καὶ δίκαι' ἔχουσιν ὧν τὸν
[1397] εὖ φρονοῦντ' ἀντέχεσθαι δεῖ, καὶ τὴν παρρησίαν
τὴν ἐκ τῆς ἀληθείας ἠρτημένην οὐκ ἔστι τἀληθὲς
δηλοῦν ἀποτρέψαι. οὐδὲ γὰρ πάντας ἐξαρέσασθαι

ᵃ Kennedy quotes Cicero, *De Amic.* xiii. 47 " solem enim
e mundo tollere videntur qui amicitiam e vita tollunt."
According to Aristotle's *Rhetoric* i. 7 and iii. 10, Pericles had
once said in a funeral speech it was " as if the spring had
been taken out of the year."

any rate, since fate removed them, not one of those remaining has made a stand against the foe. While I desire that my words may be free from offence, it seems to me that if one should declare that the valour of these men was the very life of Greece he would speak the truth ; for at one and the same time their 24 spirits were separated from their dear bodies and the self-esteem of Greece was taken from her. We shall therefore seem guilty perhaps of a bold exaggeration, but still it must be uttered : for just as, if the light of day were removed out of this universe of ours,[a] all the remnant of life would be harsh and irksome, so, now that these men have been taken from us, all the old-time radiance of the Greeks is sunk in gloom and profound obscurity.

While it stands to reason that many influences 25 helped to make them what they were, not least was their virtue ascribable to our form of government.[b] For though absolute governments dominated by a few create fear in their citizens, they fail to awaken the sense of shame. Consequently, when the test of war comes, everyone lightheartedly proceeds to save himself, knowing full well that if only he succeeds in appeasing his masters by presents or any other civility whatsoever, even though he becomes guilty of the most revolting conduct, only slight reproach will attach to him thereafter. Democracies, how- 26 ever, possess many other just and noble features, to which right-minded men should hold fast, and in particular it is impossible to deter freedom of speech, which depends upon speaking the truth, from exposing the truth. For neither is it possible for

[b] This topic is treated in the *Menex.* 238 B—239 D. Blass compares XX. 108, but the similarity is not impressive.

τοῖς αἰσχρόν τι ποιήσασιν δυνατόν, ὥσθ' ὁ μόνος
τἀληθὲς ὄνειδος λέγων λυπεῖ· καὶ γὰρ οἱ μηδὲν
ἂν εἰπόντες αὐτοὶ βλάσφημον, ἄλλου γε λέγοντος
χαίρουσιν ἀκούοντες. ἃ φοβούμενοι πάντες εἰκότως τῇ τῶν μετὰ ταῦτ' ὀνειδῶν αἰσχύνῃ τόν τ'
ἀπὸ τῶν ἐναντίων κίνδυνον προσιόντ' εὐρώστως
ὑπέμειναν, καὶ θάνατον καλὸν εἵλοντο μᾶλλον ἢ
βίον αἰσχρόν.

27 Ἃ μὲν οὖν κοινῇ πᾶσιν ὑπῆρχε τοῖσδε τοῖς ἀνδράσιν εἰς τὸ καλῶς ἐθέλειν ἀποθνῄσκειν εἴρηται,
γένος, παιδεία, χρηστῶν ἐπιτηδευμάτων συνήθεια,
τῆς ὅλης πολιτείας ὑπόθεσις· ἃ δὲ κατὰ φυλὰς
παρεσκεύασ' ἑκάστους εὐρώστους εἶναι, ταῦτ' ἤδη
λέξω. ᾔδεσαν πάντες Ἐρεχθεῖδαι τὸν ἐπώνυμον
αὐτῶν Ἐρεχθέα, εἵνεκα τοῦ σῶσαι τὴν χώραν
τὰς αὑτοῦ παῖδας, ἃς Ὑακινθίδας καλοῦσιν, εἰς
προῦπτον θάνατον δόντ' ἀναλῶσαι. αἰσχρὸν οὖν
ἡγοῦντο, τὸν μὲν ἀπ' ἀθανάτων πεφυκότα πάντα
ποιεῖν εἵνεκα τοῦ τὴν πατρίδ' ἐλευθερῶσαι, αὐτοὶ δὲ
φανῆναι θνητὸν σῶμα ποιούμενοι περὶ πλείονος ἢ
28 δόξαν ἀθάνατον. οὐκ ἠγνόουν Αἰγεῖδαι Θησέα τὸν

ᵃ Under an oligarchy, the speaker means, it is possible for
the wrongdoer to seal the mouths of the small ruling clique
by means of bribes, but under a democracy it is impossible
to buy the silence of thousands of citizens. The reference is
to oligarchic governments set up by the Spartans in subject
states. Pericles praised the Athenian form of government as
against the Spartan, Thucyd. ii. 37-39.

ᵇ The fear of exposure as a factor in democratic government is mentioned by Pericles, Thucyd. ii. 37. 3, and by
Hyper. 25. Blass compares XXII. 31.

ᶜ The list which here begins is our chief authority for the
names and order of precedence of the ten Athenian tribes as
established by Cleisthenes in 508 B.C. The particular myths

those who commit a shameful act to appease all the citizens,[a] so that even the lone individual, uttering the deserved reproach, makes the guilty wince : for even those who would never speak an accusing word themselves are pleased at hearing the same, provided another utters it. Through fear of such condemnation, all these men, as was to be expected, for shame at the thought of subsequent reproaches,[b] manfully faced the threat arising from our foes and chose a noble death in preference to life and disgrace.

The considerations that actuated these men one and all to choose to die nobly have now been enumerated,—birth, education, habituation to high standards of conduct, and the underlying principles of our form of government in general. The incentives that challenged them severally to be valiant men, depending upon the tribes to which they belonged, I shall next relate.[c] All the Erechtheidae were well aware that Erechtheus, from whom they have their name, for the salvation of this land gave his own daughters, whom they call Hyacinthides, to certain death, and so expended their lives. Therefore they regarded it as shameful, after a being born of immortal gods had sacrificed everything for the liberation of his native land, that they themselves should have been found to have placed a higher value upon a mortal body than upon immortal glory.[d] Neither were the Aegeidae ignorant that Theseus, the son of Aegeus,

that suit the context, however, are for the most part obscure and of relatively recent origin. For example, the older legends speak of but one daughter of Erechtheus as being sacrificed. The later version is known to Cicero, *Tusc. Disp.* i. 48. 116.

[d] Hyper. 24 reads in part θνητοῦ σώματος ἀθάνατον δόξαν ἐκτήσαντο, " gained immortal glory at the price of a mortal body."

Αἰγέως πρῶτον ἰσηγορίαν καταστησάμενον τῇ
πόλει. δεινὸν οὖν ἡγοῦντο τὴν ἐκείνου προδοῦναι
προαίρεσιν, καὶ τεθνάναι μᾶλλον ᾑροῦντο ἢ κατα-
λυομένης ταύτης παρὰ τοῖς Ἕλλησι ζῆν φιλοψυχή-
σαντες. παρειλήφεσαν Πανδιονίδαι Πρόκνην καὶ
Φιλομήλαν τὰς Πανδίονος θυγατέρας, ὡς ἐτιμωρή-
[1398] σαντο Τηρέα διὰ τὴν εἰς αὐτὰς ὕβριν. οὐ βιωτὸν
οὖν ἐνόμιζον αὐτοῖς, εἰ μὴ συγγενῆ φανήσονται τὸν
θυμὸν ἔχοντες ἐκείναις, ἐφ' οἷς τὴν Ἑλλάδ' ἑώρων
ὑβριζομένην.

29   Ἠκηκόεσαν Λεωντίδαι μυθολογουμένας τὰς Λεώ
κόρας, ὡς ἑαυτὰς ἔδοσαν σφάγιον τοῖς πολίταις
ὑπὲρ τῆς χώρας. ὅτε δὴ γυναῖκες ἐκεῖναι τοιαύτην
ἔσχον ἀνδρείαν, οὐ θεμιτὸν αὐτοῖς ὑπελάμβανον
χείροσιν ἀνδράσιν οὖσιν ἐκείνων φανῆναι. ἐμέμνηντ'
Ἀκαμαντίδαι τῶν ἐπῶν ἐν οἷς Ὅμηρος εἵνεκα
τῆς μητρός φησιν Αἴθρας Ἀκάμαντ' εἰς Τροίαν
στεῖλαι. ὁ μὲν οὖν παντὸς ἐπειρᾶτο κινδύνου τοῦ
σῶσαι τὴν ἑαυτοῦ μητέρ' εἵνεκα· οἱ δὲ τοὺς οἴκοι
σύμπαντας γονέας πῶς οὐκ ἔμελλον ὑπὲρ τοῦ σῶσαι
30 πάντα κίνδυνον ὑπομένειν; οὐκ ἐλάνθανεν Οἰνεί-
δας ὅτι Κάδμου μὲν Σεμέλη, τῆς δ' ὃν οὐ πρέπον
ἔστ' ὀνομάζειν ἐπὶ τοῦδε τοῦ τάφου, τοῦ δ' Οἰνεὺς

---

^a According to Plutarch, *Theseus* xxv., it was equality
between newcomers and natives that Theseus established;
the word ἰσονομία usually means equality before the law and
is almost a synonym for democracy.

^b Procnê is said to have murdered her own son Itys and
to have served his flesh to her husband Tereus in revenge for
his treachery to herself and his cruelty to Philomela. It is
curious that the speaker seems less shocked by this crime than
by the innocent tale of Alopê, § 31, below.

^c Aethra is mentioned in the *Iliad* iii. 144, but the rest of
the story is not Homeric. This Acamas is unknown to

for the first time established equality in the State.[a]
They thought it, therefore, a dreadful thing to be
false to the principles of that ancestor, and they
preferred to be dead rather than through love of life
to survive among the Greeks with this equality lost.
The Pandionidae had inherited the tradition of
Procnê and Philomela, the daughters of Pandion,
who took vengeance on Tereus for his crime against
themselves.[b] Therefore they decided that life was
not worth living unless they, akin by race, should
have proved themselves to possess equal spirit with
those women, when confronted by the outrage they
saw being committed against Greece.

The Leontidae had heard the stories related of the 29
daughters of Leô, how they offered themselves to the
citizens as a sacrifice for their country's sake. When,
therefore, such courage was displayed by those
women, they looked upon it as a heinous thing if they,
being men, should have proved to possess less of
manhood. The Acamantidae did not fail to recall
the epics in which Homer says that Acamas sailed for
Troy for the sake of his mother Aethra.[c] Now, since
he braved every danger for the sake of saving his own
mother, how were these men not bound to face every
danger for the sake of saving their parents one and
all at home? It did not escape the Oeneidae that 30
Semelê was the daughter of Cadmus, and of her was
born one whom it would be sacrilegious to name at
this tomb,[d] and by him Oeneus was begotten, who was

Homer, though he mentions two other individuals of the same
name. It was later myths that told of the rescue of Aethra
after the fall of Troy by her two grandsons, not sons, Acamas
and Demophon.

[d] Dionysus, or Bacchus, god of wine, who, as an Olympian,
could not associate with death.

γέγονεν, ὃς ἀρχηγὸς αὐτῶν ἐκαλεῖτο. κοινοῦ δ'
ὄντος ἀμφοτέραις ταῖς πόλεσιν τοῦ παρόντος κινδύνου, ὑπὲρ ἀμφοτέρων ἅπασαν ᾤοντο δεῖν ἀγωνίαν ἐκτεῖναι. ᾔδεσαν Κεκροπίδαι τὸν ἑαυτῶν
ἀρχηγόν, τὰ μὲν ὡς ἔστι δράκων, τὰ δ' ὡς ἔστιν
ἄνθρωπος λεγόμενον, οὐκ ἄλλοθέν ποθεν ἢ τῷ
τὴν σύνεσιν μὲν αὐτοῦ προσομοιοῦν ἀνθρώπῳ, τὴν
ἀλκὴν δὲ δράκοντι. ἄξια δὴ τούτων πράττειν ὑπ-
31 ελάμβανον αὐτοῖς προσήκειν. ἐμέμνηνθ' Ἱπποθων-
τίδαι τῶν Ἀλόπης γάμων, ἐξ ὧν Ἱπποθῶν ἔφυ,
καὶ τὸν ἀρχηγὸν ᾔδεσαν· ὧν[1]—τὸ πρέπον φυλάττων
ἐγὼ τῷδε τῷ καιρῷ τὸ σαφῶς εἰπεῖν ὑπερβαίνω—
[1399] ἄξια δὴ τούτων ᾤοντο δεῖν ποιοῦντες ὀφθῆναι.
οὐκ ἐλάνθανεν Αἰαντίδας ὅτι τῶν ἀριστείων στερη-
θεὶς Αἴας ἀβίωτον ἡγήσατο τὸν βίον αὑτῷ. ἡνίκ'
οὖν ὁ δαίμων ἄλλῳ τἀριστεῖ' ἐδίδου, τότε τοὺς
ἐχθροὺς ἀμυνόμενοι τεθνάναι δεῖν ᾤοντο, ὥστε
μηδὲν ἀνάξιον αὑτῶν παθεῖν. οὐκ ἡμνημόνουν
Ἀντιοχίδαι Ἡρακλέους ὄντ' Ἀντίοχον. δεῖν οὖν

---

[1] ὧν r (cod. Parisinus): ὃν rel.

---

[a] Two demes in Attica were named Oenoë, which was
sufficient to justify the invention of a hero Oeneus, but he is
not to be confused with the Homeric hero of this name who
was associated with Calydon in Aetolia and with Argos.
The word means " wineman," from οἶνος. At Athens the
anniversary of this hero fell in the month Gamelion, like the
Lenaea of Dionysus. It was natural, therefore, to call him
the son of the god, but the relationship plays no part in
recorded myths.

[b] The suggestion is that the Oeneidae would have felt
equally bound to fight on behalf of Thebes, of which the
founder was Cadmus, and on behalf of Athens, one of whose
heroes was Oeneus, great-grandson of Cadmus. This is the
weakest link in this series.

called the founder of their race.[a] Since the danger in question was common to both States, on behalf of both they thought themselves bound to endure any anguish to the end.[b] The Cecropidae were well aware that their founder was reputed to have been part dragon, part human, for no other reason than this, that in understanding he was like a man, in strength like a dragon. So they assumed that their duty was to perform feats worthy of both. The Hippothoöntidae bore in mind the marriage of Alopê, from which Hippothoön was born, and they knew also who their founder was ; about these matters—to avoid impropriety on an occasion like this [c] I forbear to speak plainly—they thought it was their duty to be seen performing deeds worthy of these ancestors. It did not escape the Aeantidae that Ajax, robbed of the prize of valour, did not consider his own life worth living.[d] When, therefore, the god was giving to another the prize of valour, at once they thought they must die trying to repel their foes so as to suffer no disgrace to themselves. The Antiochidae were not unmindful that Antiochus was the son of

[c] Alopê's son was said to have been twice exposed, and twice rescued and suckled by a mare. The use of mare's milk as a food prevailed among the Scythians, as the Greeks knew well from their colonists in the region of the Black Sea, if not from Herodotus iv. 2 ; Gylon, grandfather of Demosthenes, had lived in the Crimea and was said to have married a Thracian wife. The orator was sometimes twitted by his opponents about his Thracian blood. He may have been sensitive. Consequently the attitude here revealed might be construed as evidence for the genuineness of the speech.

[d] Ajax, worsted by Odysseus in a contest for possession of the arms of Achilles, was said to have slain himself : Homer, *Odyssey* xi. 541-567; the story of his madness and of slaughtering flocks and herds as if they were his enemies is not Homeric: Sophocles, *Ajax*.

ἡγήσαντ᾽ ἢ ζῆν ἀξίως τῶν ὑπαρχόντων ἢ τεθνάναι
καλῶς.

32 Οἱ μὲν οὖν ζῶντες οἰκεῖοι τούτων ἐλεινοί, τοιούτων ἀνδρῶν ἐστερημένοι καὶ συνηθείας πολλῆς καὶ
φιλανθρώπου διεζευγμένοι, καὶ τὰ τῆς πατρίδος
πράγματ᾽ ἔρημα καὶ δακρύων καὶ πένθους πλήρη·
οἱ δ᾽ εὐδαίμονες τῷ δικαίῳ λογισμῷ. πρῶτον μὲν
ἀντὶ μικροῦ χρόνου πολὺν καὶ τὸν ἅπαντ᾽ εὔκλειαν
ἀγήρω καταλείπουσιν, ἐν ᾗ καὶ παῖδες οἱ τούτων
ὀνομαστοὶ τραφήσονται, καὶ γονεῖς οἱ τούτων
περίβλεπτοι γηροτροφήσονται, παραψυχὴν τῷ πέν-
33 θει τὴν τούτων εὔκλειαν ἔχοντες. ἔπειτα νόσων
ἀπαθεῖς τὰ σώματα καὶ λυπῶν ἄπειροι τὰς ψυχάς,
ἃς ἐπὶ τοῖς συμβεβηκόσιν οἱ ζῶντες ἔχουσιν, ἐν
μεγάλῃ τιμῇ καὶ πολλῷ ζήλῳ τῶν νομιζομένων
τυγχάνουσιν. οὓς γὰρ ἅπασα μὲν ἡ πατρὶς θάπτει
δημοσίᾳ, κοινῶν δ᾽ ἐπαίνων μόνοι τυγχάνουσι,
ποθοῦσι δ᾽ οὐ μόνον συγγενεῖς καὶ πολῖται, ἀλλὰ
πᾶσαν ὅσην Ἑλλάδα χρὴ προσειπεῖν, συμπεπένθηκε
δὲ καὶ τῆς οἰκουμένης τὸ πλεῖστον μέρος, πῶς οὐ
34 χρὴ τούτους εὐδαίμονας νομίζεσθαι; οὓς παρέδρους
εἰκότως ἄν τις φήσαι τοῖς κάτω θεοῖς εἶναι,

---

[a] The mother of Antiochus was Meda, daughter of Phylas,
king of the Dryopes, but the story was unimportant and little
known.

[b] Compare Hyper. 24 " Are we not to think them fortunate
because their valour was proven rather than unfortunate because their lives were lost ? "

[c] With εὔκλειαν ἀγήρω compare Thucyd. ii. 43. 2 ἀγήρων
ἔπαινον and Hyper. 42 εὐδοξίαν ἀγήρατον.

[d] This topic is touched upon in Hyper. 27.

[e] Thucyd. ii. 44. 4 " and be comforted by the fair fame of
these your sons."

Heracles.[a] They concluded therefore that they must either live worthily of their heritage or die nobly.

Now, though the living kinsmen of these dead 32 deserve our sympathy, bereaved of such brave men and divorced from close and affectionate association, and though the life of our native land is desolate and filled with tears and mourning, nevertheless these dead by a just calculation are happy.[b] First of all, bartering little for much, a brief time for all eternity, they leave behind them an ageless fame[c] in which the children of these men shall be reared in honour and the parents of these men shall enjoy distinction[d] and tender care in their old age, cherishing the fame of these men as an assuagement of their sorrow.[e] In 33 the second place, immune from disease of body and beyond the reach of anguish of spirit,[f] such as the living must suffer because of the misfortunes which have befallen, they to-day receive high honour and inspire great emulation while they are accorded the customary obsequies.[g] How, then, since the whole country unites in according them a public burial, and they alone receive the words of universal praise, while their kinsmen and fellow-citizens are not alone in mourning them, but every land that has the right to be called Hellas and the greater part of the whole world mourns with them,[h] how can we do otherwise than consider them blessed of fortune ? With ex- 34 cellent reason one might declare them to be now seated beside the gods below, possessing the same

---

[f] In Hyper. 43 may be found ἀπηλλαγμένοι εἰσὶ νόσων καὶ λύπης, as Blass observes.

[g] Annual sacrifices were performed at the public sepulchre in Athens. They were followed by athletic contests.

[h] Thucyd. ii. 43. 3 " for the whole world is the sepulchre of famous men."

τὴν αὐτὴν τάξιν ἔχοντας τοῖς προτέροις ἀγαθοῖς
[1400] ἀνδράσιν ἐν μακάρων νήσοις. οὐ γὰρ ἰδών τις
οὐδὲ περὶ ἐκείνων ταῦτ᾽ ἀπήγγελκεν, ἀλλ᾽ οὓς οἱ
ζῶντες ἀξίους ὑπειλήφαμεν τῶν ἄνω τιμῶν, τούτους τῇ δόξῃ καταμαντευόμενοι κἀκεῖ τῶν αὐτῶν
τιμῶν ἡγούμεθ᾽ αὐτοὺς τυγχάνειν.

35 Ἔστι μὲν οὖν ἴσως χαλεπὸν τὰς παρούσας
συμφορὰς λόγῳ κουφίσαι, δεῖ δ᾽ ὅμως πειρᾶσθαι
καὶ πρὸς τὰ παρηγοροῦντα τρέπειν τὴν ψυχήν, ὡς
τοὺς τοιούτους ἄνδρας γεγεννηκότας καὶ πεφυκότας
αὐτοὺς ἐκ τοιούτων ἑτέρων, καλόν ἐστι τὰ δείν᾽
εὐσχημονέστερον τῶν ἄλλων φέροντας ὁρᾶσθαι καὶ
36 πάσῃ τύχῃ χρωμένους ὁμοίους εἶναι. καὶ γὰρ
ἐκείνοις ταῦτ᾽ ἂν εἴη μάλιστ᾽ ἐν κόσμῳ καὶ τιμῇ,
καὶ πάσῃ τῇ πόλει καὶ τοῖς ζῶσι ταῦτ᾽ ἂν ἐνέγκοι
πλείστην εὐδοξίαν. χαλεπὸν πατρὶ καὶ μητρὶ παίδων στερηθῆναι καὶ ἐρήμοις εἶναι τῶν οἰκειοτάτων
γηροτρόφων· σεμνὸν δέ γ᾽ ἀγήρως τιμὰς καὶ μνήμην ἀρετῆς δημοσίᾳ κτησαμένους ἐπιδεῖν, καὶ
37 θυσιῶν καὶ ἀγώνων ἠξιωμένους ἀθανάτων. λυπη-
ρὸν παισὶν ὀρφανοῖς γεγενῆσθαι πατρός· καλὸν δέ
γε κληρονομεῖν πατρῴας εὐδοξίας. καὶ τοῦ μὲν
λυπηροῦ τούτου τὸν δαίμον᾽ αἴτιον εὑρήσομεν ὄντα,
ᾧ φύντας ἀνθρώπους εἴκειν ἀνάγκη, τοῦ δὲ τιμίου

rank as the brave men who have preceded them in the islands of the blest. For though no man has been there to see or brought back this report concerning them, yet those whom the living have assumed to be worthy of honours in the world above, these we believe, taking for oracle our own opinion, receive the same honours also in the world beyond.[a]

While it is perhaps difficult[b] to mitigate the present 35 misfortunes by the spoken word, nevertheless it is our duty to endeavour to turn our minds to comforting thoughts, reflecting that it is a beautiful thing for parents who have begotten men like these, and themselves were born of others like unto them, to be seen enduring their affliction more decorously than the rest of mankind, and, no matter what fortune befalls, to be like them ; for to the departed such 36 conduct would seem most becoming in you and honourable to them, and to the whole State and to the living it would bring the greatest glory.[c] It is a grievous thing for fathers and mothers to be deprived of their children and in their old age to lack the care of those who are nearest and dearest to them. Yes, but it is a proud privilege to behold them possessors of deathless honours and a memorial of their valour erected by the State, and deemed deserving of sacrifices and games for all future time. It is 37 painful for children to be orphaned of a father. Yes, but it is a beautiful thing to be the heir of a father's fame. And of this pain we shall find the deity to be the cause, to whom mortal creatures must yield, but

[a] A similar sentiment is found in Hyper. 43.
[b] Blass compares Hyper. 41 χαλεπὸν μὲν ἴσως ἐστί.
[c] This topic is treated at greater length in the *Menex.* 247 D—248 C.

καὶ καλοῦ τὴν τῶν ἐθελησάντων καλῶς ἀποθνήσκειν αἵρεσιν.

Ἐγὼ μὲν οὖν οὐχ ὅπως πολλὰ λέξω, τοῦτ' ἐσκεψάμην, ἀλλ' ὅπως τἀληθῆ. ὑμεῖς δ' ἀποδυράμενοι καὶ τὰ προσήκονθ' ὡς χρὴ καὶ νόμιμα ποιήσαντες ἄπιτε.

of the glory and honour the source is found in the choice of those who willed to die nobly.

As for myself, it has not been my concern how I might make a long speech, but how I might speak the truth. And now do you, having spent your grief and done your part as law and custom require, disperse to your homes.

THE EROTIC ESSAY

INTRODUCTION

In the life and literature of Greece during the classical period there was scant toleration for romantic love as understood by modern races of the western world. The emotions and sentiments that are nowadays assigned to the realm of romance were then associated with attachments between people of the same sex, an ugly consequence of the segregation of men and women in social life and education. Sappho addressed love poems to her girl friends and numberless poets in analogous strains told of the love of man for man.

The hazards of these attachments were reluctantly accepted as facts but never entirely condoned by thoughtful and responsible citizens. Hopeful thinkers essayed to plead for love as an instrument of moral and intellectual uplift. The topic was so entrenched in the popular interest that even Plato discussed it, the *Lysis* being especially illuminating. A series of speeches on the theme is contained in the *Symposium*. A similar work by Xenophon bears this title. In the *Phaedrus* of Plato are found three speeches on love, the first of these being represented as the composition of the orator Lysias. Even Plutarch, later by almost five centuries, produced an erotic essay, which seems modern by comparison.

In the same general class with these writings falls the *Erotic Essay* ascribed to Demosthenes. Blass

joins with ancient and modern critics in declaring it
to be a forgery. He points out that in style it re-
sembles the *Funeral Speech* but is quite unlike any
work of the orator that is known to be genuine. He
finds that the author gives evidence of being familiar
with the *Phaedrus* and he cites numerous resemblances
to the writings of Isocrates. As in the case of the
Funeral Speech these parallels do not prove to be
impressive upon close examination. On the other
hand, their presence allows the reader to assume that
the composition belongs to the time of Demosthenes
and even Blass concedes that the idiom of the piece
is free from offence. It will be justifiable, therefore,
to refrain from hasty condemnation and to leave the
verdict open. The history of literature is not without
its surprises and paradoxes.

The style, as in the case of the *Funeral Speech*, is
epideictic. This means that the writer aims to
awaken admiration rather than to produce conviction.
He feels at liberty to resort to figurative language
such as would be out of place in forensic or deliberative oratory. In order that his sentences may run
with smoothness when read aloud he will avoid vowel
terminations before initial vowels in following words,
though the commoner monosyllables may be excep-
tions to this rule. Occasionally he may employ
rhythmical clausulae and these in turn may balance
one another with or without antithesis of meaning.
In the footnotes attention will be called to some
examples of these features of the style.

There is a brief discussion by Blass, vii. pp. 406-408.
A commentary will be found in Dindorf's *Demosthenes*
vii. pp. 1413-1425.

LXI

ΕΡΩΤΙΚΟΣ

'Αλλ' ἐπειδήπερ ἀκούειν βούλει τοῦ λόγου, δείξω
σοι καὶ ἀναγνώσομαι. δεῖ δέ σε τὴν προαίρεσιν
αὐτοῦ πρῶτον εἰδέναι. βούλεται μὲν γὰρ ὁ τὸν
λόγον ποιῶν ἐπαινεῖν 'Επικράτην, ὃν ᾤετο πολλῶν
καὶ καλῶν κἀγαθῶν ὄντων νέων ἐν τῇ πόλει χαριέ-
στατον εἶναι, καὶ πλέον τῇ συνέσει προέχειν ἢ τῷ
κάλλει τῶν ἡλικιωτῶν. ὁρῶν δ' ὡς ἔπος εἰπεῖν
τὰ πλεῖστα τῶν ἐρωτικῶν συνταγμάτων αἰσχύνην
μᾶλλον ἢ τιμὴν περιάπτοντα τούτοις περὶ ὧν ἐστι
γεγραμμένα, τοῦθ' ὅπως μὴ πείσεται πεφύλακται,
καὶ ὅπερ καὶ πεπεῖσθαί φησι τῇ γνώμῃ, τοῦτο καὶ
γέγραφεν, ὡς δίκαιος ἐραστὴς οὔτ' ἂν ποιήσειεν
2 οὐδὲν αἰσχρὸν οὔτ' ἀξιώσειεν. ὁ μὲν οὖν ὥσπερ
εἰ μάλιστ' ἂν ἐρωτικὸν λάβοις τοῦ λόγου, περὶ
τοῦτ' ἔστιν· ὁ δ' ἄλλος λόγος τὰ μὲν αὐτὸν ἐπαι-
νεῖ τὸν νεανίσκον, τὰ δ' αὐτῷ συμβουλεύει περὶ
παιδείας τε καὶ προαιρέσεως τοῦ βίου. πάντα δὲ
ταῦτα γέγραπται τὸν τρόπον ὅν τις ἂν εἰς βιβλίον
καταθεῖτο. τοῖς μὲν γὰρ λεκτικοῖς τῶν λόγων

---

[a] It was at the house of a certain Epicrates that Lysias was
supposed to have delivered his love-speech : Plato, *Phaedrus*
227 B.

[b] This topic is treated by Cicero, *De Amic.* xii.

[c] The author plainly hints at a threefold partition of his

LXI

THE EROTIC ESSAY

WELL, since you wish to hear the essay, I shall bring it out and read it aloud ; but first you must understand its purpose. The writer's desire is to praise Epicrates,[a] whom he thought to be the most charming young man in the city, although there were many fine gentlemen among those of his own age, and to surpass them even more in understanding than in beauty of person. Observing also that, generally speaking, most erotic compositions attach shame rather than honour to those about whom they are written, he has taken precautions that this should not happen in his case, and has written only what he says he is convinced of by his judgement, believing that an honest lover would neither do anything shameful nor request it.[b]   Now, 2 that part of my essay which you may find to be the most erotic, so to speak, is on this topic, but the rest of it in part praises the lad himself and in part counsels him about his education and his design for living.[c] The whole essay is written as one would put it into a book, because discourses intended to be delivered

theme : the erotic part, §§ 3-9, eulogy, §§ 10-32, and the protrepticus, §§ 36-55.   Blass sees a twofold division only, eulogy and protrepticus. In either case the remaining sections serve as introduction, transition and epilogue. Exhortations to the study of philosophy were called "protreptics."

DEMOSTHENES

ἁπλῶς καὶ ὁμοίως οἷς ἂν ἐκ τοῦ παραχρῆμά τις
εἴποι πρέπει γεγράφθαι, τοῖς δ' εἰς τὸν πλείω
χρόνον τεθησομένοις ποιητικῶς καὶ περιττῶς ἁρ-
μόττει συγκεῖσθαι· τοὺς μὲν γὰρ πιθανούς, τοὺς δ'
ἐπιδεικτικοὺς εἶναι προσήκει. ἵν' οὖν μὴ παρὰ τὸν
λόγον σοι λέγω μηδ' ἃ γιγνώσκω περὶ τούτων
[1402] αὐτὸς διεξίω, πρόσεχ' ὡς αὐτοῦ τοῦ λόγου ἤδη
ἀκουσόμενος, ἐπειδὴ καὶ αὐτὸς ἥκει, ὃν ἐβουλήθην
ἀκούειν, Ἐπικράτης.

3   Ὁρῶν ἐνίους τῶν ἐρωμένων καὶ κάλλους μετ-
εσχηκότων οὐδετέρᾳ τῶν εὐτυχιῶν τούτων ὀρθῶς
χρωμένους, ἀλλ' ἐπὶ μὲν τῇ τῆς ὄψεως εὐπρεπείᾳ
σεμνυνομένους, τὴν δὲ πρὸς τοὺς ἐραστὰς ὁμιλίαν
δυσχεραίνοντας, καὶ τοσοῦτον διημαρτηκότας τοῦ
τὰ βέλτιστα κρίνειν, ὥστε διὰ τοὺς λυμαινομένους
τῷ πράγματι καὶ πρὸς τοὺς μετὰ σωφροσύνης
πλησιάζειν ἀξιοῦντας δυσκόλως διακειμένους, ἡγησάμην τοὺς μὲν τοιούτους οὐ μόνον αὐτοῖς ἀλυ-
σιτελῶς ἔχειν, ἀλλὰ καὶ τοῖς ἄλλοις μοχθηρὰς
4 συνηθείας ἐνεργάζεσθαι, τοῖς δὲ καλῶς φρονοῦσιν
οὐκ ἐπακολουθητέον εἶναι τῇ τούτων ἀπονοίᾳ,
μάλιστα μὲν ἐνθυμουμένοις, ὅτι τῶν πραγμάτων
οὔτε καλῶν οὔτ' αἰσχρῶν ἀποτόμως ὄντων, ἀλλὰ
παρὰ τοὺς χρωμένους τὸ πλεῖστον διαλλαττόντων,
ἄλογον μιᾷ γνώμῃ περὶ ἀμφοτέρων χρῆσθαι, ἔπειθ'

---

[a] There is a reference to these two styles in Isocr. *Panegyr.*
11, as Blass notes.   The epideictic is akin to poetry in the use
of figures of speech (see § 11) ; the reference of " ornately "
is chiefly to rhythm.   In both the *Funeral Speech* and the
Erotic Essay there is careful avoidance of hiatus ; rhyth-

44

ought to be written simply and just as one might speak offhand, while those of the other kind, which are planned to last longer, are properly composed in the manner of poetry and ornately.[a] For it is the function of the former to win converts and of the latter to display one's skill. Accordingly, to avoid spoiling the essay for you or rehearsing my own opinions about these questions, I ask you to lend your attention, since you are immediately going to hear the essay itself, because Epicrates is also at hand, whom I wished to hear it.

Observing that certain of those who are loved and 3 possess their share of good looks make the right use of neither one of these blessings, but put on grand airs because of the comeliness of their appearance and exhibit reluctance to associate with their admirers,[b] and so far fail in judging what is best that, because of those who pervert the thing, they assume a surly attitude toward those also who desire to associate with them from pure motives, I concluded that such young men not only defeat their own interests but also engender evil habits in the rest, and that the 4 high-minded should not follow their foolish example, bearing in mind particularly that, since actions are not absolutely either honourable or shameful but for the most part vary according to the persons concerned,[c] it is unreasonable to adopt the same attitude toward both classes of men, and secondly,

mical clausulae are not infrequent; Gorgianic parallel clausulae occur (§ 32).
[b] The Greek word means "lover" or "sweetheart," applied to men as well as women.
[c] The same distinction is made in synonymous terms, Isocr. *Archid.* 60.

DEMOSTHENES

ὅτι πάντων ἀτοπώτατόν ἐστι, ζηλοῦν μὲν τοὺς
πλείστους φίλους καὶ βεβαιοτάτους ἔχοντας, ἀπο-
δοκιμάζειν δὲ τοὺς ἐραστάς, ὃ μόνον ἴδιον ἔθνος
οὐχ ἅπασιν ἀλλὰ τοῖς καλοῖς καὶ σώφροσιν οἰ-
κειοῦσθαι πέφυκεν.

5 Ἔτι δὲ τοῖς μὲν μηδεμίαν πω τοιαύτην φιλίαν
ἑορακόσι καλῶς ἀποβᾶσαν, ἢ σφόδρα κατεγνωκόσιν
αὑτῶν ὡς οὐκ ἂν δυνηθεῖεν σωφρόνως τοῖς ἐντυγ-
χάνουσιν ὁμιλεῖν, ἴσως οὐκ ἄλογον ταύτην ἔχειν τὴν
διάνοιαν· τοῖς δ' ὥσπερ σὺ διακειμένοις, καὶ μήτε
παντάπασιν ἀνηκόοις οὖσιν ὅσαι δὴ χρεῖαι δι' ἔρω-
[1403] τος χωρὶς αἰσχύνης ηὐξήθησαν, καὶ μετὰ τῆς
ἀκριβεστάτης εὐλαβείας τὸν ἄλλον χρόνον βεβιωκό-
σιν, οὐδ' ὑποψίαν ἔχειν εὔλογον ὡς ἄν τι πράξειαν
6 αἰσχρόν. διὸ δὴ καὶ μᾶλλον ἐπήρθην τοῦτον γράψαι
τὸν λόγον, ἡγούμενος δυοῖν τοῖν καλλίστοιν οὐ
διαμαρτήσεσθαι. τὰ μὲν γὰρ ὑπάρχοντά σοι ἀγαθὰ
διελθών, ἅμα σέ τε ζηλωτὸν καὶ ἐμαυτὸν οὐκ
ἀνόητον ἐπιδείξειν ἐλπίζω, εἴ σε τοιοῦτον ὄντ'
ἀγαπῶ· συμβουλεύσας δ' ἃ μάλιστα κατεπείγει,
νομίζω τῆς μὲν εὐνοίας τῆς ἐμῆς δεῖγμα, τῆς δὲ
κοινῆς φιλίας ἀφορμὴν ἀμφοτέροις εἰσοίσειν.

7 Καίτοι μ' οὐ λέληθεν, ὅτι χαλεπὸν μέν ἐστι καὶ
τὴν σὴν φύσιν ἀξίως τῶν ὑπαρχόντων διελθεῖν, ἔτι
δ' ἐπικινδυνότερον τὸ συμβουλεύειν μέλλονθ' αὑτὸν
ὑπεύθυνον τῷ πεισθέντι καταστῆσαι. ἀλλὰ νομίζω
τοῖς μὲν δικαίως ἐγκωμίων τυγχάνουσι περι-

ᵃ He means the prejudice against any compromise with
associations that might lead to homosexuality, variously
known as boy-love, Greek love or Doric love.

46

that it is the height of absurdity to envy those who have a host of firm friends but to repulse their admirers, who are a separate group and alone feel drawn by nature, not toward all, but only to the beautiful and modest.

Moreover, although those who have never yet seen 5 such a friendship turn out well or have severely condemned themselves on the ground that they would be incapable of associating innocently with casual acquaintances, it is perhaps not unreasonable to entertain this prejudice [a]; but for those so disposed as yourself, who have not utterly refused to hear how very many benefits accrue through love without shame and have lived the rest of their lives with the utmost circumspection, it is not reasonable to have even a suspicion that they would do anything shameful. Consequently I have felt all the more 6 moved to write this essay, feeling sure I should not fail to secure two most honourable rewards.[b] For when I have described the good qualities you possess, I hope that at one and the same time I shall prove you to be worthy of admiration and myself not senseless if I love you, being what you are ; and secondly, in tendering the advice that is most urgently needed I believe I shall present proof of my own goodwill and furnish a basis for our mutual friendship.

And yet it does not escape me that it is difficult to 7 describe your character in keeping with your deserts and that it is more hazardous still to give advice when the adviser is bound to make himself answerable for his advice to the one who accepts it.[c] It is my judgement, however, that, while it becomes the recipients

[b] The use of the dual savours of poetry.
[c] Blass notes a parallel in XVIII. 189, but it is remote.

γενέσθαι τῆς τῶν ἐπαινούντων δυνάμεως προσήκειν
τῇ τῆς ἀληθείας ὑπερβολῇ, τῆς δὲ συμβουλῆς οὐ
διαμαρτήσεσθαι, συνειδὼς ὅτι διὰ μὲν ἀνοήτων
καὶ παντελῶς ὑπ᾽ ἀκρασίας διεφθαρμένων οὐδὲ
τῶν καθ᾽ ὑπερβολὴν ὀρθῶς βουλευθέντων οὐδὲν
ἂν καλῶς ἐξενεχθείη, διὰ δὲ τῶν σωφρόνως καὶ
καθαρῶς ζῆν αἱρουμένων οὐδὲ τὰ μετρίως ἐσκεμ-
μένα διαμαρτάνεσθαι πέφυκεν.

8   Τὰς μὲν οὖν ἐλπίδας ἔχων τοιαύτας ἐγχειρῶ τῷ
λόγῳ· ἡγοῦμαι δὲ πάντας ἂν ὁμολογῆσαί μοι, τοῖς
τηλικούτοις μάλιστα κατεπείγειν κάλλος μὲν ἐπὶ
τῆς ὄψεως, σωφροσύνην δ᾽ ἐπὶ τῆς ψυχῆς, ἀνδρείαν
δ᾽ ἐπ᾽ ἀμφοτέρων τούτων, χάριν δ᾽ ἐπὶ τῶν λόγων
διατελεῖν ἔχουσιν. ὧν τὰ μὲν τῆς φύσεως οὕτω
καλῶς ἡ τύχη σοι παραδέδωκεν ὥστε περίβλεπτον
[1404] καὶ θαυμαζόμενον διατελεῖν, τὰ δ᾽ αὐτὸς παρὰ τὴν
ἐπιμέλειαν εἰς τοῦτο προάγων[1] ἥκεις ὥστε μηδέν᾽
9 ἄν σοι τῶν εὖ φρονούντων ἐπιτιμῆσαι. καίτοι τί
χρὴ τὸν τῶν μεγίστων ἐπαίνων ἄξιον; οὐχ ὑπὸ
μὲν τῶν θεῶν ἠγαπημένον φαίνεσθαι, παρὰ δὲ τοῖς
ἀνθρώποις τὰ μὲν δι᾽ αὑτόν, τὰ δὲ διὰ τὴν τύχην
θαυμάζεσθαι; καθ᾽ ὅλου μὲν τοίνυν τῶν ὑπαρχόντων σοι πρὸς ἀρετὴν ἴσως ὕστερον ἁρμόσει τὰ
πλείω διελθεῖν· ἃ δ᾽ ἑκάστου τούτων ἐγκώμι᾽ εἰπεῖν
ἔχω, ταῦτα δηλῶσαι πειράσομαι μετ᾽ ἀληθείας.

10   Ἄρξομαι δὲ πρῶτον ἐπαινεῖν, ὅπερ πρῶτον ἰδοῦσιν ἅπασιν ἔστι γνῶναί σου, τὸ κάλλος, καὶ τούτου

[1] προαγαγὼν Blass et al.

48

of merited eulogies to baffle by the excess of their real virtue the ability of those who praise them, yet in my counsel I shall not miss the mark, being well aware that no advice could be innocently carried out if proffered by men who are senseless and quite ruined by incontinence, not even if they advise supremely well, but that not even the advice that is only moderately pondered can altogether miss the mark if tendered by men who choose to live pure and self-disciplined lives.

Cherishing such hopes I enter upon my theme. All 8 men would agree with me, I believe, that it is of the utmost importance for young men of your age to possess beauty in respect of person, self-discipline in respect of soul, and manliness in respect of both, and consistently to possess charm in respect of speech. As for these two kinds of qualities, natural and acquired, Fortune has so generously blessed you with nature's gifts that you consistently enjoy distinction and admiration, and the other kind you are bringing to such perfection through your own diligence that no fair-minded person could have fault to find with you. And yet what ought he to possess who is 9 worthy of the highest eulogies? [a] Must he not manifestly be loved by the gods and among men be admired, for some qualities on his own account, for others because of his good fortune? Now the longer list of your virtuous qualities it will perhaps be fitting to describe summarily later on, but the praise I have to utter for each of the gifts of Fortune I shall now try to declare with truthfulness.

I shall begin by praising that quality of yours which 10 all who see you will recognize first, your beauty, and

[a] These identical words are found in Isocr. *De Bigis* 30.

τὸ χρῶμα, δι' οὗ καὶ τὰ μέλη καὶ ὅλον τὸ σῶμα
φαίνεται. ᾧ τίν' ἁρμόττουσαν εἰκόν' ἐνέγκω σκοπῶν οὐχ ὁρῶ, ἀλλὰ παρίσταταί μοι δεῖσθαι τῶν
ἀναγνόντων τόνδε τὸν λόγον σὲ θεωρῆσαι καὶ ἰδεῖν,
ἵνα συγγνώμης τύχω μηδὲν ὅμοιον ἔχων εἰπεῖν.
11 τῷ γὰρ ἂν εἰκάσειέ τις, ὃ θνητὸν ὂν ἀθάνατον τοῖς
ἰδοῦσιν ἐργάζεται πόθον, καὶ ὁρώμενον οὐκ ἀπο-
πληροῖ, καὶ μεταστὰν μνημονεύεται, καὶ τὴν τῶν
θεῶν ἀξίαν ἐπ' ἀνθρώπου φύσιν ἔχει, πρὸς μὲν τὴν
εὐπρέπειαν ἀνθηρόν, πρὸς δὲ τὰς αἰτίας ἀνυπονόη-
τον; ἀλλὰ μὴν οὐδὲ ταῦτ' ἔστιν αἰτιάσασθαι πρὸς
τὴν σὴν ὄψιν, ἃ πολλοῖς ἤδη συνέπεσε τῶν κάλλους
12 μετασχόντων. ἢ γὰρ δι' ἀρρυθμίαν τοῦ σχήματος
ἅπασαν συνετάραξαν τὴν ὑπάρχουσαν εὐπρέπειαν,
ἢ δι' ἀτύχημά τι καὶ τὰ καλῶς πεφυκότα συνδι-
έβαλον αὐτῷ. ὧν οὐδενὶ τὴν σὴν ὄψιν εὕροιμεν ἂν
[1405] ἔνοχον γεγενημένην· οὕτω γὰρ σφόδρ' ἐφυλάξατο
πάσας τὰς τοιαύτας κῆρας ὅστις ποτ' ἦν θεῶν ὁ
τῆς σῆς ὄψεως προνοηθείς, ὥστε μηδὲν μέμψεως
ἄξιον, τὰ δὲ πλεῖστα περίβλεπτά σου καταστῆσαι.
13 καὶ μὲν δὴ καὶ τῶν ὁρωμένων ἐπιφανεστάτου μὲν
ὄντος τοῦ προσώπου, τούτου δ' αὐτοῦ τῶν ὀμ-
μάτων, ἔτι μᾶλλον ἐν τούτοις ἐπεδείξατο τὴν
εὔνοιαν ἣν εἶχεν εἰς σὲ τὸ δαιμόνιον. οὐ γὰρ μόνον
πρὸς τὸ τὰ κατεπείγονθ' ὁρᾶν αὐτάρκη παρέσχηται,
ἀλλ' ἐνίων οὐδ' ἐκ τῶν πραττομένων γιγνωσκο-
μένης τῆς ἀρετῆς, σοῦ διὰ τῶν τῆς ὄψεως σημείων
τὰ κάλλιστα τῶν ἠθῶν ἐνεφάνισε, πρᾶον μὲν καὶ
φιλάνθρωπον τοῖς ὁρῶσι, μεγαλοπρεπῆ δὲ καὶ

the hue of your flesh, by virtue of which your limbs and your whole body are rendered resplendent. Wondering what fitting comparison for this I may offer, I find none, but it is my privilege to request those who read this essay to see you and contemplate you, so that I may be pardoned for declaring that I have no suitable simile. For to what could any- 11 one liken something mortal which arouses immortal longing in the beholder, the sight of which does not satiate, and when removed from sight lingers in the memory, which in human form possesses a natural beauty worthy of the gods, like a flower in its comeliness, beyond suspicion of imperfections? Furthermore, it is impossible to impute to your person even those blemishes which in the past have marred many another who has shared in beauty. For either through 12 ungainliness of mien they have ruined all their natural comeliness or through some unfortunate mannerism have involved their natural attractions in the same disfavour. By none of these could we find your person afflicted, for whichever of the gods it was that took forethought for your person has so diligently guarded you against all such mishaps as to leave nothing calling for criticism and to render your general appearance superb. Moreover, since the face is the most con- 13 spicuous of the parts that are seen, and of the face itself the eyes, even more in these did the god reveal the goodwill that he had toward you. For he not only furnished you with eyes adequate to perform the necessary functions but, although the virtue of some men is not recognized even from their actions, of your character he has placed in a clear light the fine qualities through the evidence of your glance, displaying it as gentle and kind toward those who look at

51

σεμνὸν τοῖς ὁμιλοῦσιν, ἀνδρεῖον δὲ καὶ σώφρονα
πᾶσιν ἐπιδείξας.

14 Ὃ καὶ μάλιστ' ἄν τις θαυμάσειεν· τῶν γὰρ ἄλλων
ἐπὶ μὲν τῆς πραότητος ταπεινῶν, ἐπὶ δὲ τῆς σεμνό-
τητος αὐθαδῶν ὑπολαμβανομένων, καὶ διὰ μὲν
τὴν ἀνδρείαν θρασυτέρων, διὰ δὲ τὴν ἡσυχίαν ἀβελ-
τέρων εἶναι δοκούντων, τοσαύτας ὑπεναντιώσεις
πρὸς ἄλληλα λαβοῦσ' ἡ τύχη πρὸς τὸ δέον ἅπανθ'
ὁμολογούμεν' ἀπέδωκεν, ὥσπερ εὐχὴν ἐπιτελοῦσα,
ἢ παράδειγμα τοῖς ἄλλοις ὑποδεῖξαι βουληθεῖσα,
ἀλλ' οὐ θνητήν, ὡς εἴθιστο, φύσιν συνιστᾶσα.

15 Εἰ μὲν οὖν οἷόν τ' ἦν ἐφικέσθαι τῷ λόγῳ τοῦ
κάλλους τοῦ σοῦ, ἢ τοῦτ' ἦν μόνον τῶν σῶν ἀξι-
έπαινον, οὐδὲν ἂν παραλιπεῖν ᾠόμεθα δεῖν ἐπαινοῦντες τῶν προσόντων σοι· νῦν δὲ δέδοικα μὴ πρός
τε τὰ λοίπ' ἀπειρηκόσι χρησώμεθα τοῖς ἀκροαταῖς,

16 καὶ περὶ τούτου μάτην τερθρευώμεθα. πῶς γὰρ
ἄν τις ὑπερβάλοι τῷ λόγῳ τὴν σὴν ὄψιν, ἧς μηδ' ἃ
τέχνη πεποίηται τῶν ἔργων τοῖς ἀρίστοις δημι-
ουργοῖς δύναται ὑπερτεῖναι; καὶ θαυμαστὸν οὐδέν·
τὰ μὲν γὰρ ἀκίνητον ἔχει τὴν θεωρίαν, ὥστ' ἄδηλον
εἶναι τί ποτ' ἂν ψυχῆς μετασχόντα φανείη, σοῦ δὲ
τὸ τῆς γνώμης ἦθος ἐν πᾶσιν οἷς ποιεῖς μεγάλην
εὐπρέπειαν ἐπαυξάνει τῷ σώματι. περὶ μὲν οὖν
τοῦ κάλλους πολλὰ παραλιπών, τοσαῦτ' ἐπαινέσαι
ἔχω.

17 Περὶ δὲ τῆς σωφροσύνης κάλλιστον μὲν τοῦτ'
ἔχοιμ' ἂν εἰπεῖν, ὅτι τῆς ἡλικίας τῆς τοιαύτης
εὐδιαβόλως ἐχούσης, σοὶ μᾶλλον ἐπαινεῖσθαι συμ-

you, dignified and serious toward those who converse with you, manly and proper to all men.

And here is a matter that may be particularly sur- 14 prising. For while other men are assumed to be mean-spirited because they are gentle and to be arrogant because they are dignified, and are thought overbearing because they are manly, and stupid because they keep quiet, Fortune in your case has taken qualities so mutually contradictory and caused them all to be properly harmonized, as if fulfilling a prayer or wishing to set an example for others, but not framing a mere mortal nature, as was her usual way.

Now if it were possible to do justice to such beauty 15 as yours in words, or if this were the only quality of yours worthy of praise, we should think it necessary to omit praise of none of your good points ; but as things are, I am afraid that we may find our hearers refusing to hear praise of your other merits and that we may defeat ourselves by harping on this theme. For how could anyone overdo the verbal description 16 of your appearance, since not even works of art executed by the skill of the best masters could do more than justice to it ? Nor is this astonishing ; for works of art have a motionless aspect, so that it is uncertain what they would look like if they possessed life, but your personality enhances in your every action the superb comeliness of your body. Only this much, therefore, I have to say in praise of your beauty, omitting a great deal.

As for discreetness of conduct, it is my privilege to 17 pass the finest of compliments, namely, that though such youthfulness readily invites scandal, it has been your lot to be praised instead. For so far from over-

βέβηκεν. οὐ γὰρ μόνον οὐδὲν ἐξαμαρτάνειν, ἀλλὰ
καὶ φρονιμώτερον ἢ κατὰ τὴν ὥραν ζῆν προῄρησαι.
καὶ τούτου μέγιστον τεκμήριον ἡ πρὸς τοὺς ἀνθρώπους ὁμιλία· πολλῶν γὰρ ἐντυγχανόντων σοι
καὶ παντοδαπὰς φύσεις ἐχόντων, ἔτι δὲ προσαγο-
μένων ἁπάντων ἐπὶ τὰς ἑαυτῶν συνηθείας, οὕτω
καλῶς προέστης τῶν τοιούτων ὥστε πάντας τὴν
18 πρὸς σὲ φιλίαν ἠγαπηκότας ἔχειν. ὃ σημεῖον τῶν
ἐνδόξως καὶ φιλανθρώπως ζῆν προαιρουμένων
ἐστίν. καίτοι τινὲς ηὐδοκίμησαν ἤδη τῶν τε συμ-
βουλευσάντων ὡς οὐ χρὴ τὰς τῶν τυχόντων ὁμιλίας
προσδέχεσθαι, καὶ τῶν πεισθέντων τούτοις· ἢ γὰρ
πρὸς χάριν ὁμιλοῦντα τοῖς φαύλοις ἀναγκαῖον
εἶναι διαβάλλεσθαι παρὰ τοῖς πολλοῖς, ἢ διευλαβού-
μενον τὰς τοιαύτας ἐπιπλήξεις ὑπ' αὐτῶν τῶν
19 ἐντυγχανόντων δυσχεραίνεσθαι συμπίπτειν. ἐγὼ
δὲ διὰ τοῦτο καὶ μᾶλλον οἶμαί σε δεῖν ἐγκωμιάζειν,
ὅτι τῶν ἄλλων ἕν τι τῶν ἀδυνάτων οἰομένων εἶναι
[1407] τὸ τοῖς ἁπάντων τρόποις ἀρέσκειν, σὺ τοσοῦτο
τούτων διήνεγκας ὥστε τῶν χαλεπῶν καὶ δυσκόλων
ἁπάντων περιγεγενῆσθαι, τοῦ μὲν συνεξαμαρτάνειν
τισὶν οὐδ' ὑποψίαν ἐνδοὺς τοῖς ἄλλοις, τῆς δὲ πρὸς
αὐτοὺς δυσχερείας τῇ τῶν τρόπων εὐαρμοστίᾳ
κρατήσας.

20 Πρὸς τοίνυν τοὺς ἐραστάς, εἰ χρὴ καὶ περὶ τούτων εἰπεῖν, οὕτω καλῶς μοι δοκεῖς καὶ σωφρόνως
ὁμιλεῖν, ὥστε τῶν πλείστων οὐδ' ὃν ἂν προέλωνται
μετρίως ἐνεγκεῖν δυναμένων, σοὶ πᾶσι καθ' ὑπερβολὴν ἀρέσκειν συμβέβηκεν. ὃ τῆς σῆς ἀρετῆς

stepping the mark, you have chosen to live more prudently than is expected of your years. Of this the most convincing evidence is your deportment toward others ; for although many make your acquaintance, and reveal characters of every kind and sort, and all seek to entice you into intimacies, you have so managed such people that all are content to feel friendship for you. This is an index of those 18 whose choice it is to live in the esteem and affection of men. And yet some men in the past have been well thought of who have advised against welcoming the company of all comers, as is also true of some who have taken their advice. For they claim that it is necessary either to humour low-minded people and so be maligned among the multitude, or else to be constantly on guard against such reproaches and so incur the dislike of such acquaintances themselves. Personally I think you deserve to be eulogized all 19 the more for this reason, that, while the other lads think it one of the impossible things to please men of every type,[a] you have so surpassed these as to have risen superior to all the difficult and troublesome people, allowing the others no reason even for suspecting immoral relations with any and overcoming your annoyance with them by the adaptability of your manners.

Now touching your admirers, if it is right to speak 20 also of these, you seem to me to deport yourself so admirably and sensibly toward them, that, though most of them cannot be patient even with the object of their preference, you succeed in pleasing them all exceedingly. And this is a most unmistakable proof

[a] Blass calls attention to this same thought in *Epist.* iii. 27, but Theognis 23-26 shows it to be an ancient commonplace.

σημεῖον ἐναργέστατόν ἐστιν. ὧν μὲν γὰρ δίκαιον
καὶ καλόν, οὐδεὶς ἄμοιρος αὐτῶν παρὰ σοῦ καθ-
έστηκεν· ἃ δ' εἰς αἰσχύνην ἥκει, τούτων οὐδ' εἰς
ἐλπίδ' οὐδεὶς ἔρχεται· τοσαύτην τοῖς μὲν τῶν
βελτίστων ὀρεγομένοις ἐξουσίαν, τοῖς δ' ἀποθρα-
σύνεσθαι βουλομένοις ἀτολμίαν ἡ σὴ σωφροσύνη
21 παρεσκεύακεν. ἔτι τοίνυν τῶν πλείστων ἐκ τῆς
σιωπῆς ὅταν ὦσι νέοι, τὴν τῆς σωφροσύνης δόξαν
θηρωμένων, σὺ τοσοῦτον τῇ φύσει διενήνοχας ὥστ'
ἐξ ὧν λέγεις καὶ ὁμιλεῖς τοῖς ἐντυγχάνουσι μηδὲν
ἐλάττω τὴν περὶ σεαυτὸν εὐδοξίαν ἢ διὰ πάντα τὰ
λοιπὰ πεποιῆσθαι· τοσαύτη πειθὼ καὶ χάρις καὶ
ἐν οἷς σπουδάζεις ἐστί σου καὶ ἐν οἷς παίζεις. καὶ
γὰρ εὐήθης ἀναμαρτήτως, καὶ δεινὸς οὐ κακοήθως,
καὶ φιλάνθρωπος ἐλευθερίως, καὶ τὸ σύνολον τοιοῦτος εἶ, οἷος ἂν ἐξ Ἀρετῆς υἱὸς Ἔρωτι γένοιτο.
22 Τὴν τοίνυν ἀνδρείαν—οὐδὲ γὰρ τοῦτ' ἄξιόν ἐστι
παραλιπεῖν, οὐχ ὡς οὐ πολλὴν ἐπίδοσιν ἐχούσης ἔτι
τῆς σῆς φύσεως, καὶ τοῦ μέλλοντος χρόνου πλείους
ἀφορμὰς παραδώσοντος λόγων τοῖς ἐπαινεῖν σε
[1408] βουλομένοις, ἀλλ' ὡς καλλίστων ὄντων τῶν μετὰ
ταύτης τῆς ἡλικίας ἐπαίνων, ἐν ᾗ τὸ μηδὲν ἐξαμαρτάνειν τοῖς ἄλλοις εὐκτόν ἐστι—σοῦ δ' ἐπὶ πολλῶν
μὲν ἄν τις καὶ ἑτέρων τὴν ἀνδρείαν διέλθοι, μάλιστα
δ' ἐπὶ τῆς ἀσκήσεως, ἧς καὶ πλεῖστοι γεγένηνται
23 μάρτυρες. ἀνάγκη δ' ἴσως πρῶτον εἰπεῖν, ταύτην[1]
τὴν ἀγωνίαν ὡς καλῶς προείλου. τὸ γὰρ ὀρθῶς,
ὅ τι πρακτέον ἐστί, νέον ὄντα δοκιμάσαι, καὶ ψυχῆς
ἀγαθῆς καὶ γνώμης φρονίμου κοινόν ἐστι σημεῖον·

[1] αὐτὴν Blass.

---

[a] This is the language of poetry as predicted in § 2.

of your goodness ; for not one finds himself disappointed of favours from you which it is just and fair to ask, but no one is permitted even to hope for such liberties as lead to shame. So great is the latitude your discreetness permits to those who have the best intentions ; so great is the discouragement it presents to those who would fling off restraint. Furthermore, 21 while the majority of men, when young, seek a reputation for prudence by keeping silent, you are so superior to them in natural gifts that you gain men's good opinion of you not less by your speech and demeanour in casual company than by all your other merits ; so great is the grace and charm of your words whether in jest or in earnest. For you are ingenuous without any mistakes, clever without being malicious, kindly without sacrifice of independence, and, taking all in all, like a child of Virtue sired by Love.[a]

Turning now to courage—for it will not do to omit 22 this either, not because I would intimate that your character does not still admit of great development nor that the future will fail to furnish richer material for eulogy to those who wish to praise you, but rather that words of praise mean most at your age when to do no wrong is the best hope for other lads— your courage a man might extol on many other grounds but especially because of your training for athletic sports, of which you have a multitude of witnesses. And perhaps it is in place first to say that 23 you have done well in choosing this kind of contest. For to judge rightly when one is young what line of action one should pursue [b] is the token of an honest

[b] Blass notes a similarity in the *Funeral Speech* 17 ; not impressive.

δι' ὧν οὐδέτερον παραλιπεῖν ἄξιον τὸν τῆς προαιρέσεως ἔπαινον.

Συνειδὼς τοίνυν τῶν μὲν ἄλλων ἀθλημάτων καὶ δούλους καὶ ξένους μετέχοντας, τοῦ δ' ἀποβαίνειν μόνοις μὲν τοῖς πολίταις ἐξουσίαν οὖσαν, ἐφιεμένους δὲ τοὺς βελτίστους, οὕτως ἐπὶ τοῦτον τὸν 24 ἀγῶν' ὥρμησας. ἔτι δὲ κρίνων τοὺς μὲν τὰ δρομικὰ γυμναζομένους οὐδὲν πρὸς ἀνδρείαν οὐδ' εὐψυχίαν ἐπιδιδόναι, τοὺς δὲ τὴν πυγμὴν καὶ τὰ τοιαῦτ' ἀσκήσαντας πρὸς τῷ σώματι καὶ τὴν γνώμην διαφθείρεσθαι, τὸ σεμνότατον καὶ κάλλιστον τῶν ἀγωνισμάτων καὶ μάλιστα πρὸς τὴν σαυτοῦ φύσιν ἁρμόττον ἐξελέξω, τῇ μὲν συνηθείᾳ τῶν ὅπλων καὶ τῇ τῶν δρόμων φιλοπονίᾳ τοῖς ἐν τῷ πολέμῳ συμβαίνουσιν ὡμοιωμένον, τῇ δὲ μεγαλοπρεπείᾳ καὶ τῇ σεμνότητι τῆς παρασκευῆς πρὸς τὴν τῶν 25 θεῶν δύναμιν εἰκασμένον, πρὸς δὲ τούτοις ἡδίστην μὲν θέαν ἔχον, ἐκ πλείστων δὲ καὶ παντοδαπῶν συγκείμενον, μεγίστων δ' ἄθλων ἠξιωμένον· πρὸς γὰρ τοῖς τιθεμένοις τὸ γυμνασθῆναι καὶ μελετῆσαι [1409] τοιαῦτα, οὐ μικρὸν ἆθλον προφανήσεται τοῖς καὶ μετρίως ἀρετῆς ἐφιεμένοις. τεκμήριον δὲ μέγιστον ἄν τις ποιήσαιτο τὴν Ὁμήρου ποίησιν, ἐν ᾗ καὶ τοὺς Ἕλληνας καὶ τοὺς βαρβάρους μετὰ τοιαύτης παρασκευῆς πολεμήσαντας πεποίηκεν ἀλλήλοις· ἔτι

ᵃ The contestants were called " apobates," *desultores, i.e.*
" dismounters." The drivers seem to have dismounted at

soul and of sound judgement alike, and on neither ground would it be right to omit praise of your choice.

You, therefore, being well aware that slaves and aliens share in the other sports but that dismounting is open only to citizens and that the best men aspire to it, have eagerly applied yourself to this sport.[a] Discerning, moreover, that those who train for the foot-races add nothing to their courage nor to their morale either, and that those who practise boxing and the like ruin their minds as well as their bodies, you have singled out the noblest and grandest of competitive exercises and the one most in harmony with your natural gifts, one which approximates to the realities of warfare through the habituation to martial weapons and the laborious effort of running, in the magnificence and majesty of the equipment simulates the might of the gods,[b] presents besides the most delectable spectacle, embraces the largest number and the greatest variety of features and has been deemed worthy of the most valuable prizes. For, apart from those offered, getting the drill and practice in such exercises itself will possess glamour as no paltry prize in the eyes of those who are even moderately ambitious for excellence. The best evidence for this may be found in the poetry of Homer, in which he represents the Greeks and barbarians warring against one another with this equipment.[c]

times and raced with the teams. Dionysius of Halicarn. *Roman Antiq.* vii. 73 ; E. Norman Gardiner, *Greek Athletic Sports and Festivals*, pp. 237-239.

[b] Certain gods were represented as using chariots, particularly Ares and Poseidon.

[c] Homeric warriors employed charioteers, dashed recklessly among the foe to spread dismay, and finally dismounted to engage in single combat : *Iliad* xvi., especially 712-867.

δὲ καὶ νῦν τῶν πόλεων τῶν Ἑλληνίδων οὐ ταῖς
ταπεινοτάταις, ἀλλὰ ταῖς μεγίσταις ἐν τοῖς ἀγῶσι
χρῆσθαι σύνηθές ἐστιν.

26 Ἡ μὲν οὖν προαίρεσις οὕτω καλὴ καὶ παρὰ πᾶσιν
ἀνθρώποις ἠγαπημένη· νομίζων δ' οὐδὲν εἶναι
προὔργου τῶν σπουδαιοτάτων ἐπιθυμεῖν, οὐδὲ
καλῶς πρὸς ἅπαντα πεφυκέναι τὸ σῶμα, μὴ τῆς
ψυχῆς φιλοτίμως παρεσκευασμένης, τὴν μὲν φιλο-
πονίαν εὐθέως ἐν τοῖς γυμνασίοις ἐπιδειξάμενος
οὐδ' ἐν τοῖς ἔργοις ἐψεύσω, τὴν δ' ἄλλην ἐπιφά-
νειαν τῆς σαυτοῦ φύσεως καὶ τὴν τῆς ψυχῆς ἀν-
27 δρείαν ἐν τοῖς ἀγῶσι μάλιστ' ἐνεδείξω. περὶ ὧν
ὀκνῶ μὲν ἄρξασθαι λέγειν, μὴ λειφθῶ τῷ λόγῳ
τῶν τότε γεγενημένων, ὅμως δ' οὐ παραλείψω· καὶ
γὰρ αἰσχρόν, ἃ θεωροῦντας ἡμᾶς εὐφραίνει, ταῦτ'
ἀπαγγεῖλαι μὴ θέλειν.

Ἅπαντας μὲν οὖν εἰ διεξιοίην τοὺς ἀγῶνας, ἴσως
ἂν ἄκαιρον μῆκος ἡμῖν ἐπιγένοιτο τῷ λόγῳ· ἑνὸς δ',
ἐν ᾧ πολὺ διήνεγκας, μνησθεὶς ταῦτά τε δηλώσω
καὶ τῇ τῶν ἀκουόντων δυνάμει συμμετρότερον
28 φανήσομαι χρώμενος. τῶν γὰρ ζευγῶν ἀφεθέντων,
καὶ τῶν μὲν προορμησάντων, τῶν δ' ὑφηνιοχου-
μένων, ἀμφοτέρων περιγενόμενος, ὡς ἑκατέρων
προσῆκε, τὴν νίκην ἔλαβες, τοιούτου στεφάνου
τυχών, ἐφ' ᾧ, καίπερ καλοῦ τοῦ νικᾶν ὄντος, κάλλιον ἐδόκει καὶ παραλογώτερον εἶναι τὸ σωθῆναι.
[1410] φερομένου γὰρ ἐναντίου μέν σοι τοῦ τῶν ἀντιπάλων
ἅρματος, ἁπάντων δ' ἀνυπόστατον οἰομένων εἶναι

---

[a] Athens and Thebes.

[b] Blass notes the expression of a similar fear in the *Funeral
Speech* 6 and in Isocr. *Panegyr.* 66, but surely it is a commonplace.

I may add that even now it is customary to employ it in contests in Greek cities, and not in the meanest cities but in the greatest.[a]

So admirable is your choice of sport and so approved 26 among all men. Believing also, as you do, that it is futile to desire the things most worth while, or yet to be physically endowed for all sorts of feats, unless the soul has been prepared for an ambitious career, at the very outset you exhibited diligence in the training grounds, nor in the real tests were you disappointing, but you gave extraordinary proof of the distinction of your natural gifts and particularly of the courage of your soul in the games. I hesitate 27 to begin treating this topic for fear words may fail me in the description of what took place on that occasion, but nevertheless I shall not pass it over; for it is a shame to refuse a report of what enthralls us as spectators.

Were I to describe all the contests an unseemly length would perhaps accrue to this essay,[b] but by recalling a single example in which you especially distinguished yourself I shall demonstrate the same truth and be found to make a more reasonable use of the patience of my hearers. When the teams had 28 been started and some had leaped to the fore and some were being reined in, you, prevailing over both, first one and then the other,[c] in proper style, seized the victory, winning that envied crown in such fashion that, glorious as it was to win it, it seemed the more glorious and astounding that you came off safely. For when the chariot of your opponents was bearing down upon you head-on and all thought the

[c] Blass notes the same phrase in Isocr. *Panegyr.* 72; it may have been technical in the language of ancient sport.

61

τὴν τῶν ἵππων δύναμιν, ὁρῶν αὐτῶν[1] ἐνίους καὶ
μηδενὸς δεινοῦ παρόντος ὑπερηγωνιακότας, οὐχ
ὅπως ἐξεπλάγης ἢ κατεδειλίασας, ἀλλὰ τῇ μὲν
ἀνδρείᾳ καὶ τῆς τοῦ ζεύγους ὁρμῆς κρείττων ἐγέ-
νου, τῷ δὲ τάχει καὶ τοὺς διηυτυχηκότας τῶν
29 ἀνταγωνιστῶν παρῆλθες. καὶ γάρ τοι τοσοῦτον
μετήλλαξας τῶν ἀνθρώπων τὰς διανοίας ὥστε,
πολλῶν θρυλούντων ὡς ἐν τοῖς ἱππικοῖς ἀγῶσιν
ἡδίστην θέαν παρέχεται τὰ ναυαγοῦντα, καὶ δοκούντων ἀληθῆ ταῦτα λέγειν, ἐπὶ σοῦ τοὐναντίον
τοὺς θεατὰς φοβεῖσθαι πάντας μή τι συμπέσῃ τοιοῦτον περὶ σέ· τοσαύτην εὔνοιαν καὶ φιλονικίαν[2]
ἡ σὴ φύσις αὐτοῖς παρέσχεν.

30 Εἰκότως· καλὸν μὲν γὰρ καὶ τὸ καθ' ἕν τι περίβλεπτον γενέσθαι, πολὺ δὲ κάλλιον τὸ πάντα περι-
λαβεῖν ἐφ' οἷς ἄν τις νοῦν ἔχων φιλοτιμηθείη.
δῆλον δ' ἐκεῖθεν· εὑρήσομεν γὰρ Αἰακὸν μὲν καὶ
Ῥαδάμανθυν διὰ σωφροσύνην, Ἡρακλέα δὲ καὶ
Κάστορα καὶ Πολυδεύκην δι' ἀνδρείαν, Γανυμήδην
δὲ καὶ Ἄδωνιν καὶ ἄλλους τοιούτους διὰ κάλλος
ὑπὸ θεῶν ἀγαπηθέντας. ὥστ' ἔγωγ' οὐ θαυμάζω
τῶν ἐπιθυμούντων τῆς σῆς φιλίας, ἀλλὰ τῶν μὴ
τὸν τρόπον τοῦτον διακειμένων· ὅπου γὰρ ἑνὸς
ἑκάστου τῶν προειρημένων μετασχόντες τινὲς τῆς
τῶν θεῶν ὁμιλίας ἠξιώθησαν, ἦ που τοῦ γ' ἁπάντων
κυρίου καταστάντος εὐκτὸν θνητῷ φύντι φίλον
31 γενέσθαι. δίκαιον μὲν οὖν καὶ πατέρα καὶ μητέρα
καὶ τοὺς ἄλλους οἰκείους τοὺς σοὺς ζηλοῦσθαι,
[1411] τοσοῦτον ὑπερέχοντος σοῦ τῶν ἡλικιωτῶν ἀρετῇ,

---

[1] αὐτῶν Post.
[2] φιλονικίαν Post ; φιλονεικίαν codd. opt. ; φιλοτιμίαν vulg.,
Rennie.

momentum of your horses beyond checking, you, aware that some drivers, though no danger should threaten, become overanxious for their own safety, not only did not lose your head or your nerve, but by your courage got control of the impetus of your team and by your speed passed even those contenders whose luck had suffered no setback. What 29 is more, you caused such a revolution in men's minds that, though many keep insisting that nothing in equestrian contests affords such delight as a crash, and seem to speak the truth, in your case all the spectators, on the contrary, were afraid that some such accident might befall you. Such goodwill and eagerness for your success did your personality awaken in them.

They had good reason to feel so, for while it is a 30 splendid thing to become distinguished for some one excellence, it is still more splendid to combine all the qualities of which a man of sense might justly feel proud. From the following examples this will be clear : we shall find that Aeacus and Rhadamanthys were beloved by the gods for their discretion, Heracles, Castor and Pollux for their courage, and Ganymedes, Adonis, and others like them for their beauty, so that I at any rate am not astonished at those who covet your friendship but at those who are not so disposed. For when some, through sharing in one or another of the qualities I have mentioned, have been deemed worthy of the company of the gods, surely to a mere mortal it is the height of desire to become the friend of one who has become the proud possessor of all good qualities. Certainly your 31 father and mother and the rest of your kinsmen are rightly envied because you so far surpass those of

πολὺ δὲ μᾶλλον οὓς σὺ ὁ τῶν τηλικούτων ἀγαθῶν
ἠξιωμένος σαυτοῦ προκρίνας ἀξίους εἶναι φίλους ἐξ
ἁπάντων αἱρῇ. τοὺς μὲν γὰρ ἡ τύχη σοι μετόχους
κατέστησε, τοὺς δ᾽ ἡ σφετέρα καλοκἀγαθία προσ-
32 συνέστησεν· οὓς οὐκ οἶδα πότερον ἐραστὰς ἢ μόνους
ὀρθῶς γιγνώσκοντας προσαγορεῦσαι χρή. δοκεῖ
γάρ μοι καὶ κατ᾽ ἀρχὰς ἡ τύχη, τῶν μὲν φαύλων
καταφρονοῦσα, τὰς δὲ τῶν σπουδαίων ἀνδρῶν
διανοίας ἐρεθίσαι βουληθεῖσα, τὴν σὴν φύσιν οὐ
πρὸς ἡδονὴν ἐξαπατηθῆναι καλὴν ποιῆσαι, ἀλλὰ
πρὸς ἀρετὴν εὐδαιμονῆσαι χρήσιμον.

33 Πολλὰ δ᾽ ἔχων ἔτι περὶ σοῦ διελθεῖν, αὐτοῦ
καταλύσειν μοι δοκῶ τὸν ἔπαινον, δεδιὼς μὴ καθ᾽
ὑπερβολὴν τῆς ἀνθρωπίνης φύσεως ὑπὲρ σοῦ δια-
λέγεσθαι δόξω· τοσοῦτον γὰρ ὡς ἔοικεν ἡ τῶν
λόγων δύναμις ἔλαττον ἔχει τῆς ὄψεως ὥστε, τοῖς
μὲν ὁρατοῖς οὐδεὶς ἀπιστεῖν ἀξιοῖ, τοὺς δὲ τούτων
ἐπαίνους οὐδ᾽ ἂν ἐλλείπωσιν ἀληθεῖς εἶναι νομί-
34 ζουσι. παυσάμενος οὖν περὶ τούτων, ἤδη πειρά-
σομαί σοι συμβουλεύειν ἐξ ὧν ἂν ἐντιμότερον ἔτι
τὸν σαυτοῦ βίον καταστήσειας. βουλοίμην δ᾽ ἄν σε
μὴ πάρεργον ποιήσασθαι τὸ προσέχειν τὸν νοῦν τοῖς
μέλλουσι ῥηθήσεσθαι, μηδ᾽ ὑπολαμβάνειν τοῦθ᾽,
ὡς ἄρ᾽ ἐγὼ τούτοις κέχρημαι τοῖς λόγοις οὐ τῆς
σῆς ὠφελίας ἕνεκα, ἀλλ᾽ ἐπιδείξεως ἐπιθυμῶν, ἵνα
μήτε διαμάρτῃς τῆς ἀληθείας, μήτ᾽ ἀντὶ τῶν βελτίστων τὰ τυχόνθ᾽ ἑλόμενος χεῖρον περὶ σαυτοῦ

---

[a] This sentence exhibits rhythmical clausulae and Gorgianic parallelism of structure along with assonance of the

your own age in excellence, but still more enviable are those whom you, who have been deemed worthy of such blessings, select from the whole number to be your friends, judging them worthy of your companionship. And since Fortune has appointed the former to share your affection, but the latter their own fine qualities have recommended in addition, I do not 32 know whether to call these young men admirers or unique for their sound judgement. For, as I think, Fortune, scorning base men and wishing to arouse the minds of the good, at the very outset made your nature beautiful, not for a life of pleasure, to be beguiled thereto, but serviceable for a virtuous life, to have happiness therein.[a]

Although I have still much to say in praise of you, 33 I think I shall cease my eulogy at this point, fearing that I may seem to plead your cause in terms exceeding human limitations. For so far, as it seems, does the power of words fall short of that of vision that, while none would think of mistrusting the evidence of his eyes, people think the praise of things men say they have seen, even if it falls short of the truth, to be incredible. Accordingly, I shall leave this topic 34 and now endeavour to counsel you on the means of rendering your life still more worthy of esteem. To the words I am about to utter I would not have you give heed as to a matter of trivial importance, nor to leap to the conclusion that I have, after all, addressed you thus, not for your good, but from a desire to display my skill; otherwise you may miss the truth and, by choosing hapazard counsel in place of the best, fall short of the best in judging your own

vowel $\bar{e}$. It is suggested that the Greek version be read aloud.

35 βουλεύσῃ. καὶ γὰρ τοῖς μὲν ἀφανῆ καὶ ταπεινὴν
[1412] τὴν φύσιν ἔχουσιν, οὐδ᾽ ὅταν μὴ καλῶς τι πράξωσιν
ἐπιπλήττομεν, τοῖς δ᾽ ὥσπερ σὺ περιβλέπτοις γεγενημένοις, καὶ τὸ παραμελῆσαί τινος τῶν καλλίστων αἰσχύνην φέρει. ἔτι δ᾽ οἱ ἐπὶ τῶν ἄλλων
λόγων ψευσθέντες, καθ᾽ ἑνὸς μόνου πράγματος οὐ
τὰ κράτιστ᾽ ἔγνωσαν· οἱ δὲ τῆς τῶν ἐπιτηδευμάτων
συμβουλίας διαμαρτόντες ἢ καταφρονήσαντες, παρ᾽
ὅλον τὸν βίον τῆς ἑαυτῶν ἀγνωσίας ὑπομνήματ᾽
ἔχουσιν.

36 Τούτων μὲν οὖν οὐδὲν δεῖ σε παθεῖν, σκοπεῖσθαι
δὲ τί τῶν ἀνθρωπείων μεγίστην δύναμιν ἔχει, καὶ
τίνος καλῶς μὲν ἀποβάντος πλεῖστ᾽ ἂν κατορθοῖμεν,
διαφθαρέντος δὲ μέγιστ᾽ ἂν βλαπτοίμεθα παρὰ τὸν
βίον· οὐ γὰρ ἄδηλον ὅτι τούτου καὶ μάλιστ᾽ ἐπιμέλειαν ποιητέον, ὃ μεγίστην ῥοπὴν ἐφ᾽ ἑκάτερον
37 ἐργάζεσθαι πέφυκεν. τῶν μὲν τοίνυν ἐν ἀνθρώποις
διάνοιαν ἁπάντων εὑρήσομεν ἡγεμονεύουσαν, ταύτην δὲ φιλοσοφίαν μόνην παιδεῦσαί τ᾽ ὀρθῶς καὶ
γυμνάσαι δυναμένην. ἧς οἶμαί σε δεῖν μετασχεῖν,
καὶ μὴ κατοκνῆσαι μηδὲ φυγεῖν τὰς ἐνούσας ἐν
αὐτῇ πραγματείας, ἐνθυμούμενον ὅτι διὰ μὲν ἀργίας
καὶ ῥᾳθυμίας καὶ τὰ παντελῶς ἐπιπολῆς δυσχείρωτ᾽
ἐστί, διὰ δὲ καρτερίας καὶ φιλοπονίας οὐδὲν τῶν
38 ὄντων ἀγαθῶν ἀνάλωτον πέφυκε, καὶ διότι πάντων
ἀλογώτατόν ἐστι, πρὸς μὲν χρηματισμὸν καὶ ῥώμην
καὶ τὰ τοιαῦτα φιλοτίμως ἔχειν καὶ πολλὰς ὑπομένειν κακοπαθείας, ἃ πάντα θνήτ᾽ ἐστὶ καὶ τῇ
διανοίᾳ δουλεύειν εἴωθε, τὴν δ᾽ ἐπιστατοῦσαν μὲν

interests. For we do not reproach men of humble 35
and insignificant natural gifts even when they commit
a dishonourable act, but to those who, like yourself,
have attained distinction, even a bit of negligence in
some matter of high honour brings disgrace.[a] Again,
those who go astray in other domains fail merely to
make the best decision in some single, isolated
matter, but those who miss the right advice on the
conduct of life, or scorn it, have reminders of their
own folly to live with their whole life long.

Now you must not fall into any of these errors but 36
rather seek to discover what is of supreme consequence
in human affairs, and what it is that turning out well
would do us the most good, but turning out badly
would hurt us most along life's pathway. For it
requires no proof that upon this factor we must ex-
pend the greatest care, which more than anything
else possesses the power to tip the scale to one side
or the other. Now of the powers residing in human 37
beings we shall find that intelligence leads all the
rest and that philosophy alone is capable of educating
this rightly and training it. In this study I think
you ought to participate, and not balk at or flee
from the labours involved in it, reflecting that through
idleness and indolence even quite superficial things
become difficult, while through persistence and
diligence none of the worth-while things is unattain-
able, and that of all things the most irrational is to 38
be ambitious for wealth, bodily strength, and such
things, and for their sakes to submit to many hard-
ships, all of which prizes are perishable and usually
slaves to intelligence, but not to aim at the improvement of the mind, which has supervision over all other

[a] See p. 64, note a.

τῶν ἄλλων, συνδιατελοῦσαν δὲ τοῖς ἔχουσιν, ὅλου
[1413] δ' ἡγεμονεύουσαν τοῦ βίου μὴ ζητεῖν ὅπως διακεί-
39 σεται βέλτιον. καίτοι καλὸν μὲν καὶ παρὰ τύχην
ἐν τοῖς σπουδαιοτάτοις θαυμάζεσθαι, πολὺ δὲ κάλλιον διὰ τὴν ἐπιμέλειαν τὴν αὑτοῦ μηδενὸς τῶν
ἐνδόξων ἄμοιρον γενέσθαι· τῆς μὲν γὰρ ἐνίοτε καὶ
τοῖς φαύλοις μετασχεῖν συνέβη, τῆς δ' οὐκ ἔστιν
ἄλλοις μετουσία πλὴν τοῖς ἐν ἀνδραγαθίᾳ δια-
φέρουσιν.

40 Ἀλλὰ μὴν περί γε τῆς φιλοσοφίας ἀκριβῶς μὲν
ἕκαστα διελθεῖν ἡγοῦμαι τὸν μέλλοντα χρόνον ἡμῖν
ἐπιτηδειοτέρους καιροὺς παραδώσειν· συντόμως δ'
εἰπεῖν οὐδὲ νῦν οὐδὲν κωλύσει περὶ αὑτῆς. ἐν οὖν
πρῶτον ἐκεῖνό σε δεῖ καταμαθεῖν ἀκριβῶς, ὅτι πᾶσα
μὲν παιδεία δι' ἐπιστήμης καὶ μελέτης τινὸς συν-
έστηκεν, ἡ δὲ φιλοσοφία καὶ μᾶλλον τῶν ἄλλων·
ὅσῳ γὰρ ἀκριβεστέρους¹ ἔχει τοὺς ἐφεστῶτας, τοσ-
41 ούτῳ κάλλιον αὐτὴν συγκεῖσθαι προσήκει. καίτοι
τί ποτ' ἂν βουληθείημεν, τῆς μὲν διανοίας ἐπὶ τοῦ
λέγειν καὶ βουλεύεσθαι τεταγμένης, τῆς δὲ φιλοσοφίας ἑκατέρου τούτων ἐμπειρίαν παραδιδούσης, μὴ
ταύτην κατασχεῖν τὴν πραγματείαν, δι' ἧς ἀμφοτέρων τούτων ἐγκρατῶς ἕξομεν; τότε γὰρ εἰκὸς
καὶ τὸν βίον ἡμῶν μεγίστην ἐπίδοσιν λαβεῖν ὅταν,
τῶν κρατίστων ὀρεγόμενοι, τὰ μὲν διδακτὰ τέχνῃ,
τὰ δὲ λοιπὰ γυμνασίᾳ καὶ συνηθείᾳ κατασχεῖν δυ-
42 νηθῶμεν. οὐ γὰρ δήπου τοῦτό γ' ἔστιν εἰπεῖν ὡς

¹ φρονιμωτέρους Blass, Rennie.

ᵃ The oldest of the Greek-letter fraternities in the univer-

powers, abides continually with those who possess it, and guides the whole life.[a]   And yet, although it is a 39 fine thing to be admired among high-minded people even on account of fortuitous success, it is much finer through care bestowed upon one's self to gain a share in all the accomplishments that are esteemed ; for often it has fallen to the lot of vulgar men to share in the former but none have a part in the latter except those who excel in real manliness.

However, touching the subject of philosophy, some 40 future occasion will afford me more suitable opportunities to review carefully the particulars, but the outlines of it nothing will prevent me from running over at once. This one point, therefore, you must grasp clearly at the outset, that all education consists of the gaining of skill by a combination of theory and practice,[b] and this is even more true of philosophy than of any other studies, for the synthesis of learning and practice is likely to be more perfect in proportion as the instructors are more clear on this point. And 41 yet, since intelligence commands the province of speaking and deliberating, and philosophy confers facility in each of these, what reason can there be why we should refuse to get a firm grasp of this study, through which we shall become masters of both alike ? Because life may then too be expected to make a great advance for us when we reach out for the things of supreme importance and find ourselves able to secure by rule and precept such as can be taught and the rest by practice and habituation. It certainly is not 42 permissible to make the assertion that it is not through

sities of the U.S. (1776), ΦΒΚ, took its name from φιλοσοφία βίου κυβερνήτης.
   [b] This idea recurs in §§ 41 and 47.

οὐδὲν πρὸς τὸ φρονεῖν εὖ παρὰ τὴν ἐπιστήμην δια-
φέρομεν ἀλλήλων· ὅλως μὲν γὰρ ἅπασα φύσις
βελτίων γίγνεται παιδείαν προσλαβοῦσα τὴν προσ-
ήκουσαν, πολὺ δὲ μάλισθ' ὅσαις ἐξ ἀρχῆς εὐφυέστε-
[1414] ρον τῶν ἄλλων ἔχειν ὑπῆρξε· τοῖς μὲν γὰρ αὐτῶν
μόνον βελτίοσι γίγνεσθαι, τοῖς δὲ καὶ τῶν ἄλλων
συμβαίνει διενεγκεῖν.

43 Εὖ δ' ἴσθι τὴν μὲν ἐκ τῶν πράξεων ἐμπειρίαν
γιγνομένην σφαλερὰν οὖσαν καὶ πρὸς τὸν λοιπὸν
βίον ἀχρήστως ἔχουσαν, τὴν δ' ἐκ τοῦ φιλοσοφεῖν
παιδείαν πρὸς ἅπαντα ταῦτ' εὐκαίρως συγκεκρα-
μένην. καίτοι τινὲς ἤδη καὶ δι' εὐτυχίαν πραγμάτων γυμνασθέντες ἐθαυμάσθησαν· σοὶ δὲ προσήκει
τούτων μὲν καταφρονεῖν σαυτοῦ δ' ἐπιμέλειαν
ἔχειν· οὐ γὰρ αὐτοσχεδιάζειν ἀλλ' ἐπίστασθαί σε
δεῖ περὶ τῶν μεγίστων, οὐδ' ἐπὶ τῶν καιρῶν μελε-
τᾶν ἀλλ' ἀγωνίζεσθαι καλῶς ἐπίστασθαι.

44 Νόμιζε δὲ πᾶσαν μὲν τὴν φιλοσοφίαν μεγάλα
τοὺς χρωμένους ὠφελεῖν, πολὺ δὲ μάλιστα τὴν περὶ
τὰς πράξεις καὶ τοὺς πολιτικοὺς λόγους ἐπιστήμην.
τῆς γὰρ γεωμετρίας καὶ τῆς ἄλλης τῆς τοιαύτης
παιδείας ἀπείρως μὲν ἔχειν αἰσχρόν, ἄκρον δ'
ἀγωνιστὴν γενέσθαι ταπεινότερον τῆς σῆς ἀξίας·
ἐν ἐκείνῃ δὲ τὸ μὲν διενεγκεῖν ζηλωτόν, τὸ δ'
45 ἄμοιρον γενέσθαι παντελῶς καταγέλαστον. γνοίης
δ' ἂν ἐξ ἄλλων τε πολλῶν, καὶ παραθεωρήσας τοὺς

---

[a] Blass compares Isocr. *Antid.* 189-192, with which may
be compared in turn Cicero, *Pro Archia* vii. 15.

[b] Blass cites Isocr. *Antid.* 267, where the statement is

acquired knowledge that we surpass one another in sound judgement; for, speaking generally, all natural ability is improved by the addition of the appropriate education,[a] and this is especially true of talents which at the outset are inherently superior to the rest, because the one kind is capable only of improving upon itself while the other may also surpass the rest.

Be well assured also that the facility acquired solely 43 from practical experience is treacherous and useless for subsequent needs of life, but the education secured through the pursuit of philosophy is happily blended for all these needs. There is no denying, of course, that in the past some men who got practical training just by good luck in action have won admiration, but for you the proper thing is to disregard these men and to take yourself seriously in hand. For in matters of the utmost importance you should not be extemporizing instead of really knowing what to do or in emergencies be studying your arguments instead of really knowing how to debate an issue on its merits.

Be convinced too that all philosophical learning 44 confers precious benefits upon those who take advantage of it, but especially is this true of the knowledge that deals with practical affairs and political discussions. No doubt it is disgraceful to be quite ignorant of geometry and other such subjects of study, but to become a topmost contender in this field is too low an ambition for merit like yours.[b] In that kind of philosophy, however, not only is it a worthy ambition to excel, but to remain ignorant is altogether ridiculous. You may infer this to be true on many other grounds 45 and especially by scanning the careers of those who

made that cultural studies do not directly prepare the candidate for public life but do increase his power to learn.

πρὸ σαυτοῦ γεγενημένους ἐνδόξους ἄνδρας. τοῦτο
μὲν Περικλέα τὸν συνέσει πλεῖστον τῶν καθ' αὑτὸν
διενεγκεῖν δόξαντα πάντων, ἀκούσει πλησιάσαντ'
Ἀναξαγόρᾳ τῷ Κλαζομενίῳ καὶ μαθητὴν ἐκείνου
γενόμενον ταύτης τῆς δυνάμεως μετασχόντα· τοῦτο
δ' Ἀλκιβιάδην εὑρήσεις φύσει μὲν πρὸς ἀρετὴν
πολλῷ χεῖρον διακείμενον, καὶ τὰ μὲν ὑπερηφάνως,
[1415] τὰ δὲ ταπεινῶς, τὰ δ' ὑπερακρατῶς ζῆν προῃρη-
μένον, ἀπὸ δὲ τῆς Σωκράτους ὁμιλίας πολλὰ μὲν
ἐπανορθωθέντα τοῦ βίου, τὰ δὲ λοιπὰ τῷ μεγέθει
46 τῶν ἄλλων ἔργων ἐπικρυψάμενον. εἰ δὲ δεῖ μὴ
παλαιὰ λέγοντας διατρίβειν, ἔχοντας ὑπογυιοτέροις
παραδείγμασι χρῆσθαι, τοῦτο μὲν Τιμόθεον οὐκ ἐξ
ὧν νεώτερος ὢν ἐπετήδευσεν, ἀλλ' ἐξ ὧν Ἰσοκράτει
συνδιατρίψας ἔπραξε, μεγίστης δόξης καὶ πλείστων
τιμῶν εὑρήσεις ἀξιωθέντα· τοῦτο δ' Ἀρχύταν τὴν
Ταραντίνων πόλιν οὕτω καλῶς καὶ φιλανθρώπως
διοικήσαντα κύριον αὐτῆς καταστάντα ὥστ' εἰς
ἅπαντας τὴν ἐκείνου μνήμην διενεγκεῖν· ὃς ἐν ἀρχῇ
καταφρονούμενος ἐκ τοῦ Πλάτωνι πλησιάσαι τοσ-
47 αύτην ἔλαβεν ἐπίδοσιν. καὶ τούτων οὐδὲν ἀλόγως
ἀποβέβηκε· πολὺ γὰρ ἂν ἦν ἀτοπώτερον εἰ τὰ μὲν
μικρὰ δι' ἐπιστήμης καὶ μελέτης ἠναγκαζόμεθ'

---

[a] Blass notes the same information in Isocr. *Antid.* 235.

[b] Isocrates employs the same words of Persian satraps,
Panegyr. 152, as Blass notes.

[c] The phrase " closer to our own times " is defined by the
mention of Timotheüs, who died in 355 B.C., just after Demosthenes entered public life. The author, whether the orator
or a forger, belongs to the second half of the fourth century.

[d] Timotheüs, son of Conon, was called by Cornelius Nepos
the last Athenian general worthy of mention. Demosthenes
regularly spoke of him with admiration.

[e] There is a brief life of Archytas by Diogenes Laertius.

have become eminent before your time. You will hear first that Pericles, who is thought to have far surpassed all men of his age in intellectual grasp, addressed himself to Anaxagoras of Clazomenae and only after being his pupil [a] acquired this power of judgement. You will next discover that Alcibiades, though his natural disposition was far inferior in respect to virtue and it was his pleasure to behave himself now arrogantly, now obsequiously,[b] now licentiously, yet, as a fruit of his association with Socrates, he made correction of many errors of his life and over the rest drew a veil of oblivion by the greatness of his later achievements. But not to 46 spend our time rehearsing ancient examples while others are available closer to our own times,[c] you will discover that Timotheüs was deemed worthy of the highest repute and numerous honours, not because of his activities as a younger man, but because of his performances after he had studied with Isocrates.[d] You will discover also that Archytas of Tarentum became ruler of his city and managed its affairs so admirably and so considerately as to spread the record of that achievement to all mankind; yet at first he was despised and he owed his remarkable progress to studying with Plato.[e] Of these examples 47 not one worked out contrary to reason [f]; for it would be much stranger if we were obliged to achieve paltry ends through gaining skill that combines theory and

---

which may be consulted in the Loeb translation. It is not known positively that he was a pupil of Plato, but he was his friend : Plato, *Epist.* vii. 338 c, 350 A ; xiii. 360 c. His adherence was to the school of Pythagoras.

[f] With a difference of one word this sentence is found in Isocr. *Panegyr.* 150, as Blass notes. It looks, however, like a commonplace.

ἐπιτελεῖν, τὰ δὲ μέγιστ᾽ ἄνευ ταύτης τῆς πραγματείας ἐδυνάμεθα πράττειν.

Περὶ μὲν οὖν τούτων οὐκ οἶδ᾽ ὅ τι δεῖ πλείω
λέγειν· οὐδὲ γὰρ ἐξ ἀρχῆς ὡς παντελῶς ἀπείρως
ἔχοντός σου περὶ αὐτῶν ἐμνήσθην, ἀλλ᾽ ἡγούμενος
τὰς τοιαύτας παρακλήσεις τοὺς μὲν ἀγνοοῦντας
48 προτρέπειν τοὺς δ᾽ εἰδότας παροξύνειν. μηδὲν δ᾽
ὑπολάβῃς τοιοῦτον, ὡς ἄρ᾽ ἐγὼ ταῦτ᾽ εἴρηκα δι-
δάξειν αὐτὸς ἐπαγγελλόμενός σέ τι τούτων· οὐ γὰρ
ἂν αἰσχυνθείην εἰπών, ὅτι πολλὰ μαθεῖν αὐτὸς ἔτι
δέομαι, καὶ μᾶλλον ἀγωνιστὴς προῄρημαι τῶν
πολιτικῶν ἢ διδάσκαλος εἶναι τῶν ἄλλων.   οὐχ
ὡς ἀναινόμενος δὲ ταῦτα διορθοῦμαι τὴν τῶν σοφι-
στεύειν ἑλομένων δόξαν, ἀλλ᾽ ὅτι τἀληθὲς τοῦτον
49 ἔχον τυγχάνει τὸν τρόπον· ἐπεὶ σύνοιδά γε πολλοὺς
[1416] μὲν ἐξ ἀδόξων καὶ ταπεινῶν ἐπιφανεῖς διὰ τῆς
πραγματείας ταύτης γεγενημένους, Σόλωνα δὲ καὶ
ζῶντα καὶ τελευτήσαντα μεγίστης δόξης ἠξιωμένον·
ὃς οὐκ ἀπεληλαμένος τῶν ἄλλων τιμῶν, ἀλλὰ τῆς
μὲν ἀνδρείας τὸ πρὸς Μεγαρέας τρόπαιον ὑπόμνημα
50 καταλιπών, τῆς δ᾽ εὐβουλίας τὴν Σαλαμῖνος κο-
μιδήν, τῆς δ᾽ ἄλλης συνέσεως τοὺς νόμους οἷς ἔτι
καὶ νῦν οἱ πλεῖστοι τῶν Ἑλλήνων χρώμενοι δια-
τελοῦσιν.   ὅμως τοσούτων αὐτῷ καλῶν ὑπαρχόντων,

ᵃ Writings that urged young men to study philosophy
formed a distinct literary genre among the ancients under the
name " protreptics." The *Epistle to Menoeceus* of Epicurus
is an extant example.

practice, but were capable of accomplishing the big things without this effort.

Now I do not know what call there is to say more on these topics, for not even at the outset did I introduce them because I assumed you were absolutely ignorant, but because I thought that such exhortations both arouse those who lack knowledge and spur on those who possess it.[a] And do not make any such 48 assumption as this, that in speaking these words I am presumably offering to teach you any of these branches myself, for I should feel no shame in saying that there is still much I need myself to learn, and that I have chosen rather to be a contender in political life than a teacher of the other arts.[b] Not that in disavowing these subjects of instruction I am impugning the reputation of those who have chosen the profession of sophist, but my reason is that the truth of the matter happens to be as follows : for I am 49 aware, of course, that many men have risen to eminence from humble and obscure estate through the practice of this art, and that Solon, both living and dead, was deemed worthy of the highest renown. He was not disqualified for the other honours [c] but left behind him a memorial of his courage in the trophy of victory over the Megarians, of his astute- 50 ness in the recovery of Salamis, and of general sagacity in the laws which the majority of the Greeks continue using to this day. Yet in spite of these great claims to distinction he set his heart upon

[b] This self-characterization has been thought by some to point to Androtion as the author, but the grounds seem slight to Blass, p. 407 and note 2.

[c] This statement hints at the long contested question, whether practical statesmanship could be combined with philosophical insight.

75

ἐπ' οὐδενὶ μᾶλλον ἐσπούδασεν ἢ τῶν ἑπτὰ σοφι-
στῶν ὅπως γένηται, νομίζων τὴν φιλοσοφίαν οὐκ
ὄνειδος ἀλλὰ τιμὴν τοῖς χρωμένοις φέρειν, καλῶς
ἐγνωκὼς αὐτὸ τοῦτ' οὐχ ἧττον ἢ καὶ τἄλλ' ἐφ'
οἷς διήνεγκεν.

51 Ἐγὼ μὲν οὖν οὔτ' αὐτὸς ἄλλως γιγνώσκω, σοί τε
παραινῶ φιλοσοφεῖν, μεμνημένῳ τῶν ἐξ ἀρχῆς
ὑπαρξάντων σαυτῷ· τούτου γὰρ ἕνεκα διῆλθον ἐν
ἀρχῇ τοῦ λόγου κἀγὼ περὶ αὐτῶν, οὐχ ὡς ἐκ τοῦ
τὴν σὴν φύσιν ἐπαινεῖν ἀνακτήσεσθαί σε προσδοκῶν,
ἀλλ' ἵνα μᾶλλον προτρέψω σε πρὸς τὴν φιλοσοφίαν,
ἐὰν μὴ παρὰ μικρὸν ποιήσῃ μηδ' ἐπὶ τοῖς ὑπ-
άρχουσιν ἀγαθοῖς μέγα φρονήσας τῶν μελλόντων
52 ὀλιγωρήσῃς. μηδ' εἰ τῶν ἐντυγχανόντων κρείττων
εἶ, μηδὲν τῶν ἄλλων ζήτει διενεγκεῖν, ἀλλ' ἡγοῦ
κράτιστον μὲν εἶναι τὸ πρωτεύειν ἐν ἅπασι, τούτου
δ' ὀρεγόμενον ὀφθῆναι μᾶλλον συμφέρειν ἢ προ-
έχοντ' ἐν τοῖς τυχοῦσι. καὶ μὴ καταισχύνῃς τὴν
φύσιν, μηδὲ ψευσθῆναι ποιήσῃς τῶν ἐλπίδων τοὺς
[1417] ἐπὶ σοὶ μέγα φρονοῦντας, ἀλλ' ὑπερβαλέσθαι πειρῶ
τῇ σαυτοῦ δυνάμει τὴν τῶν εὐνουστάτων ἐπιθυμίαν.

53 καὶ νόμιζε τοὺς μὲν ἄλλους λόγους, ὅταν ἐπιεικῶς
ἔχωσι, τοῖς εἰποῦσι δόξαν περιτιθέναι, τὰς δὲ συμβουλίας τοῖς πεισθεῖσιν ὠφέλειαν καὶ τιμὴν προσ-
άπτειν· καὶ τὰς μὲν περὶ τῶν ἄλλων κρίσεις τὴν

---

[a] This statement is absurd. The legend of the Seven
Sages became current only in the fourth century : Plato,
Protagoras 343 A. In Isocr. *Antid.* 235 also Solon is called
" one of the seven sophists." Originally this term suggested
no disrespect.

nothing so much as becoming one of the Seven Sages,[a] believing that philosophy was no reproach but that it brought honour to those who pursued it, having been no less wise in this very judgement than in the others in which he showed himself superior.

My own judgement is not different from Solon's 51 and I recommend to you to study philosophy, bearing in mind the advantages you have possessed from the beginning. Indeed it was with this purpose in view I ran through the list of them myself in the first part of my essay,[b] not expecting to make a conquest of you by praising your natural gifts, but that I may the better urge you to take up philosophy if you shall escape the error of putting a low value on it, or, through pride in your present advantages, of undervaluing the advantages yet to be gained. Again, even 52 if you are better than the common run of men,[c] do not seek to be superior in no respect to the talented remainder, but deem it the highest purpose to be first among all, and that it is more to your advantage to be seen striving for this than merely being foremost among the rank and file. And do not bring shame upon your natural gifts or cause to be cheated of their hopes those who are proud of you, but endeavour by your own ability to surpass the desires of those who have your interests most at heart. And bear in mind that speeches of the other 53 kinds, when they fulfil their purpose, only crown their authors with glory, but that good counsels attach benefit and honour to those who hearken to them ; and that the decisions we make about all other

[b] §§ 10-32.
[c] Isocr. *Evagoras* 81 begins with similar words, as Blass notes : " nor must you be content if you are already superior to those who are here present . . ."

αἴσθησιν ἣν ἔχομεν δηλοῦν, τὰς δὲ τῶν ἐπιτηδευμάτων αἱρέσεις τὴν ὅλην φύσιν ἡμῶν δοκιμάζειν.
ἐν οἷς ἅμα κρίνων αὐτὸς κριθήσεσθαι προσδόκα
παρὰ πᾶσι, κἀμὲ τὸν οὕτως ἐγκωμιάσαντά σ᾽ ἑτοί-
54 μως ἐν ἀγῶνι γενήσεσθαι τῆς δοκιμασίας. δι᾽ ἃ
δεῖ σε τῶν ἐπαίνων ἄξιον εἶναι δόξαντα κἀμὲ τῆς
σῆς φιλίας ἀνεπιτίμητον εἶναι.[1]

Οὐχ οὕτω δ᾽ ἄν σε προθύμως ἐπὶ τὴν φιλοσοφίαν
παρεκάλουν, εἰ μὴ τῆς μὲν εὐνοίας τῆς ἐμῆς τοῦτον
ἄν σοι κάλλιστον ἔρανον εἰσενεγκεῖν ᾤμην, τὴν δὲ
πόλιν ἑώρων διὰ μὲν ἀπορίαν τῶν καλῶν κἀγαθῶν
ἀνδρῶν τοῖς τυχοῦσι πολλάκις χρωμένην, διὰ δὲ
τὰς τούτων ἁμαρτίας αὐτὴν ταῖς μεγίσταις ἀτυ-
55 χίαις περιπίπτουσαν. ἵν᾽ οὖν ἡ μὲν τῆς σῆς ἀρετῆς,
σὺ δὲ τῶν παρὰ ταύτης τιμῶν ἀπολαύσῃς, προθυ-
μότερόν σοι παρεκελευσάμην. καὶ γὰρ οὐδ᾽ ἐπὶ
σοὶ νομίζω γενήσεσθαι ζῆν ὡς ἔτυχεν, ἀλλὰ προσ-
τάξειν σοι τὴν πόλιν τῶν αὑτῆς τι διοικεῖν, καὶ
ὅσῳ τὴν φύσιν ἐπιφανεστέραν ἔχεις, τοσούτῳ μει-
ζόνων ἀξιώσειν καὶ θᾶττον βουλήσεσθαι πεῖράν σου
λαμβάνειν. καλὸν οὖν παρεσκευάσθαι τὴν γνώμην,
ἵνα μὴ τότε πλημμελῇς.

56 Τὸ μὲν οὖν ἐμὸν ἦν ἔργον εἰπεῖν ἅ σοι συμφέρειν
ἡγοῦμαι πεπρᾶχθαι, σὸν δὲ βουλεύσασθαι περὶ αὐτῶν. προσήκει δὲ καὶ τοὺς ἄλλους τοὺς ζητοῦντας

---

[1] ποιεῖν Blass ; ἀφεῖναι Rennie. Post suggests διὰ σὲ γὰρ
δεῖ τῶν κ.τ.λ.

---

[a] Blass notes the occurrence of this sentence in Isocr.
Archid. 87, with ἐπὶ τὸν πόλεμον instead of ἐπὶ τὴν φιλοσοφίαν.

matters make plain the power of perception we possess, but that the choices we make of careers put our whole character to the test. And as you pass judgement in these matters, count upon being judged at the same time yourself by all men, and do not forget that I, who have been so ready to praise you, will also be involved in the hazard of the test. The proofs by which you must be judged 54 worthy of my praises must also acquit me of all censure for the friendship I bear you.

I would not be pressing you so urgently to study philosophy [a] unless I thought that in this I was making you a most precious contribution as evidence of my goodwill, and unless I observed that our city often makes use of ordinary men for lack of men of the best type, and through their bungling incurs the gravest misfortunes. So, then, in order that our city may 55 enjoy abilities such as yours and you the honours which these abilities deserve, I have urged you with some vehemence. Neither do I think that it will be in your power to live as chance decrees, but that the city will appoint you to be in charge of some department of her business, and in proportion as your natural gifts are the more conspicuous it will judge you worthy of greater responsibilities and will the sooner desire to make trial of you. The wise plan, therefore is to train your mind that you may not fail when that day comes.

Now it has been my part to tell you [b] what studies 56 I think it is to your advantage to have pursued, but it is yours to decide concerning them. There is an obligation also on the rest, those who seek to be on

[b] Blass notes a similarity in Isocr. *Evagoras* 80 ; seemingly a commonplace of the protreptic genre.

[1418] οἰκείως πρὸς σὲ διακεῖσθαι, μὴ τὰς ἐπιπολαίους
ἡδονὰς καὶ διατριβὰς ἀγαπᾶν, μηδ' ἐπὶ ταύτας
προκαλεῖσθαι, ἀλλὰ φιλοπονεῖν καὶ σκοπεῖν ὅπως
τὸν σὸν βίον ὡς λαμπρότατον καταστήσουσιν· αὐτοί
τε γὰρ οὕτως ἂν μάλιστ' ἐπαινοῖντο καὶ σοὶ πλεί-
57 στων ἀγαθῶν αἴτιοι γένοιντο. μέμφομαι μὲν οὖν
οὐδὲ νῦν οὐδένα τῶν σοὶ πλησιαζόντων· καὶ γάρ
μοι δοκεῖ τῆς ἄλλης εὐτυχίας τῆς σῆς καὶ τοῦθ' ἓν
εἶναι, τὸ μηδενὸς φαύλου τυχεῖν ἐραστοῦ, ἀλλ' οὓς
ἄν τις ἕλοιτο βουλόμενος φίλους ἐκ τῶν ἡλικιωτῶν
ἐκλέγεσθαι· παραινῶ μέντοι σοι φιλοφρονεῖσθαι μὲν
πρὸς ἅπαντας τούτους καὶ ἔχειν ἡδέως, πείθεσθαι
δὲ τοῖς πλεῖστον νοῦν ἔχουσιν αὐτῶν, ἵνα καὶ τούτοις αὐτοῖς ἔτι σπουδαιότερος δοκῇς εἶναι καὶ τοῖς
ἄλλοις πολίταις. εὐτύχει.

intimate terms with you, not to be content with superficial pleasures and pastimes, nor to summon you to these, but to consider diligently how they may render your career most brilliant. By so doing they would bring most credit to themselves and become instruments of the greatest service to you. Neither am I 57 now finding fault with any one of those who keep company with you, for this also seems to me one element of your general good fortune, that you have found no base admirer, but select as friends from the young men of your own age such only as any man would gladly choose. I urge you, however, while being friendly and agreeable to all of these, to heed those of them who have the most sense, so that you may seem even more worthy of respect to this particular group and to the rest of the citizens. Farewell.

EXORDIA

INTRODUCTION

THE following fifty-six selections, as their collective
title, *Prooemia* or *Exordia*, indicates, are the opening
paragraphs of speeches. Some of them appear elsewhere as the beginnings of extant orations of Demosthenes. These will be noted as they occur in the
translation.

Many are so general in character that they might
have been used on any occasion to introduce any
subject. In this there is nothing surprising. On one
occasion Cicero embarrassed himself by attaching the
same introduction to two different essays; this
happened because he kept a volume of them at hand
(*Ad Att.* xvi. 6. 4). Suidas informs us that the orators
Antiphon, Thrasymachus and Cephalus also possessed
such collections. The same is related of Critias.

Cicero (*De Oratore* ii. 80) assigns a threefold function to the exordium: to gain the goodwill of the
audience and to render it open-minded and attentive.
This description hardly squares with the practice
exemplified in this collection. Athenian democracy
is sharply criticized: members of the Assembly are
unwilling to face the facts; they favour speakers
who tell them what they like to hear; they shout
down unpopular speakers who might have something
worth-while to say; they act impulsively on bad
advice and then punish the advisers; they listen to

speakers who advocate oligarchy; they submit to being abused from the bema. The speakers, in turn, are inclined to say what is pleasant rather than what is true, to be actuated by partisan motives, and to seek to add to their own reputations at the expense of the common good.

The general tone, however, reveals a stubborn faith in democratic government. The faults of citizens and legislators are stressed for the sake of emphasizing their responsibilities. No sympathy is revealed with oligarchic sentiments such as are found in the *Athenian Constitution* of the Pseudo-Xenophon.

The Greek term *prooemium* is associated also with poetry and music; it means " prelude," thus suggesting the key-note of the performance that follows. For this reason Quintilian preferred it to the Latin *exordium*, which signifies merely " beginning." His theory is set forth in his *Institutes* iv. 1. Brief mention is found in Aristotle's *Rhetoric* iii. 14. 7-8.

The subject has not interested English-speaking scholars. Brief notes may be found in Dindorf's *Demosthenes* vii. 1426-1442. There is a dissertation by R. Swoboda, *De Demosthenis quae feruntur prooemiis*, Vienna, 1887; the author rejects them. Blass (iii. 322-328) is inclined to accept them; he calls attention to the close relationship of the subject matter to that of the Public Orations preceding 349 B.C. It may be added that Nos. 26-29 are found in Oxyrhynchus Papyrus i. 53 of the first or second century A.D.

Arabic numerals have been used for references to the Exordia, Roman numerals for the Orations.

ΠΡΟΟΙΜΙΑ ΔΗΜΗΓΟΡΙΚΑ [1]

Α

Εἰ μὲν περὶ καινοῦ τινος πράγματος προυτίθετ᾽, ὦ ἄνδρες Ἀθηναῖοι, λέγειν, ἐπισχὼν ἂν ἕως οἱ πλεῖστοι τῶν εἰωθότων γνώμην ἀπεφήναντο, εἰ μὲν ἤρεσκέν τί μοι τῶν ῥηθέντων, ἡσυχίαν ἦγον, εἰ δὲ μή, τότ᾽ ἂν καὐτὸς ἐπειρώμην ἃ γιγνώσκω λέγειν· ἐπειδὴ δ᾽ ὑπὲρ ὧν πολλάκις εἰρήκασιν οὗτοι πρότερον, περὶ τούτων νυνὶ σκοπεῖτε, ἡγοῦμαι καὶ πρῶτος ἀναστὰς εἰκότως ἂν μετὰ τούτους δοκεῖν λέγειν. 2 εἰ μὲν οὖν εἶχε καλῶς τὰ πράγματα οὐδ᾽ ἂν ἔδει βουλεύεσθαι· ἐπειδὴ δ᾽ ὡς ἅπαντες ὁρᾶτ᾽ ἔχει [1419] δυσκολίαν, ὡς ἐκ τοιούτων πειράσομαι συμβουλεύειν ἃ κράτιστ᾽ εἶναι νομίζω. πρῶτον μὲν οὖν ὑμᾶς ἐκεῖνο ἐγνωκέναι δεῖ ὡς οὐδὲν ὧν ἐποιεῖτ᾽ ἐπὶ τοῦ πολεμεῖν ὄντες τοῦ λοιποῦ πρακτέον ἐστίν, ἀλλὰ πάντα τἀναντία· εἰ γὰρ ἐκεῖνα φαῦλα πεποίηκε τὰ πράγματα, τἀναντί᾽ εἰκὸς βελτίω ποιῆ- 3 σαι. ἔπειτα νομιστέον οὐχ ὃς ἂν ὑμῖν ἢ μηδὲν ἢ μικρὰ προστάττῃ, τοῦτον ὀρθῶς λέγειν· ὁρᾶτε γὰρ ὡς ἐκ τῶν τοιούτων ἐλπίδων καὶ λόγων εἰς πᾶν

---

[1] Title lacking in best ms. : " Oratorical Preludes."

[a] The beginning of *Phil.* i. differs but slightly from this.

EXORDIA

1 [a]

IF it had been proposed to discuss some new measure, men of Athens, I should have waited until most of the regular speakers had declared their opinions, and if any of their views had pleased me, I should have held my peace ; otherwise, I should then have attempted to say what I myself think. But since you are now considering matters on which these speakers have often spoken before, I feel that, even if the first to rise, I may reasonably appear to be speaking after them. Now, if our interests were prospering, there 2 would be no need to deliberate ; but since, as you all observe, they are in straits, I shall try, on that assumption, to advise what I consider best. In the first place, you ought to recognize that none of the policies you pursued while engaged in the war are to be used henceforth, but quite their opposites.[b] For if those policies have brought your fortunes low, it is very likely that their opposites will improve them.[c] Next, you must consider that it is not the speaker who 3 places upon you little or no burden who is in the right, for you see that, as a consequence of such optimistic speeches, our present condition has reached the

[b] Similar advice is given in VIII. 38. *Cf. Olynth.* ii. 23.
[c] This advice is satirically tendered to Dionysus by Euripides in Aristoph. *Frogs* 1446-1450.

προελήλυθε μοχθηρίας τὰ παρόντα· ἀλλ' ὃς ἂν τὸ
χαρίζεσθαι παρείς, ἃ δεῖ καὶ δι' ὧν παυσαίμεθ' ἂν
αἰσχύνην ὀφλισκάνοντες καὶ ζημιούμενοι, ταῦτα
λέγῃ. καὶ γὰρ ὡς ἀληθῶς, εἰ μὲν ὅσ' ἂν τῷ λόγῳ
τις ὑπερβῇ λυπῆσαι μὴ βουλόμενος καὶ τὰ πράγμαθ' ὑπερβήσεται, δεῖ πρὸς ἡδονὴν δημηγορεῖν· εἰ
δ' ἡ τῶν λόγων χάρις, ἂν ᾖ μὴ προσήκουσα, ἔργῳ
ζημία γίγνεται, αἰσχρόν ἐστι φενακίζειν ἑαυτούς,
καὶ μετὰ τῆς ἐσχάτης ἀνάγκης πρᾶξαι ταῦθ' ἃ
πάλαι θέλοντας προσῆκεν ποιεῖν.

B

Οὐχὶ ταὐτὰ γιγνώσκειν, ὦ ἄνδρες Ἀθηναῖοι, παρίσταταί μοι, ὅταν τε τὸ τῆς πολιτείας ὄνομ' ὑμῶν
ἀκούσω, καὶ ὅταν τὸν τρόπον ὃν προσφέρονταί τινες
ὑμῶν τοῖς ὑπὲρ ταύτης λέγουσιν ἴδω. τὴν μὲν γὰρ
πολιτείαν δημοκρατίαν, ὥσπερ ἅπαντες ἴστ', ὀνο-
μάζετε· τῶν δὲ τἀναντία ταύτῃ λεγόντων ἐνίους
2 ἥδιον ἀκούοντας ὁρῶ. ὃ καὶ θαυμάζω τίς ποθ' ἡ
πρόφασις. πότερον προῖκα λέγειν ταῦτ' αὐτοὺς
[1420] οἴεσθε; ἀλλ' οἱ τῶν ὀλιγαρχιῶν, ὑπὲρ ὧν οὗτοι
λέγουσι, κύριοι καὶ πλείω σιωπῇ[1] μᾶλλον ἂν δοῖεν.
ἀλλὰ βελτίω ταῦτ' εἶναι τῶν ἑτέρων ὑπειλήφατε;
βελτίων ἄρ' ὑμῖν ὀλιγαρχία δημοκρατίας φαίνεται.
ἀλλ' αὐτοὺς εἶναι βελτίους ἡγεῖσθε; καὶ τίς ἂν

----

[1] σιωπῆς edd.

----

[a] The danger of speaking to please only is mentioned in
Phil. iii. 63-64 and *Olynth.* iii. 3.
[b] *Cf. Phil.* i. 38.
[c] The beginning of *Olynth.* iii. is similar but the occasion
different.

limit of wretchedness, but rather the speaker who, putting aside the thought of pleasing you, shall tell you what ought to be done and by what means we may cease bringing disgrace upon ourselves and incurring losses.[a] For, to speak truthfully, if all that a man passes over in his speech through reluctance to pain you is going to be passed over also by the course of events, it is right to harangue you for your pleasure; but if the charm of words, when unbecoming the occasion, becomes a penalty in action,[b] it is shameful to cheat yourselves, and to do only under the utmost necessity what you should have done voluntarily long before.

2 [c]

THE same thoughts do not present themselves to me, men of Athens, when I hear you refer by name to our form of government and again when I see the manner in which some of you treat those who speak in its defence. As you all know, the name you give to our government is democracy, but I see that some of you listen with more pleasure to those who advocate the opposite to it. I wonder just what their motive 2 may be. Or do you imagine they are making these speeches gratis? Well, the masters of the oligarchies, whose cause these men are pleading, might quietly increase their fees.[d] But honestly, have you assumed that their principles are better than the other kind? So oligarchy, presumably, looks better to you than democracy! Then do you think the men themselves are better? And yet who could

[a] This is ironical, explaining πρόφασις; virtual reported speech.

χρηστὸς ὑφ' ὑμῶν νομίζοιτ' εἰκότως, ἐναντία τῇ
καθεστώσῃ πολιτείᾳ δημηγορῶν; οὐκοῦν λοιπὸν
ἁμαρτάνειν ὑμᾶς ὅταν οὕτως ἔχητε τὴν γνώμην.
τοῦτο τοίνυν φυλάττεσθε μὴ πάσχειν, ὦ ἄνδρες
Ἀθηναῖοι, ὅπως μή ποτε τοῖς ἐπιβουλεύουσιν λαβὴν
δώσετε, εἶτα τότ' αἰσθήσεσθ' ἡμαρτηκότες ἡνίκ'
3 οὐδ' ὁτιοῦν ὑμῖν πλέον ἔσται.[1] τὸ μὲν οὖν, ὦ ἄνδρες
Ἀθηναῖοι, μὴ πάνθ' ὡς ἂν ἡμεῖς βουλοίμεθ' ἔχειν,
μήτε παρ' αὐτοῖς ἡμῖν μήτε παρὰ τοῖς συμμάχοις,
ἴσως οὐδέν ἐστι θαυμαστόν· πολλῶν γὰρ τὸ τῆς
τύχης αὐτόματον κρατεῖ, καὶ πολλαὶ προφάσεις τοῦ
μὴ πάντα κατὰ γνώμην συμβαίνειν ἀνθρώποις οὖσι.
τὸ δὲ μηδ' ὁτιοῦν μεταλαμβάνειν τὸν δῆμον, ἀλλὰ
τοὺς ἀντιπράττοντας περιεῖναι, τοῦτο καὶ θαυμαστόν, ὦ ἄνδρες Ἀθηναῖοι, καὶ φοβερὸν τοῖς εὖ φρονοῦσιν, ὡς ἐγὼ κρίνω. ἡ μὲν οὖν ἀρχὴ παντός
ἐσθ' αὕτη μοι τοῦ λόγου.

Γ

Ἀντὶ πολλῶν, ὦ ἄνδρες Ἀθηναῖοι, χρημάτων τὸ
μέλλον συνοίσειν περὶ ὧν νυνὶ τυγχάνετε σκοποῦντες
οἶμαι πάντας ἂν ὑμᾶς ἑλέσθαι. ὅτε τοίνυν τοῦθ'
οὕτως ἔχει, προσήκει παρέχειν ἐθέλοντας ἀκούειν
ὑμᾶς αὐτοὺς τῶν βουλομένων συμβουλεύειν· οὐ γὰρ
μόνον εἴ τι χρήσιμον ἐσκεμμένος ἥκει τις, τοῦτ' ἂν
ἀκούσαντες λάβοιτε, ἀλλὰ καὶ τῆς ὑμετέρας τύχης
ὑπολαμβάνω πολλὰ τῶν δεόντων ἐκ τοῦ παραχρῆμ'

---

[1] Blass prints the rest as a separate exordium, bracketing
οὖν.

reasonably be regarded by you as honest when he speaks in public against the interest of the established government ? Therefore it remains to conclude that you are mistaken when you hold this opinion. Consequently, be on your guard against falling into this error, men of Athens, so that you shall not some day give those who are plotting against you an opening, and only then learn that you have made a mistake, when it will no longer be of the least advantage to you. Now, the fact that everything is not going as 3 we might wish, men of Athens, either at home or among our allies, is perhaps not astonishing ; for in many things the whim of Fortune prevails and there are many plausible reasons why everything does not turn out according to plan, men being but men. Yet for the common people to have no portion at all and their opponents a superabundance is something to astound and alarm intelligent men, as I judge it, men of Athens. This, then, is the starting point of my entire speech.

3 [a]

I BELIEVE, men of Athens, that in preference to a large sum of money you would choose the plan that will pay you in the matters you are now considering. This being so, it is then your duty to show yourselves willing hearers of your prospective counsellors ; for not only in the event of someone having come here with a useful idea thought out, would you, having listened, have the benefit of it, but I also assume it to be part of your good fortune that many timely suggestions would occur to some men on the

[a] The beginning of *Olynth.* i. differs but slightly.

[1421] ἐνίοις ἐπελθεῖν ἂν εἰπεῖν, ὥστ' ἐξ ἁπάντων ῥᾳδίαν τὴν τοῦ συμφέροντος ὑμῖν αἵρεσιν γίγνεσθαι.

Δ

Ἔστιν, ὦ ἄνδρες Ἀθηναῖοι, δίκαιον, ἐπειδὴ ἐφ' ὑμῖν ἐστιν ἑλέσθαι τῶν ῥηθέντων ὅ τι ἂν βούλησθε, ἁπάντων ἀκοῦσαι. καὶ γὰρ πολλάκις συμβαίνει τὸν αὐτὸν ἄνθρωπον τοῦτο μὲν μὴ λέγειν ὀρθῶς, ἕτερον δέ τι· ἐκ μὲν οὖν τοῦ θορυβεῖν τάχ' ἂν δυσχεράναντες πολλῶν χρησίμων ἀποστερηθείητε, ἐκ δὲ τοῦ μετὰ κόσμου καὶ σιγῆς ἀκοῦσαι, καὶ τὰ καλῶς ἔχονθ' ἅπαντα ποιήσετε, κἂν δοκῇ τις παραληρεῖν, παραλείψετε. ἐγὼ μὲν οὖν οὔτ' εἴωθα μακρολογεῖν, οὔτ' ἄν, εἰ τὸν ἄλλον εἰώθειν χρόνον, νῦν ἐχρησάμην τούτῳ, ἀλλ' ἃ συμφέρειν ὑμῖν νομίζω, ταῦθ' ὡς ἂν δύνωμαι διὰ βραχυτάτων ἐρῶ πρὸς ὑμᾶς.

Ε

Ὁρῶ μέν, ὦ ἄνδρες Ἀθηναῖοι, παντάπασι πρόδηλον ὄν, οὕς τ' ἂν ἀκούσαιτε λόγους ἡδέως, καὶ πρὸς οὓς οὐκ οἰκείως ἔχετε· οὐ μὴν ἀλλὰ τὸ μὲν λέγειν ἅ τις οἴεται χαριεῖσθαι, τῶν παρακρούσασθαί τι βουλομένων εἶναι νομίζω, τὸ δ' ὑφίστασθαι, περὶ ὧν πέπεικεν ἑαυτὸν συμφέρειν τῇ πόλει, καὶ θορυβηθῆναι κἂν ἄλλο τι βούλησθ' ὑμεῖς, εὔνου καὶ 2 δικαίου τοῦτο πολίτου κρίνω. βουλοίμην δ' ἂν ὑμᾶς, εἰ καὶ μηδὲ δι' ἓν τῶν ἄλλων, δι' ἐκεῖνο ὑπομεῖναι τοὺς λόγους ἀμφοτέρων, ἵν' ἐὰν μὲν ὀρθότερον φανῇ τις λέγων ὧν ὑμεῖς ὡρμήκατε,

92

spur of the moment, so that from the whole number the choice of the advantageous is made easier for you.

4

IT is your duty, men of Athens, to listen to every proposal made, since it is your prerogative to adopt whichever of them you choose. For it often happens that the same person is wrong on one point and right on another ; and so by shouting him down when displeased you may perhaps deprive yourselves of many useful ideas, whereas by attending with decorum and in silence, you will act on every sound proposal, and if you think someone is making a foolish suggestion, you will ignore it. As for me, I am not accustomed to make long speeches, and even if previously I had been in the habit, I should not have taken this occasion to do so ; instead, I shall tell you as briefly as I can what I consider to be in your interests.

5

I OBSERVE, men of Athens, that there is no mistaking what kind of speeches you would like to hear and to what kind you are averse. Yet to say what one thinks will find favour I consider to be the badge of those who wish to work some deception, whereas to endure, when one is speaking for measures he is convinced are advantageous to the State, either your heckling or what else you choose to do, I judge to be the part of a loyal and honest citizen. And I should 2 like to have you bear patiently with the speeches of both sides to this end, if for no other, in order that, if someone shall be found to offer a proposal better than those upon which you are intent, you may avail

χρήσησθε τούτῳ, ἂν δ' ἀπολειφθῇ καὶ μὴ δύνηται
διδάξαι, δι' αὐτόν, ἀλλὰ μὴ δι' ὑμᾶς οὐκ ἐθέλοντας
ἀκούειν τοῦτο πεπονθέναι δοκῇ. ἔτι δ' οὐδὲ πάθοιτ'
ἂν ἀηδὲς τοσοῦτον εἰ πολλά τινος ληροῦντος ἀκού-
[1422] σαιτε, ὅσον εἰ τῶν δεόντων τι λέγειν ἔχοντός τινος
3 εἰπεῖν κωλύσαιτε. ἡ μὲν οὖν ἀρχὴ τοῦ δοκιμάζειν
ὀρθῶς ἅπαντ' ἐστὶ μηδὲν οἴεσθαι πρότερον γιγνώσκειν πρὶν μαθεῖν, ἄλλως τε καὶ συνειδότας πολλάκις ἤδη πολλοὺς μετεγνωκότας. ἂν τοίνυν ὑμεῖς
ταῦθ' ὑπάρξητε νῦν πεπεισμένοι, οἴομαι μετὰ
βραχέων λόγων καὶ αὐτὸς ἀντιλέγειν εἰκότως
δόξειν καὶ ὑμῖν τὰ βέλτιστα φανεῖσθαι λέγων.

ς

Πολλῶν, ὦ ἄνδρες Ἀθηναῖοι, λόγων εἰρημένων
παρὰ πάντων τῶν συμβεβουλευκότων, οὐδὲν ὑμᾶς
ὁρῶ νῦν ὄντας ἐγγυτέρω τοῦ τί πρακτέον εὑρῆσθαι,
ἢ πρὶν εἰς τὴν ἐκκλησίαν ἀναβῆναι. αἴτιον δὲ τούτου ταῦθ' ὅπερ οἶμαι τοῦ κακῶς ἔχειν τὰ ὅλα· οὐ
γὰρ παραινοῦσιν ὑμῖν ὑπὲρ τῶν παρόντων οἱ λέγοντες ἀλλ' ἑαυτῶν κατηγοροῦσι καὶ λοιδοροῦνται,
ὡς μὲν ἐγὼ κρίνω, συνεθίζοντες ὑμᾶς ἄνευ κρίσεως,
ὅσων εἰσὶν αἴτιοι κακῶν, ἀκούειν, ἵν' ἄν ποτ' ἄρ'
εἰς ἀγῶνα καθιστῶνται, μηδὲν ἡγούμενοι καινὸν
ἀκούειν, ἀλλ' ὑπὲρ ὧν ὠργίσθε πολλάκις, πραότεροι
δικασταὶ καὶ κριταὶ γίγνησθε τῶν πεπραγμένων
2 αὐτοῖς. τὴν μὲν οὖν αἰτίαν δι' ἣν ταῦτα ποιοῦσιν,

yourselves of it, but, if he falls short and is unable to make his point, that he may seem to have suffered this repulse through his own fault and not because of your refusing to listen. Furthermore, your experience would not be so disagreeable if you should listen to some fool making a long speech as it would if you prevented a man from speaking who had something timely to propose. In all matters, of 3 course, the first step toward right judgement is never to imagine you understand before learning, especially knowing as you do that many men before now have often changed their minds. If, then, you on your part are now convinced of these truths, I think that I on my part shall seem justified in speaking briefly in opposition and be found to propose the plans that are best for you.

6

ALTHOUGH many speeches have been made, men of Athens, by all your counsellors, I do not see that you are now any nearer to discovering what ought to be done than before you came up to the Assembly. The cause of this, in my opinion, is the same as the cause of the wretched plight of our affairs in general, that the speakers do not offer advice about the business before you, but accuse and revile one another, accustoming you, in my judgement, to hearing, without process of law, all the mischief of which they are the cause, in order that if, after all, they do come to face the test some day, you, thinking you are hearing nothing new, but only the charges over which you have often been angry, may so become more merciful jurors and judges of their misdeeds. Perhaps it 2

ἴσως ἀνόητον ἀκριβῶς ζητεῖν εἴη ἂν ἐν τῷ παρόντι·
ὅτι δ' ὑμῖν οὐχὶ συμφέρει, διὰ τοῦτ' ἐπιτιμῶ. ἐγὼ
δ' οὔτε κατηγορήσω τήμερον οὐδενός, οὔθ' ὑπο-
σχήσομαι τοιοῦτον οὐδὲν ὃ μὴ παραχρῆμ' ἐπιδείξω,
οὐδ' ὅλως τῶν αὐτῶν τούτοις οὐδὲν ποιήσω· ἀλλ'
ἃ βέλτιστα μὲν τοῖς πράγμασι, συμφέροντα δὲ τοῖς
βουλευομένοις ὑμῖν ἡγοῦμαι, ταῦθ' ὡς ἂν δύνωμαι
διὰ βραχυτάτων εἰπὼν καταβήσομαι.

Z

[1423] Οἱ μὲν ἐπαινοῦντες, ὦ ἄνδρες Ἀθηναῖοι, τοὺς
προγόνους ὑμῶν, λόγον εἰπεῖν μοι δοκοῦσι προαιρεῖσθαι κεχαρισμένον, οὐ μὴν συμφέροντά γ'
ἐκείνοις οὓς ἐγκωμιάζουσι ποιεῖν. περὶ γὰρ
πραγμάτων ἐγχειροῦντες λέγειν, ὧν οὐδ' ἂν εἷς
ἀξίως ἐφικέσθαι τῷ λόγῳ δύναιτο, αὐτοὶ μὲν τοῦ
δύνασθαι λέγειν δόξαν ἐκφέρονται, τὴν δ' ἐκείνων
ἀρετὴν ἐλάττω τῆς ὑπειλημμένης παρὰ τοῖς ἀκούουσιν φαίνεσθαι ποιοῦσιν. ἐγὼ δ' ἐκείνων μὲν
ἔπαινον τὸν χρόνον ἡγοῦμαι μέγιστον, οὗ πολλοῦ
γεγενημένου, μείζω τῶν ὑπ' ἐκείνων πραχθέντων
2 οὐδένες ἄλλοι παραδείξασθαι δεδύνηνται, αὐτὸς δὲ
πειράσομαι τὸν τρόπον εἰπεῖν ὅν μοι δοκεῖτε μάλιστα δύνασθαι παρασκευάσασθαι. καὶ γὰρ οὕτως
ἔχει· εἰ μὲν ἡμεῖς ἅπαντες λέγειν δεινοὶ φανείημεν,
οὐδὲν ἂν τὰ ὑμέτερ' εὖ οἶδ' ὅτι βέλτιον σχοίη· εἰ
δὲ παρελθὼν εἰς ὁστισοῦν δύναιτο διδάξαι καὶ πεῖσαι τίς παρασκευὴ καὶ πόση καὶ πόθεν πορισθεῖσα
χρήσιμος ἔσται τῇ πόλει, πᾶς ὁ παρὼν λέλυται

---

[a] The beginning of XIV is identical.

would be foolish at the moment to inquire into the exact reason why they do this ; but because it harms you, for this reason I censure them. For my own part, I will accuse no one to-day nor will I sponsor any charge that I shall not make good on the spot, nor, in general, will I do any of the things which these men do ; but when I have stated as briefly as I can what I think best for your interests and most profitable for you who deliberate, I will step down.

7 [a]

THOSE who praise your forefathers, men of Athens, in my judgement choose a charming theme upon which to speak, and yet I do not think they do a favour to those whom they extol. For instance, when they undertake to tell of the deeds of those men, to which no speaker could do justice, while winning for themselves a reputation for ability to speak, they cause the valour of those men to seem to their hearers less than had been supposed. As for me, I consider the greatest commendation of those heroes to be the test of time, for although a long interval has gone by, no others have been able to exhibit greater deeds than those performed by them, and I shall myself merely 2 try to tell you after what manner I think you will be best able to make your preparations. For this is the situation ; though we should all prove ourselves to be clever speakers, I know well that your interests would not be advanced in the slightest, but if just one speaker, no matter who, should come forward and be able to demonstrate convincingly what kind of preparation, and how great, and provided from what funds, would be to the State's advantage, all our

97

φόβος. ἐγὼ δὴ τοῦτ', ἂν ἄρ' οἷός τ' ὦ, πειράσομαι
ποιῆσαι, μικρὰ προειπὼν ὑμῖν ὡς ἔχω γνώμης περὶ
τῶν πρὸς τὸν βασιλέα.

H

Ἀμφότεροί μοι δοκοῦσιν ἁμαρτάνειν, ὦ ἄνδρες
Ἀθηναῖοι, καὶ οἱ τοῖς Ἀρκάσιν καὶ οἱ τοῖς Λακεδαιμονίοις συνειρηκότες. ὥσπερ γὰρ ἀφ' ἑκατέρων
ἥκοντες, οὐχ ὑμῶν ὄντες, πρὸς οὓς ἀμφότεροι
πρεσβεύονται, κατηγοροῦσι καὶ διαβάλλουσιν ἀλλήλους. ἦν δὲ τοῦτο μὲν τῶν ἀφιγμένων ἔργον, τὸ
δὲ κοινῶς ὑπὲρ τῶν πραγμάτων λέγειν καὶ τὰ
[1424] βέλτισθ' ὑπὲρ ὑμῶν σκοπεῖν ἄνευ φιλονικίας, τῶν
2 ἐνθάδε συμβουλεύειν ἀξιούντων. νῦν δ', εἴ τις
αὐτῶν ἀφέλοι τὸ γιγνώσκεσθαι καὶ τὸ τῇ φωνῇ
λέγειν ἀττικιστί, πολλοὺς ἂν οἴομαι τοὺς μὲν
Ἀρκάδας, τοὺς δὲ Λάκωνας αὐτῶν εἶναι νομίσαι.

Ἐγὼ δ' οἶδα μὲν ὡς χαλεπὸν τὰ βέλτιστα λέγειν
ἐστίν· συνεξηπατημένων γὰρ ὑμῶν, καὶ τῶν μὲν
ταυτί, τῶν δὲ ταυτὶ βουλομένων, ἐὰν τὰ μεταξύ τις
ἐγχειρῇ λέγειν κᾆθ' ὑμεῖς μὴ περιμείνητε μαθεῖν,
χαριεῖται μὲν οὐδετέροις, διαβλήσεται δὲ πρὸς
3 ἀμφοτέρους· οὐ μὴν ἀλλ' αἱρήσομαι μᾶλλον αὐτός,
ἐὰν ἄρα τοῦτο πάθω, δοκεῖν φλυαρεῖν, ἢ παρ' ἃ
βέλτιστα νομίζω προέσθαι τισὶν ὑμᾶς ἐξαπατῆσαι.
τὰ μὲν οὖν ἄλλ' ὕστερον, ἂν ὑμῖν βουλομένοις ᾖ,

---

a Of Persia, known also as " the great king."
b The beginning of XVI is identical.

present apprehension is as good as dispelled. This I shall try to do, if, after all, I am able, having first told you briefly how my opinion stands with respect to our relations with the King.[a]

8 [b]

BOTH parties seem to me to be in the wrong, men of Athens, both those who have supported the Arcadians and those who have supported the Spartans. For, just as if they had come here from one or the other of the two countries and were not of your own citizen body, to which both embassies are appealing, they are denouncing and abusing one another. This, however, was a concern of the visiting envoys, while to discuss the questions in the common interest and to consider your own interest without self-seeking is the duty of those who see fit to offer advice here in Athens. Yet as things now are, if one could cancel 2 the fact of their being known and their using the Attic speech, many people, I believe, would think the one group Arcadians and the other Spartans !

I know myself how difficult it is to propose the best procedure, for when you have been deceived and some of you want this and others that, if someone undertakes to suggest a compromise and then you do not wait to learn the facts, he will please neither party and will be put in the wrong with both sides. Nevertheless, I shall choose to be thought to talk 3 nonsense, if that, after all, is to be my fate, rather than to abandon you to certain people to be deceived in violation of what I consider best for you. And so, with your permission, I shall go into other

99

λέξω· ἐκ δὲ τῶν ὁμολογουμένων ὑπ' αὐτῶν ἄρξομαι,
ἃ κράτιστα νομίζω, διδάσκειν.

Θ

Οὐχὶ ταὐτὰ γιγνώσκων ἐνίοις τῶν εἰρηκότων
ἀνέστηκ', ὦ ἄνδρες Ἀθηναῖοι. οὐ μὴν οὐδὲ τούτους αἰτιάσομαι κακίᾳ τἀναντία τοῖς βελτίστοις
εἰρηκέναι, ἀλλ' ὅτι πολλοὶ τοῦ τὰ πράγματα κρίνειν
ἀμελήσαντες, τοὺς λόγους σκοπεῖν οὓς ἐροῦσιν εἰώ-
θασι, κἂν τούτοις ἀφθόνοις ἐντύχωσιν, ἑτοίμως
δημηγορεῖν, οὐκ ὀρθῶς ἐγνωκότες, οὐδὲ λογιζόμενοι παρ' ἑαυτοῖς ὅτι πολλῶν πράξεων ἐν πολλῷ
χρόνῳ πᾶσι πεπραγμένων, καὶ διὰ τοὺς καιροὺς
ἐνίων ὑπεναντίων αὐταῖς, ἂν τὰς ἑτέρας τις ὑπερ-
βαίνων τὰς ἑτέρας λέγῃ, λήσει τὸ ῥᾷστον τῶν
2 ἔργων ποιῶν, αὐτὸν ἐξαπατῶν. οἱ μὲν οὖν οὕτω
χρώμενοι τῷ συμβουλεύειν δοκοῦσί μοι τὴν ἀπὸ
τῶν ῥηθέντων τοῦ δύνασθαι λέγειν δόξαν γιγνο-
[1425] μένην αὐτοῖς ἱκανὴν φιλοτιμίαν ἡγεῖσθαι· ἐγὼ δὲ
νομίζω χρῆναι τὸν πόλει περὶ πραγμάτων ἐπι-
χειροῦντα συμβουλεύειν, μᾶλλον ὅπως τὰ δόξαντα
συνοίσει σκοπεῖν, ἢ πῶς οἱ παραχρῆμα λόγοι χάριν
ἕξουσι. δεῖ γὰρ τοῖς ἐπὶ τῶν λόγων εὐδοκιμοῦσι
συμφέροντός τινος ἔργου πρᾶξιν προσεῖναι, ἵνα μὴ
νῦν μόνον ἀλλ' ἀεὶ τὰ ῥηθέντα καλῶς ἔχῃ.

details later, and proceed to explain what I think is best, starting from the premises upon which both sides agree.

9

I HAVE taken the floor, men of Athens, because I do not hold the same views as some of those who have spoken. Still I shall not allege that these men out of villainy have expressed sentiments opposed to your best interests, but I say that many, while neglecting to judge events critically, make a practice of considering the words they will use, and if they chance to find an ample supply of these, of haranguing the people without more ado. In this they are wrong nor do they reflect in their own minds that, since it is the experience of all that over a long period many plans have worked out happily and some of them, because of the times, quite contrary to their promise, if some speaker cites the one kind and passes over the other, he will unconsciously be doing the easiest thing in the world, deceiving himself. Now those 2 who thus use the privilege of advising you seem to me to look upon the reputation for eloquence accruing to them from their speeches as an adequate ambition, but it is my opinion that the man who proposes to advise the State on matters of policy should rather consider how the measures adopted shall prove of benefit, and not how his remarks of the moment may find favour. For those who win esteem by their words ought to add to it the accomplishment of some useful work in order that not only now, but for all time, their utterances may have merit.

DEMOSTHENES

I

Εἰ μὲν ἐγνώκατ᾽, ὦ ἄνδρες Ἀθηναῖοι, τί βέλτιστον ὂν τυγχάνει πρᾶξαι περὶ τῶν παρόντων, ἁμάρ-
τημα τὸ συμβουλεύειν προτιθέναι· ἃ γὰρ αὐτοὶ
πρὶν ἀκοῦσαι δοκιμάζετε συμφέρειν, τί δεῖ ταῦτ᾽
ἀκούοντας μάτην ἐνοχλεῖσθαι; εἰ δὲ σκοπεῖτε καὶ
βουλεύεσθ᾽ ὡς ἐκ τῶν ῥηθησομένων δοκιμάσαι δέον,
οὐκ ὀρθῶς ἔχει τὸ κωλύειν τοὺς βουλομένους λέγειν·
παρὰ μὲν γὰρ τῶν ὅλως ἀποστερεῖσθ᾽ ἐκ τοῦ
τοῦτο ποιεῖν, εἴ τι χρήσιμον ἐντεθύμηνται, τοὺς δ᾽
ἀφέντας ἃ τυγχάνουσιν ἐγνωκότες, ὧν ὑμᾶς ἐπι-
2 θυμεῖν οἴονται, ταῦτα ποιεῖτε συμβουλεύειν. ἔστι
δ᾽ ἁμαρτάνειν μὲν βουλομένων τὸ συναναγκάζειν
τὸν παριόνθ᾽ ἃ βούλεσθε λέγειν, βουλευομένων δ᾽
ἀκούσαντας ἃ γιγνώσκει σκοπεῖν, κἄν τι καλῶς
ἔχῃ, χρῆσθαι. λέγω δὲ ταῦτ᾽ οὐκ ἐναντία τοῖς
ὑμῖν ἀρέσκουσι μέλλων παραινεῖν, ἀλλ᾽ ἐκεῖνο
εἰδώς, ὅτι ἂν μὲν μὴ θελήσητε τῶν ἀντιλεγόντων
ἀκοῦσαι, ἐξηπατῆσθαι φήσουσιν ὑμᾶς, ἂν δ᾽ ἀκούσαντες μὴ πεισθῆτε, ἐξεληλεγμένοι παραχρῆμ᾽
ἔσονται τὰ χείρω παραινοῦντες.

ΙΑ

Οἴομαι πάντας ὑμᾶς, ὦ ἄνδρες Ἀθηναῖοι, γιγνώσκειν, ὅτι οὐ κρινοῦντες ἥκετε τήμερον οὐδένα τῶν
[1426] ἀδικούντων, ἀλλὰ βουλευσόμενοι περὶ τῶν παρόντων. δεῖ τοίνυν τὰς μὲν κατηγορίας ὑπερθέσθαι
πάσας, καὶ τότ᾽ ἐν ὑμῖν λέγειν καθ᾽ ὅτου πέπεικεν

102

10

If you have decided, men of Athens, what it is best to do in the circumstances, it is a mistake to propose debate ; for why should you be needlessly bored by listening to what you have yourselves judged to be expedient before hearing it discussed ? But if, assuming that you must reach a judgement on the basis of what shall be said, you are exploring and deliberating, it is wrong to stop those who wish to speak, since by so doing you are deprived entirely of whatever practical proposal some speakers have thought up, and you cause other speakers to abandon their own conclusions in favour of what they think you desire to hear. While to unite in forcing the 2 speaker to express your wishes shows an intention to do wrong, the willingness to deliberate is proved when you listen to his views, scan them and, if any is good, adopt it. I say this, not as one about to recommend measures opposed to those you are favouring, but as one who knows that, if you refuse to hear the opposition, they will say you have been deceived, while, if you do listen and are not persuaded, they will have been proved on the spot to be offering the worse proposals.

11

I think you all know, men of Athens, that you have not come here to-day to put any of the wrongdoers on trial but to deliberate about the present state of affairs. So it is our duty to defer all accusations and only when we put someone on trial *a* should this or

---

a The Assembly sometimes acted as a court, for example, in cases of treason.

ἕκαστος ἑαυτόν, ὅταν τινὰ κρίνωμεν· εἰ δέ τίς τι χρήσιμον ἢ συμφέρον εἰπεῖν ἔχει, τοῦτο νῦν ἀποφαίνεσθαι. τὸ μὲν γὰρ κατηγορεῖν τοῖς πεπραγμένοις ἐγκαλούντων ἐστί τὸ δὲ συμβουλεύειν περὶ τῶν παρόντων καὶ γενησομένων προτίθεται. οὐκοῦν οὐ λοιδορίας οὐδὲ μέμψεως ὁ παρὼν καιρός, ἀλλὰ συμβουλῆς εἶναί μοι δοκεῖ. διὸ πειράσομαι μὲν φυλάξασθαι, ὃ τούτοις ἐπιτιμῶ, μὴ παθεῖν αὐτός, συμβουλεῦσαι δ' ἃ κράτιστα νομίζω περὶ τῶν παρόντων.

IB

Οὐδέν' ἂν ἀντειπεῖν, ὦ ἄνδρες Ἀθηναῖοι, νομίζω, ὡς οὐ κακοῦ πολίτου καὶ φαύλου τὴν γνώμην ἀνδρός ἐστιν, οὕτω τινὰ μισεῖν ἢ φιλεῖν τῶν ἐπὶ τὰ κοινὰ προσιόντων ὥστε τοῦ τῇ πόλει βελτίστου μηδὲν φροντίζειν, ἀλλὰ τὰ μὲν πρὸς ἐπήρειαν, τὰ δὲ πρὸς φιλίαν δημηγορεῖν, ἃ ποιοῦσ' ἔνιοι τῶν δευρὶ παριόντων. ἐγὼ δὲ τούτοις μὲν τοσοῦτον ἂν εἴποιμι, ὅτι μοι δοκοῦσιν οὐδ' εἴ τι πεποιήκασι τοιοῦτον μέγισθ' ἡμαρτηκέναι, ἀλλ' ὅτι δηλοῦσιν
2 οὐδέποτ' οὐδὲ παύσασθαι παρεσκευασμένοι. ὑμῖν δὲ παραινῶ μὴ προϊεμένους ὑμᾶς αὐτοὺς ἱκανὸν τοῦτο νομίζειν, δίκην, ὅταν ὑμῖν δόξῃ, παρὰ τούτων λαβεῖν, ἀλλὰ καὶ τούτους, ὅσον ἐστὶν ἐν ὑμῖν, κωλύειν, καὶ αὐτούς, ὥσπερ ὑπὲρ πόλεως προσήκει βουλευομένους, τὰς ἰδίας ἀνελόντας φιλονικίας τὸ κοινῇ βέλτιστον σκοπεῖσθαι, ἐνθυμουμένους ὅτι οὐ-

that man speak before you against another who,
he has convinced himself, is an offender. But if
anyone has something practical or profitable to say,
now is the time to declare it. For accusation is for
those who have fault to find with past actions, but
in deliberative session the discussion is solely about
present and future actions. Therefore the present
is no occasion for abuse or blame but for taking
counsel together, it seems to me. For this reason
I shall try to guard against falling myself into the
error which I condemn in these men and to offer
the advice that I think best in the present state of
affairs.

12

I think that no man will deny, men of Athens, that
it is the mark of a disloyal citizen and a low-minded
man so to hate or favour anyone who enters into
public life that he takes no thought for the State's
best interests, but shapes his public utterances sometimes to vent his malice and sometimes to prove his
friendship, as a number of those are doing who come
forward here to speak. To these I would say no
more than this : that in my opinion, if they have
done something of the kind, their greatest offence is
not this, but rather that they show themselves unpre-
pared ever to stop doing it ! As for yourselves, I give
you this advice : do not be guilty of self-ruin and
think it enough if you punish these men when you
see fit ; but, while holding them in check so far as
lies in your power, you must yourselves, as becomes
men deliberating on behalf of the State, put aside
your own private feuds and aim at what is most to
the common good, reflecting that the punishment of

DEMOSTHENES

[1427] δείς, οὐδ᾽ ἅμα πάντες οἱ πολιτευόμενοι, τῶν νόμων, ἐφ᾽ οἷς ὑμεῖς ἐστ᾽, ἀξιόχρεώ εἰσι[1] διαφθαρέντων δίκην δοῦναι.

ΙΓ

Ἴσως ἐπίφθονον ἄν τισιν, ὦ ἄνδρες Ἀθηναῖοι, δόξειεν εἶναι, εἴ τις ὢν ἰδιώτης καὶ τῶν πολλῶν ὑμῶν εἷς, ἑτέρων συμβεβουλευκότων οἳ καὶ τῷ πάλαι πολιτεύεσθαι καὶ τῷ παρ᾽ ὑμῖν δόξαν ἔχειν προέχουσι, παρελθὼν εἴποι, ὅτι οὐ μόνον αὐτῷ δοκοῦσιν οὐκ ὀρθῶς λέγειν, ἀλλ᾽ οὐδ᾽ ἐγγὺς εἶναι τοῦ τὰ δέοντα γιγνώσκειν. οὐ μὴν ἀλλ᾽ ἔγωγ᾽ οὕτω σφόδρ᾽ οἶμαι μᾶλλον ὑμῖν συμφέροντ᾽ ἐρεῖν τούτων, ὥστε οὐκ ὀκνήσω πάνθ᾽ ἃ τυγχάνουσιν εἰρηκότες ἄξια μηδενὸς εἶναι φῆσαι. νομίζω δὲ καὶ ὑμᾶς ὀρθῶς ἂν ποιεῖν εἰ, μὴ τὸν λέγοντ᾽, ἀλλὰ τὰ συμβουλευόμενα σκοποῖτε. δεῖ γάρ, ὦ ἄνδρες Ἀθηναῖοι, τὴν παρ᾽ ὑμῶν εὔνοιαν μή τισιν, ὥσπερ ἐκ γένους, ἀλλὰ τοῖς τὰ βέλτιστ᾽ ἀεὶ λέγουσιν ὑπάρχειν.

ΙΔ

Βουλοίμην ἂν ὑμᾶς, ὦ ἄνδρες Ἀθηναῖοι, προσέχοντας ἃ μέλλω λέγειν ἀκοῦσαι· καὶ γάρ ἐστιν οὐ μικρά. ἐγὼ θαυμάζω τί δή ποτε, πρὶν μὲν εἰς τὴν ἐκκλησίαν ἀναβῆναι, ὅτῳ τις ἂν ὑμῶν ἐντύχῃ, οὗτος εὐπόρως εἰπεῖν ἔχει δι᾽ ὧν ἂν τὰ παρόντα πράγματα βελτίω γένοιτο· καὶ πάλιν αὐτίκα δὴ μάλ᾽ ἐὰν ἀπέλθητε, ὁμοίως ἕκαστος ἐρεῖ τὰ δέ-

[1] ἀξιόχρεώς ἐστιν Blass.

---

[a] Or, less probably, " the laws of which you are in charge."

106

no individual, nor even of all the politicians in a body, can square the account if once the laws should be destroyed on which your very life depends.[a]

13

PERHAPS it might seem offensive to certain persons, men of Athens, if someone, an ordinary citizen and one of the common people like yourselves, should come forward after others who are eminent for both long political experience and reputation among you have already stated their opinions, and say that he thinks the others are not only wrong but not even near to discerning what ought to be done. Nevertheless, I feel so confident that I am going to give more profitable counsel than theirs that I shall not hesitate to declare all they have said to be worthless. I think that you too would be doing well if you kept in view, not the speaker, but the advice being offered. For the right thing, men of Athens, is to extend your goodwill, not to certain persons as though by hereditary privilege, but to those who from time to time offer the best counsel.

14

I SHOULD like you to listen attentively to what I am going to say, men of Athens ; it is not unimportant. I wonder just why it is that, before we come up to the Assembly, any one of you whom a person may chance to meet is prepared to say readily by what means the present state of affairs may be improved ; and then again, the minute you leave the Assembly, each man will be just as ready to say what we ought to do.

οντα· ἐν δὲ τῷ περὶ τούτων σκοπεῖν ὄντες καὶ συνειλεγμένοι, πάντα μᾶλλον ἢ ταῦτα λεγόντων τινῶν
2 ἀκούετε. ἆρά γ', ὦ ἄνδρες Ἀθηναῖοι, γνῶναι μὲν
ἔστιν ἑκάστῳ τὰ δέονθ' ὑμῶν καὶ τὰ τῶν ἄλλων
εἰπεῖν ἐπίσταται, ποιῶν δ' αὐτὸς ἕκαστος οὐ χαίρει,
εἶτ' ἰδίᾳ μέν, ὡς ἄρ' αὐτὸς ἑτοίμως τὰ βέλτιστ' ἂν
[1428] πράττειν δόξων, τοῖς ἄλλοις ἐπιτιμᾷ, κοινῇ δ' εὐ-
λαβεῖσθε τὰ τοιαῦτα ψηφίζεσθαι δι' ὧν ἐν τῷ
3 λῃτουργεῖν τι τῶν καθηκόντων ἅπαντες ἔσεσθε; εἰ
μὲν τοίνυν μηδένα καιρὸν οἴεσθ' ἥξειν ὃς εἴσω τῆς
εἰρωνείας ἀφίξεται ταύτης, καλῶς ἂν ἔχοι τοῦτον
τὸν τρόπον διάγειν· εἰ δὲ τὰ πράγμαθ' ὁρᾶτ' ἐγγυτέρω προσάγοντα, δεῖ σκοπεῖσθαι ὅπως μὴ
πλησίον αὐτοῖς μαχεῖσθε ἃ πόρρωθεν ἔξεστι φυλάξασθαι, καὶ τοὺς νῦν περιοφθέντας ἐφηδομένους
ὕστερον ἕξετ' οἷς ἂν πάσχητε.

IE

Περὶ μὲν τῶν παρόντων, ὦ ἄνδρες Ἀθηναῖοι,
πραγμάτων τῇ πόλει, καίπερ οὐκ ἐχόντων ὡς ἔδει,
οὐ πάνυ μοι δοκεῖ τῶν χαλεπῶν εἶναι ζητῆσαι τί
ἄν τις πράξας βελτίω ποιήσειεν. ὅντινα μέντοι
χρὴ τρόπον πρὸς ὑμᾶς εἰπεῖν περὶ αὐτῶν, τοῦτο
παμπόλλην δυσκολίαν ἔχειν νομίζω, οὐχ ὡς οὐ
συνησόντων ὅ τι ἄν τις λέγῃ, ἀλλ' οὕτω πολλὰ
καὶ ψευδῆ καὶ πάντα μᾶλλον ἢ τὰ βέλτιστα τοῖς

But when we are met together and dealing with these problems, you hear anything rather than this from certain speakers. Then has each one of you, men 2 of Athens, the gift of deciding what ought to be done, and does each know how to state the duties of the rest, while he is reluctant himself to do his own, and then again, does each man as an individual, as if to give the impression of being one who would of course promptly do what is best, find fault with everyone else, but as a body are you committed to fighting shy of voting such measures as will ensure that you will one and all become engaged in performing some duty to the State ? Well then, if you really 3 think that no crisis will arrive to make a breach in this fence of evasiveness, it would be grand to carry on after this fashion. But if you see your troubles drawing nearer, you must plan that you shall not have to grapple with them at close range when it is possible to forestall them from a distance, and that you shall not have those whom you now disregard exulting later on at your discomfiture.

15

As for the problems now confronting the State, men of Athens, even though things are not as they should be, I do not consider it altogether difficult to discover by what action one may effect an improvement. I judge, on the other hand, that the manner in which I must speak to you about them means very grave irritation ; not because you will fail to understand what a person will say but because you seem to me to have become so accustomed to hearing many un-truths and anything rather than what best meets

πράγμασιν συνειθίσθαι μοι δοκεῖτ' ἀκούειν, ὥστε
δέδοικα μὴ τῷ νῦν τὰ βέλτιστ' εἰπόντι, ἣν τοῖς ἐξ-
ηπατηκόσιν προσῆκεν ἀπέχθειαν ὑπάρχειν παρ'
2 ὑμῶν, ταύτην ἀπενέγκασθαι συμβῇ. ὁρῶ γὰρ ὑμᾶς
πολλάκις οὐ τοὺς αἰτίους τῶν πραγμάτων μισοῦντας,
ἀλλὰ τοὺς ὑστάτους περὶ αὐτῶν εἰπόντας τι πρὸς
ὑμᾶς. οὐ μὴν ἀλλὰ καίπερ οὕτως ἀκριβῶς ταῦτα
λογιζόμενος, ὅμως οἶμαι πάντα παρεὶς τἆλλα,
περὶ αὐτῶν τῶν παρόντων ἃ κράτιστα νομίζω δεῖν
λέγειν.

Ιϛ

Ἐβουλόμην ἂν ὑμᾶς, ὦ ἄνδρες Ἀθηναῖοι, ᾗ πρὸς
τοὺς ἄλλους ἅπαντας εἰώθατε προσφέρεσθαι φιλαν-
θρωπίᾳ, ταύτῃ καὶ πρὸς ὑμᾶς αὐτοὺς χρῆσθαι· νυνὶ
δ' ἀμείνους ἐστὲ τὰ τῶν ἄλλων δεῖν' ἐπανορθοῦν,
[1429] ἢ τῶν ὑμῖν αὐτοῖς συμβαινόντων φροντίζειν. ἴσως
μὲν οὖν αὐτὸ τοῦτό τις ἂν φήσειε μέγιστον ἔπαινον
φέρειν τῇ πόλει, τὸ μηδενὸς εἵνεκα κέρδους ἰδίου
πολλοὺς κινδύνους ὑπὲρ αὐτοῦ τοῦ δικαίου προῃρῆ-
σθαι. ἐγὼ δὲ ταύτην τ' ἀληθῆ τὴν δόξαν εἶναι
νομίζω κατὰ τῆς πόλεως καὶ βούλομαι, κἀκεῖνο δὲ
ὑπολαμβάνω σωφρόνων ἀνθρώπων ἔργον εἶναι,
ἴσην πρόνοιαν τῶν αὐτοῖς οἰκείων ὅσην περ τῶν
ἀλλοτρίων ποιεῖσθαι, ἵνα μὴ φιλάνθρωποι μόνον,
ἀλλὰ καὶ νοῦν ἔχοντες φαίνησθε.

ΙΖ

Ἴσως, ὦ ἄνδρες Ἀθηναῖοι, προσήκει τῷ βουλομένῳ τι παραινεῖν ὑμῖν, οὕτω πειρᾶσθαι λέγειν

_____
a Cf. Olynth. i. 16.

your needs, that I fear it may be the lot of the man who now makes the best proposal to earn for his reward at your hands the hostility which would properly have been the due of those who have deceived you. For I observe that often you hate, not 2 those who are to blame for your troubles, but those who have most recently made mention of them to you.[a] Nevertheless, although I am so precisely measuring this hazard, I still think that I must put all other subjects aside and confine myself to saying what I think is the best advice about the present situation.

16

I SHOULD have wished, men of Athens, that you treat yourselves with that benevolence which you are accustomed to practise toward all other peoples. As it now is, you are better at rectifying the woes of others than you are at taking to heart the troubles which befall yourselves. Someone may perhaps say, of course, that this is exactly what brings the greatest glory to the State—to have deliberately chosen to assume many risks for the sake of sheer justice with no thought of selfish advantage. Now, while I for one believe this reputation which prevails concerning the State to be true and desire it to be, yet I assume it also to be an obligation of prudent men to exercise as much foresight in their domestic affairs as in those of strangers, so that you may show yourselves to be not only men of goodwill but sensible also.

17

PERHAPS it really is the duty, men of Athens, of one who wishes to recommend some measure to you to

ὡς καὶ δυνήσεσθ' ὑπομεῖναι· εἰ δὲ μὴ τοῦτ', ἀφέντα
τοὺς ἄλλους ἅπαντας λόγους, περὶ αὐτῶν ὧν σκοπεῖτε συμβουλεύειν, καὶ ταῦθ' ὡς διὰ βραχυτάτων.
οὐ γὰρ ἐνδείᾳ μοι δοκεῖτε λόγων οὐδὲ νῦν ὁρᾶν τὰ
πράγματα πάντα λελυμασμένα, ἀλλὰ τῷ τοὺς μὲν
ἑαυτῶν εἵνεκα δημηγορεῖν καὶ πολιτεύεσθαι, τοὺς
δὲ μήπω τούτου δεδωκότας πεῖραν, μᾶλλον ὅπως
εὖ δόξουσι λέγειν σπουδάζειν, ἢ πῶς ἔργον ἐξ ὧν
λέγουσί τι συμφέρον πραχθήσεται. ἐγὼ δ' ἵνα μὴ
λάθω τοὐναντίον οὗ φημι δεῖν αὐτὸς ποιῶν, καὶ
πλείω περὶ τῶν ἄλλων λέγων ἢ περὶ ὧν ἀνέστην
ἐρῶν, ἀφεὶς τἆλλα πάντα, ἃ παραινῶ καὶ δὴ πειράσομαι πρὸς ὑμᾶς εἰπεῖν.

ΙΗ

Δοκεῖτέ μοι δικαίως ἄν, ὦ ἄνδρες Ἀθηναῖοι,
προσέχειν τὸν νοῦν, εἴ τις ὑπόσχοιθ' ὑμῖν ταὐτὰ
δίκαια καὶ συμφέροντα δείξειν ὄνθ' ὑπὲρ ὧν βου-
[1430] λευόμεθα. ἐγὼ τοίνυν οἶμαι τοῦτο ποιήσειν οὐ
χαλεπῶς, ἂν ὑμεῖς βραχύ μοι πεισθῆτε πάνυ. μὴ
πάνθ', ὡς ἕκαστος ἔχει γνώμης ὑμῶν περὶ τῶν
παρόντων, ὀρθῶς ἐγνωκέναι πεπείσθω· ἀλλ' ἂν
παρὰ ταῦτά τι συμβαίνη λέγεσθαι, σκοπείτω πάνθ'
ὑπομείνας ἀκοῦσαι, εἶτ' ἂν ὀρθῶς εἰρῆσθαί τι δοκῇ
χρήσθω. οὐ γὰρ ἧττον ὑμέτερον τῶν χρησαμένων
ἔσται τὸ κατορθωθὲν ἢ τοῦ πρὸς ὑμᾶς εἰπόντος. ἢ

attempt to speak in such a way that you will find it possible to hear him to the end ; but otherwise his duty is to leave aside all other themes and discuss only those matters you are considering, and these as briefly as possible. For I do not think it due to any lack of speeches that now once more you observe all your affairs to be in a muddle, but the reason is that some are orating and playing politics for their own gain, and others, who have so far not given evidence of this offence, are more concerned to be thought good speakers than that some concrete good may be effected by what they say. As for me, that I may not unwittingly do the opposite of what I myself say is right, and say more about other matters than about those of which I have risen to speak, I shall disregard all other topics and endeavour to tell you forthwith what I recommend.

18

I THINK that you would rightly pay attention, men of Athens, if any man should promise to demonstrate that in the matters you are considering justice and expediency coincide. Now I believe that I shall do this without difficulty if you on your part will comply with a very slight request of mine. Let none of you, according as one or another has an opinion about the present situation, be positive that he is right in all his conclusions ; but, if it turns out that something be said against these, let him consider it, listening to all the points patiently, and then, if some suggestion seems to have been rightly made, adopt it. For the measure that succeeds will belong no less to you who adopted it than to him who proposed

113

μὲν οὖν ἀρχὴ τοῦ σκοπεῖν ὀρθῶς ἐστι μὴ βεβουλεῦ-
σθαι πρὶν ἐξ ὧν δεῖ βουλεύσασθαι ἀκοῦσαι. οὐ γὰρ
αὐτὸς οὔτε καιρὸς οὔτε τρόπος τοῦ τ᾽ ἐπικυρῶσαι
τὰ δοκοῦντα, καὶ τοῦ σκέψασθαι τί πρῶτον δοκεῖ
συμφέρειν.

ΙΘ

Μεθ᾽ ὑμῶν, ὦ ἄνδρες Ἀθηναῖοι, παρελήλυθα βου-
λευσόμενος πότερον χρή με λέγειν ἢ μή. διὸ
δ᾽ αὐτὸς τοῦτ᾽ ἀπορῶ κρῖναι φράσω πρὸς ὑμᾶς.
ἀναγκαῖον εἶναί μοι δοκεῖ τῷ μήθ᾽ αὑτῷ μήτε τισὶν
χαρίσασθαι βουλομένῳ, ἀλλ᾽ ὑπὲρ ὑμῶν εἰπεῖν ἃ
πέπεικεν ἑαυτὸν μάλιστα συμφέρειν, καὶ συνειπεῖν
ἃ καλῶς λέγουσιν ἀμφότεροι, καὶ τοὐναντίον ἀντειπεῖν ὅσα μὴ δίκαι᾽ ἀξιοῦσιν. εἰ μὲν οὖν ὑμεῖς
ὑπομείναιτ᾽ ἀκοῦσαι ταῦτ᾽ ἀμφότερα διὰ βραχέων,
πολλῷ βέλτιον ἂν περὶ τῶν λοιπῶν βουλεύσαισθε·
εἰ δὲ πρὶν μαθεῖν ἀποσταίητε, γένοιτ᾽ ἂν ἐμοὶ
μηδετέρους ἀδικοῦντι πρὸς ἀμφοτέρους διαβεβλῆ-
σθαι. τοῦτο δ᾽ οὐχὶ δίκαιός εἰμι παθεῖν. ἂν μὲν
οὖν κελεύητε, ἕτοιμός εἰμι λέγειν· εἰ δὲ μή, καὶ
σιωπᾶν ἔχει μοι καλῶς.

Κ

[1431] Καὶ δίκαιον, ὦ ἄνδρες Ἀθηναῖοι, καὶ συμφέρον
ὑμῖν ἡγοῦμαι, τὰς μὲν αἰτίας καὶ τὰς κατηγορίας
ὅταν βουλεύεσθαι δέῃ παραλείπειν, περὶ τῶν παρόντων δὲ λέγειν ὅ τι βέλτιστον ἕκαστος ἡγεῖται.

ᵃ A measure was often debated several times before being
ratified.   Debate should be leisurely, ratification prompt and
decisive : 21. 3.

it to you. Surely the first step toward sound deliberation is not to have reached a decision before you have heard the discussions upon which you should base your decision. For the occasion and the method of ratifying your resolutions and of deciding in the first instance what seems expedient are not the same.[a]

19

I HAVE come forward, men of Athens, to consult with you whether I should speak or not, and I shall explain to you for what reason I am at a loss how to decide this by myself. It is obligatory, in my opinion, that one who seeks to gratify neither himself nor certain people, but wishes to say on your behalf what he is convinced is most expedient, should both support good measures proposed by either side, and, conversely, oppose all unfair proposals which either side thinks fit to urge. Accordingly, if you should submit to hear both these lines of argument briefly, you would deliberate much better on the remaining questions ; but, if you should desert me before learning my views, it would be my lot to be put in the wrong with both sides without being guilty of injustice to either. Now, I do not deserve to be in this plight. Therefore, if you bid me, I am prepared to speak ; otherwise I am satisfied to keep silence.

20

I CONSIDER it both just and profitable, men of Athens, for you to lay aside charges and accusations when we are to deliberate, and for each one to say what he thinks is best concerning the matters before you.

ὅτι μὲν γάρ τινων αἰτίων ὄντων κακῶς τὰ πράγ-
ματ᾽ ἔχει πάντες ἐπιστάμεθα, ἐξ ὅτου δὲ τρόπου
βελτίω δύναιτ᾽ ἂν γενέσθαι, τοῦτο τοῦ συμβουλεύ-
2 οντος ἔργον εἰπεῖν. ἔπειτ᾽ ἔγωγε νομίζω καὶ κατ-
ηγόρους εἶναι τῶν ἀδικούντων χαλεπούς, οὐ τοὺς
ἐν τοιούτοις καιροῖς ἐξετάζοντας τὰ πεπραγμένα,
ὅτ᾽ οὐδεμίαν δώσουσι δίκην, ἀλλὰ τοὺς τοιοῦτό
τι συμβουλεῦσαι δυνηθέντας ἀφ᾽ οὗ βελτίω τὰ
παρόντα γένοιτ᾽ ἄν· διὰ γὰρ τούτους ἐφ᾽ ἡσυχίας
καὶ παρ᾽ ἐκείνων ἐγγένοιτ᾽ ἂν ὑμῖν δίκην λαβεῖν.
3 τοὺς μὲν οὖν ἄλλους λόγους πάντας περιέργους
ἡγοῦμαι ἃ δ᾽ ἂν οἶμαι συνενεγκεῖν περὶ ὧν νυνὶ
σκοπεῖτε, ταῦτ᾽ εἰπεῖν πειράσομαι, τοσοῦτον ἀξι-
ώσας μόνον· ἂν ἄρα του μεμνῶμαι τῶν πεπραγμένων, μὴ κατηγορίας μ᾽ ἕνεχ᾽ ἡγεῖσθε λέγειν,
ἀλλ᾽ ἵνα δείξας ἃ τόθ᾽ ἡμάρτετε, νῦν ἀποτρέψω
ταὐτὰ παθεῖν.

ΚΑ

Εἰ καὶ τὸν ἄλλον χρόνον, ὦ ἄνδρες Ἀθηναῖοι,
μηδενὶ συμπολιτευόμενοι τοσαύτην ἤγομεν ἡσυχίαν
ὅσηνπερ ἐν τῷ παρόντι, οὔτε τὰ νῦν ἂν γεγενημένα
συμβῆναι νομίζω, τῶν τ᾽ ἄλλων οἶμαι πολλὰ βέλτιον ἂν ἡμῖν ἔχειν. νῦν δ᾽ ὑπὸ τῆς ἐνίων ἀσελγείας
οὔτε παρελθεῖν οὔτ᾽ εἰπεῖν οὔθ᾽ ὅλως λόγου τυχεῖν
2 ἔστιν. ὅθεν συμβαίνει πολλὰ καὶ οὐκ ἐπιτήδει᾽

---

[a] Or, "when you are at peace."
[b] On subservience to politicians see *Olynth.* iii. 30-32.
The reference is to Aeschines ; the opening lines seem to
refer to the Amphissian War of 339 b.c. and its sequels :
XVII. 142-153.

For while we all understand that through the fault of certain men our affairs are in a bad way, it is the task of your counsellor to suggest by what means they may be improved. Moreover, I for my part regard 2 as stern accusers of the wrongdoers, not those who scrutinize their past actions on such occasions as this, when they will pay no penalty, but those who prove able to offer such advice as may effect some amelioration of our present situation ; for with the help of these men it would also be possible at your leisure [a] to bring those guilty men to justice. Ac- 3 cordingly, I consider all other topics to be out of place but shall attempt to tell you what I think would be expedient in the matters you are now considering, making this request only : if after all I do make mention of any of those things done in the past, do not think that I am speaking by way of accusation, but in order that, having shown you wherein you then erred, I may now avert your suffering the same misfortune again.

21

IF all along, men of Athens, we had been as peaceful as at this moment, playing into the hands of no politician,[b] I believe that the events which now have happened would never have taken place and that in many other respects we should be in better shape. But as it is, because of the high-handedness of some men, it is impossible either to come forward or speak, or in general to get in a word.[c] The consequences 2 of this are numerous and perhaps not to our liking.

[c] For organized interruptions in the Assembly see XIII. 20 and *Olynth.* ii. 29-30.

ἴσως. εἰ μὲν οὖν ἀεὶ ταῦτα[1] πυνθάνεσθαι καὶ
σκοπεῖν ὅ τι χρὴ ποιῆσαι καὶ πάσχειν οἷάπερ νυνὶ
[1432] βούλεσθε, ψηφιεῖσθ' ἅπερ ἐκ τῶν παρεληλυθότων
χρόνων, καθέλκειν τριήρεις, ἐμβαίνειν, εἰσφέρειν,
πάντα ταῦτ' ἤδη· ἃ τριῶν ἡμερῶν ἢ πέντε, ἂν
σιωπηθῇ τὰ παρὰ τῶν πολεμίων καὶ σχῶσιν ἡσυχίαν ἐκεῖνοι, πάλιν οὐκέτι καιρὸν εἶναι πράττειν
ὑπολήψεσθε. ὅπερ ἡνίκ' ἐν Ἑλλησπόντῳ Φίλιππον
ἠκούσαμεν συνέβη, καὶ πάλιν ἡνίκ' εἰς Μαραθῶνα
τριήρεις αἱ λῃστρίδες προσέσχον.

3   Ὡς γὰρ ἂν χρήσαιτό τις, ὦ ἄνδρες Ἀθηναῖοι,
καλῶς δυνάμει παρεσκευασμένῃ, οὕτως ὑμεῖς
εἰώθατε τῷ βουλεύεσθαι χρῆσθαι, ὀξέως. δεῖ δὲ
βουλεύεσθαι μὲν ἐφ' ἡσυχίας, ποιεῖν δὲ τὰ δόξαντα
μετὰ σπουδῆς, καὶ λογίσασθαι τοῦθ', ὅτι εἰ μὴ καὶ
τροφὴν ἱκανὴν ποριεῖτε καὶ στρατηγόν τινα τοῦ
πολέμου νοῦν ἔχοντα προστήσεσθε, καὶ μένειν ἐπὶ
τῶν οὕτω δοξάντων ἐθελήσετε, ψηφίσμαθ' ὑμῖν
περιέσται, καὶ παραναλώσετε μὲν πάνθ' ὅσ' ἂν
δαπανήσητε, βελτίω δ' οὐδ' ὁτιοῦν τὰ πράγματ'
ἔσται, κρινεῖτε δ' ὃν ἂν βούλησθ' ὀργισθέντες. ἐγὼ
δὲ βούλομαι τοὺς ἐχθροὺς ὑμᾶς ἀμυνομένους ὀφθῆναι πρότερον ἢ τοὺς πολίτας κρίνοντας· οὐ γὰρ
ἡμῖν αὐτοῖς πολεμεῖν μᾶλλον ἢ κείνοις ἐσμὲν
δίκαιοι.

4   Ἵν' οὖν μή, τὸ ῥᾷστον ἁπάντων, ἐπιτιμήσω μόνον, ὃν τρόπον ἄν μοι δοκεῖτε ταῦτα ποιῆσαι διδάξω, δεηθεὶς ὑμῶν μὴ θορυβῆσαι μηδ' ἀναβάλλειν

[1] ταῦτα edd.

---

[a] 352 b.c.; *Olynth.* iii. 4-5 and *Phil.* i. 34.
[b] Contrast Thucyd. i. 70.

Accordingly, if what you wish is to be all the time getting this kind of news, to be considering what you ought to do, and to be in such a plight as at present, you will vote the same measures as for years past—to launch triremes, to embark, to pay a special war-tax and all that sort of thing, forthwith. Then in three or five days, if rumours of hostile movements cease and our enemies become inactive, you will once more assume that there is no longer need to act. This is just what happened when we heard that Philip was in the Hellespont and again when the pirate triremes put in at Marathon.[a]

For just as a man would properly employ a force in 3 arms, men of Athens, you are accustomed to handle your deliberations, with dispatch. What you ought to do, however, is to deliberate at leisure but put your decisions into effect with speed,[b] and to make up your minds to this, that unless you shall provide an adequate food-supply and place some general of good sense in charge of the war, and be willing to abide by the decisions so taken, you will have to your credit just a lot of decrees, and while you will have squandered all that you have spent, your interests will be not a whit advanced and in angry mood you will put on trial whomever it pleases you. For my part, I wish you to be seen repelling your enemies before sitting in judgement on your fellow-citizens; for it is a crime for us to make war upon one another rather than upon them.

In order, therefore, that I may not censure only— 4 the easiest of all things[c]—I shall explain how I think you may accomplish this, requesting you not to make an uproar or get the idea that I am merely

[c] *Cf. Olynth.* i. 16.

νομίσαι με καὶ χρόνον ἐμποιεῖν. οὐ γὰρ οἱ ταχὺ
καὶ τήμερον εἰπόντες μάλιστ' εἰς τὸ δέον λέγουσιν·
οὐ γὰρ ἂν τά γ' ἤδη γεγενημένα κωλῦσαι δυνηθεῖ-
μεν τῇ νυνὶ βοηθείᾳ· ἀλλ' ὃς ἂν δείξῃ τίς πορι-
[1433] σθεῖσα παρασκευὴ διαμεῖναι δυνήσεται τέως ἂν ἢ
περιγενώμεθα τῶν ἐχθρῶν ἢ πεισθέντες διαλυσώ-
μεθα τὸν πόλεμον· οὕτω γὰρ οὐκέτι τοῦ λοιποῦ
πάσχοιμεν ἂν κακῶς.

ΚΒ

Οἶμαι πάντας ἂν ὑμᾶς, ὦ ἄνδρες Ἀθηναῖοι, ὁμο-
λογῆσαι ὅτι δεῖ τὴν πόλιν ἡμῶν, ὅταν μὲν περὶ
τῶν ἰδίων τινὸς τῶν αὑτῆς βουλεύηται, ἴσην πρόνοιαν ἔχειν τοῦ συμφέροντος ὅσηνπερ τοῦ δικαίου,
ὅταν δ' ὑπὲρ τῶν συμμαχικῶν ἢ τῶν κοινῶν, οἷον
καὶ τὸ νυνὶ παρόν, μηδενὸς οὕτως ὡς τοῦ δικαίου
φροντίζειν. ἐν μὲν γὰρ ἐκείνοις τὸ λυσιτελὲς ἐξ-
αρκεῖ, ἐν δὲ τοῖς τοιούτοις καὶ τὸ καλὸν προσεῖναι
2 δεῖ. τῶν μὲν γὰρ πράξεων, εἰς οὓς ἂν ἥκωσι,
κύριοι καθίστανται· τῆς δ' ὑπὲρ τούτων δόξης
οὐδεὶς τηλικοῦτός ἐσθ' ὅστις ἔσται κύριος, ἀλλ'
ὁποίαν τιν' ἂν τὰ πραχθέντ' ἔχῃ δόξαν, τοιαύτην οἱ
πολλοὶ περὶ τῶν πραξάντων διήγγειλαν. διὸ δεῖ
3 σκοπεῖν καὶ προσέχειν ὅπως δίκαια φανεῖται. χρῆν
μὲν οὖν οὕτως ἅπαντας ἔχειν τὴν διάνοιαν περὶ τῶν
ἀδικουμένων ὥσπερ ἄν, εἴ τι γένοιθ', ὃ μὴ συμβαίη, τοὺς ἄλλους ἀξιώσειε πρὸς αὑτὸν ἕκαστος
ἔχειν. ἐπειδὴ δὲ καὶ παρὰ τὴν αὑτῶν γνώμην

---

[a] The preceding six lines are found also in *Phil.* i. 14-15.

procrastinating and interposing delay. For it is not those who say " At once " and " To-day " who speak most to the point, for we could not prevent by the present reinforcement what has already happened ; but it will be the man who shows what armament, once furnished, will be able to hold out until we either get the upper hand of our enemies or by accepting terms bring the war to an end. For in this way we should no longer be victims of aggression in time to come.[a]

22

I BELIEVE that all of you, men of Athens, would agree that our city, when deliberating about any of her domestic affairs, should have as much concern for advantage as for justice, but when the question has to do with our allies or the general interests of Greece, as in the present instance, she ought to be mindful of nothing so scrupulously as of justice. Because in the former matters, expediency suffices, but in such as the latter, honour as well ought to play a part. For, of the actions themselves they become arbiters 2 to whom the decisions belong ; of the opinion formed of them, however, no man is so powerful as to be the arbiter ; but whatever opinion shall attach to the actions, such is that which the multitude spreads abroad concerning the actors. Therefore you must look to it diligently that your actions shall be manifestly just. By rights, of course, all men should 3 feel toward those who are wronged as each would think fit to demand of all others to feel toward himself if something should go amiss, which I pray may not happen. Since, however, certain persons, contrary to their own judgement, take the opposite

ἐναντιοῦνταί τινες, μικρὰ πρὸς τούτους εἰπών, ἃ
βέλτισθ᾽ ὑμῖν ὑπολαμβάνω, ταῦτ᾽ ἤδη συμβου-
λεύσω.

ΚΓ

Οὐ μικρὰν ἄν μοι δοκεῖτ᾽, ὦ ἄνδρες Ἀθηναῖοι,
ζημίαν νομίσαι, εἴ τις ἀηδὴς δόξα καὶ μὴ προσήκουσα τῇ πόλει παρὰ τοῖς πολλοῖς περιγίγνοιτο.
τοῦτο τοίνυν οὕτω καλῶς ἐγνωκότες, οὐκ ἀκόλουθα
ποιεῖτε τὰ λοιπά, ἀλλ᾽ ὑπάγεσθ᾽ ἑκάστοτε πράττειν
ἔνια, ἃ οὐδ᾽ ἂν αὐτοὶ φήσαιτε καλῶς ἔχειν. ἐγὼ δ᾽
οἶδα μὲν τοῦθ᾽, ὅτι τοὺς ἐπαινοῦντας ἥδιον προσ-
δέχονται πάντες τῶν ἐπιτιμώντων· οὐ μὴν οἶμαι
[1434] δεῖν, ταύτην τὴν φιλανθρωπίαν διώκων, λέγειν παρ᾽
ἃ συμφέρειν ὑμῖν ἡγοῦμαι.[1]

2   Τὴν μὲν οὖν ἀρχὴν εἰ καλῶς ἐγιγνώσκετε, οὐδὲν
δεῖν κοινῇ ποιεῖν ὑποληπτέον ἦν ὧν ἰδίᾳ μέμφεσθε,
ἵνα μὴ συνέβαινεν, ὅπερ νυνὶ γίγνεται· περιιὼν μὲν
ἕκαστος, "ὡς αἰσχρὰ καὶ δεινὰ" λέγει καὶ "μέχρι
τοῦ προβήσεται τὰ πράγματα;" συγκαθεζόμενος
δ᾽ αὐτὸς ἕκαστός ἐστι τῶν τὰ τοιαῦτα ποιούντων.
ἐγὼ μὲν οὖν ἐβουλόμην ἄν, ὥσπερ ὅτι ὑμῖν συμφέρει τοῦ τὰ βέλτιστα λέγοντος ἀκούειν οἶδα,
οὕτως εἰδέναι συνοῖσον καὶ τῷ τὰ βέλτιστ᾽ εἰπόντι·
πολλῷ γὰρ ἂν ἥδιον εἶχον. νῦν δὲ φοβοῦμαι μέν,
ὅμως δ᾽ ἅ γε πιστεύω χρηστὰ φανεῖσθαι, κἂν ὑμεῖς
μὴ πεισθῆτε, οὐκ ἀποτρέψομαι λέγειν.

---

[1] Blass prints the rest as a separate exordium, bracketing
οὖν.

---

[a] *Cf. Olynth.* i. 16.

stand, I shall first address a few words to them and thereupon offer what I assume to be the best advice for you.

23

No small detriment you would esteem it, as I believe, men of Athens, if some offensive opinion and discreditable to the city should come to prevail abroad. Now then, right as you are in this judgement, your actions in general are not consistent with it ; but time and again you are misled into doing things that not even you yourselves would say are honourable. And while I am aware that all men receive with more pleasure those who praise than those who rebuke, yet I do not think it right in quest of this goodwill to say anything but what I judge to be in your interests.[a]

If, then, at the outset your judgement had been 2 sound, there would have been no need to assume that as a body you must do what as individuals you condemn, so that this very thing should not be happening which is now going on. While every man goes about saying " How disgraceful, how shocking!" and " How long will this business go on ? ", every man sitting here with you is himself one of those who do such things. As for me, I should certainly have wished that, just as I know it pays you to listen to the speaker who makes the best proposals, so I might be sure it would also pay the one who made them ; for so I should be much happier.[b] As it now is, I have fears ; nevertheless, I shall not be deterred from saying what I am confident will prove to be best, even if you shall not be convinced.

[b] This clause is found also in *Phil.* i. 51.

ΚΔ

Εἰ καὶ μηδὲν ἄλλο τις, ὦ ἄνδρες Ἀθηναῖοι, πρότερον παρ' ὑμῖν εἰρηκὼς εἴη, νῦν γε λέγων περὶ ὧν οὐκ ὀρθῶς ἐγκαλοῦσιν οἱ πρέσβεις τῇ πόλει, παρὰ πάντων ἄν μοι δοκεῖ δικαίως συγγνώμης τυχεῖν.

Καὶ γὰρ ἐν ἄλλοις μέν τισιν ἡττᾶσθαι τῶν ἐναντίων οὐχ οὕτως ὄνειδος ὡς ἀτύχημ' ἂν φανείη· καὶ γὰρ τῇ τύχῃ καὶ τοῖς ἐφεστηκόσι καὶ πολλοῖς ἄλλοις[1] μέτεστι τοῦ καλῶς ἢ μὴ ἀγωνίσασθαι· ἐν δὲ τῷ τὰ δίκαι' ὑπὲρ αὑτῶν μὴ ἔχειν λέγειν ἀξίως τῶν ὑπαρχόντων, αὐτῆς τῆς γνώμης τῆς τῶν τοῦτο 2 παθόντων τὸ ὄνειδος εὑρήσομεν. εἰ μὲν οὖν ἕτεροί τινες ἦσαν ἐν οἷς ἐγίγνονθ' οἱ λόγοι περὶ ὑμῶν, οὔτε τούτους ἂν οἶμαι ῥᾳδίως οὕτω ψεύδεσθαι, οὔτε τοὺς ἀκούοντας πολλὰ τῶν εἰρημένων ἀνασχέσθαι. νῦν δὲ τἆλλά τ' οἶμαι τῆς ὑμετέρας πλεονεκτοῦσιν εὐηθείας ἅπαντες, καὶ δὴ καὶ τοῦτο [1435] νῦν οὗτοι· ἀκροαταῖς γὰρ ἐχρήσαντο καθ' ὑμῶν ὑμῖν, οἵοις οὐδέσιν ἂν τῶν ἄλλων, ἀκριβῶς οἶδα τοῦτ' ἐγώ.

3 Ἄξιον δ' εἶναί μοι δοκεῖ διὰ ταῦτα τοῖς θεοῖς χάριν ὑμᾶς ἔχειν, ὦ ἄνδρες Ἀθηναῖοι, καὶ τούτους μισεῖν. τὸ μὲν γὰρ ὁρᾶν τούτους τὸν Ῥοδίων δῆμον, τὸν πολὺ τούτων ποτ' ἀσελγεστέρους λόγους λέγοντα πρὸς ὑμᾶς, ἱκέτην ὑμέτερον γεγενημένον, εὐτύχημ' εἶναι νομίζω τῆς πόλεως· τὸ δὲ τοὺς

---

[1] Lacking in most codd.

[a] Chians, Byzantines and Rhodians. See XV. 3 and the Introduction to that oration.

24

Even if the speaker were one who had never spoken on another subject before you, men of Athens, surely now, discussing the groundless charges which the ambassadors *a* bring against the State, he might well, I think, meet with indulgence from all.

For in certain other contests to be worsted by one's adversaries may seem to be not so much a reproach as a misfortune, because luck and the officials in charge and many other factors play a part in the winning or the losing of a contest ; but in the event of men having no self-justification to offer worthy of the merits of their case we shall find the reproach of those found in this plight to attach to nothing but their intelligence. Surely if it had been some other 2 people before whom these speeches about you were being made, I do not think these men would be finding it so easy to lie nor would the hearers have tolerated many of their assertions. But as things now are, I think that in general all and every take advantage of your simplicity and in particular these men have done so on the present occasion ; for they have found in you such an audience for charges against yourselves as they would have found in no other people, as I know for a certainty.

And well may you, in my view, men of Athens, 3 for this turn of events be grateful to the gods and detest these men.*b* For the fact that they see the democracy of Rhodes, which used to address you much more presumptuously than these, now become your suppliant, I consider a piece of good fortune for the State ; but that these stupid men should neither

b Chians and Byzantines.

ἀνοήτους τούτους μήτε τοῦτο λογίζεσθαι, παρὸν οὕτως ἐναργὲς ἰδεῖν, μήθ' ὅτι πολλάκις καθ'
ἕν' αὐτῶν ἕκαστον ὑμεῖς σεσώκατε, καὶ πλείω
πράγματ' ἐσχήκατε τὴν τούτων θρασύτητα καὶ
κακοδαιμονίαν ἐπανορθοῦντες, ἐπειδὰν δι' ἑαυτοὺς
ἀνέλωνται πόλεμον, ἢ τὰ ὑμέτερ' αὐτῶν πράττοντες, τοῦτο παμπόλλην ὑμῖν ὀργὴν εἰκότως ἂν παρα-
4 στῆσαί μοι δοκεῖ. οὐ μὴν ἀλλ' ἴσως τούτοις μὲν
εἵμαρται μηδέποτ' εὖ πράττουσιν εὖ φρονῆσαι· ἡμῖν
δὲ προσήκει καὶ δι' ἡμᾶς αὐτοὺς καὶ διὰ τἀλλ' ἃ
πέπρακται τῇ πόλει, σπουδάσαι δεῖξαι πᾶσιν ἀνθρώποις ὅτι καὶ πρότερον καὶ νῦν καὶ ἀεὶ ἡμεῖς
τὰ δίκαια προαιρούμεθα πράττειν, ἕτεροι δέ τινες
καταδουλοῦσθαι βουλόμενοι τοὺς αὐτῶν πολίτας
διαβάλλουσι πρὸς ἡμᾶς.

ΚΕ

Εἰ μετὰ τῆς αὐτῆς γνώμης, ὦ ἄνδρες Ἀθηναῖοι,
τούς τε λόγους ἠκούετε τῶν συμβουλευόντων καὶ
τὰ πράγματ' ἐκρίνετε, πάντων ἀσφαλέστατον ἦν
ἂν τὸ συμβουλεύειν. καὶ γὰρ εὐτυχῶς καὶ καλῶς[1]
πράξασι (λέγειν γὰρ εὐφήμως πάντα δεῖ) κοίν' ἂν
ἦν τὰ τῆς αἰτίας ὑμῖν καὶ τῷ πείσαντι. νῦν δ'
ἀκούετε μὲν τῶν ἃ βούλεσθε λεγόντων ἥδιστα,
αἰτιᾶσθε δὲ πολλάκις ἐξαπατᾶν ὑμᾶς αὐτοὺς ἐὰν
2 μὴ πάνθ' ὃν ἂν ὑμεῖς τρόπον βούλησθε γένηται, οὐ
[1436] λογιζόμενοι τοῦθ', ὅτι τοῦ μὲν ζητῆσαι καὶ λογίσασθαι τὰ βέλτισθ', ὡς ἄνθρωπος, καὶ πρὸς ὑμᾶς
εἰπεῖν, αὐτὸς ἕκαστός ἐστι κύριος, τοῦ δὲ πραχθῆ-

---

[1] ἄλλως Dobree.

consider this, though it is so plain to see, nor that you have often gone to the rescue of them one after another, and that you have been put to more trouble rectifying the errors of their rashness and infatuation, whenever they have chosen to make war on their own account, than in managing your own affairs, might well have aroused in you the profoundest wrath, it seems to me.   Perhaps, however, it is the destiny of 4 these people never to be wise when prosperous.[a]   Still it is the fitting thing for you, because you are who you are and because of the past performance of the State, to make a point of demonstrating to all men that, as in former times, so now and always we prefer to practise justice, though certain others, wishing to enslave their own fellow-citizens, accuse them falsely before us.

25

If you were of the same mind, men of Athens, when listening to the speeches of those who counsel you and when judging the outcome of measures taken, offering advice would be the safest thing in the world. For if you met with good luck and success—because one must always use words of good omen—the credit for these would be common to yourselves and the sponsor.   But, as things are, you most enjoy listening to those who say what you wish to hear, yet often you charge them with deceiving you if everything does not turn out the way you would like, not taking 2 this into account, that of the task of studying and calculating the best measures, within human limitations, and of explaining them to you, each man is himself the arbiter, but of their execution and profit-

---

[a] The same charge is made in XV. 16.

ναι ταῦτα καὶ συνενεγκεῖν ἐν τῇ τύχῃ τὸ πλεῖστον
μέρος γίγνεται. ἔστι δ' ἄνθρωπον ὄντ' ἀγαπητὸν
τῆς αὐτοῦ διανοίας λόγον ὑπέχειν· τῆς δὲ τύχης
ℵ προσυποσχεῖν ἕν τι τῶν ἀδυνάτων. εἰ μὲν οὖν
εὑρημένον ἦν πῶς ἄν τις ἀσφαλῶς ἄνευ κινδύνου
δημηγοροίη, μανία παραλείπειν τοῦτον[1] ἦν τὸν
τρόπον· ἐπεὶ δ' ἀνάγκη τὸν περὶ τῶν μελλόντων
πραγμάτων γνώμην ἀποφαινόμενον κοινωνεῖν τοῖς
ἀπ' αὐτῶν γενομένοις καὶ μετέχειν τῆς ἀπὸ τούτων
αἰτίας, αἰσχρὸν ἡγοῦμαι λέγειν μὲν ὡς εὔνους, μὴ
ὑπομένειν δ', εἴ τις ἐκ τούτου κίνδυνος ἔσται.

Εὔχομαι δὲ τοῖς θεοῖς, ἃ καὶ τῇ πόλει κἀμοὶ
συμφέρειν μέλλει, ταῦτ' ἐμοί τ' εἰπεῖν ἐλθεῖν ἐπὶ
νοῦν καὶ ὑμῖν ἑλέσθαι. τὸ γὰρ πάντα τρόπον
ζητεῖν νικῆσαι, δυοῖν θάτερον, ἢ μανίας ἢ κέρδους
ἕνεκ' ἐσπουδακότος φήσαιμ' ἂν εἶναι.

Κϛ

Εἴη μέν, ὦ ἄνδρες Ἀθηναῖοι, καὶ περὶ ὧν νυνὶ
τυγχάνετ' ἐκκλησιάζοντες καὶ περὶ τῶν ἄλλων
ἁπάντων, ταὐτὰ καὶ δοκοῦντα βέλτισθ' ὑμῖν εἶναι
καὶ ὄνθ' ὡς ἀληθῶς. δεῖ μέντοι περὶ πραγμάτων
μεγάλων βουλευομένους καὶ κοινῶν, ἁπάντων ἐθέλειν ἀκούειν τῶν συμβουλευόντων, ὡς ἐμοὶ δοκεῖ,
ἐνθυμουμένους ὅτι αἰσχρόν ἐστιν, ὦ ἄνδρες Ἀθηναῖοι, νῦν μὲν βουλομένων τι παραινεῖν ἐνίων θορυβεῖν, ὕστερον δὲ κατηγορούντων τῶν αὐτῶν τούτων

---

[1] τοῦτον ἂν Blass.

[a] Demosthenes defends himself by this argument in XVIII.
192-193 : τὸ μὲν γάρ πέρας, ὡς ἂν ὁ δαίμων βουληθῇ, πάντων γί-
γνεται· ἡ δὲ προαίρεσις αὐτὴ τὴν τοῦ συμβούλου διάνοιαν δηλοῖ.

ableness the control, for the most part, lies in the power of Fortune.[a] As a human being it is enough for a man to stand accountable for his own thinking; but to stand accountable also for the play of Fortune is quite impossible. Certainly, if a way had been 3 discovered whereby a man might address the people with safety to the State and without hazard to himself, it would be madness to ignore it; but since it is a certainty that one who declares an opinion on actions about to be taken will share in the benefits therefrom accruing and participate in the credit for these benefits, I consider it shameful to speak as a loyal citizen, yet not face the test if some danger shall arise therefrom.[b]

So I pray the gods that such measures as are destined to profit both the State and myself may occur to my mind to suggest and to you to adopt. For to seek by any and every means to be on the winning side is either one of two things, I should say, a sign of mental derangement or of one who is bent on selfish gain.

26

If only it might be, men of Athens, that, when you meet to discuss the present questions or any others, the seemingly best for you and the really best might be one and the same! It is your duty, however, when deliberating on matters of supreme importance and of general concern, to be willing to listen to all your counsellors, as it seems to me, thinking it shameful, men of Athens, to create an uproar now when a number of speakers wish to propose some measure, but later to enjoy hearing these same men denounc-

[b] He refers to the anger of the Assembly.

2 τῶν πεπραγμένων ἡδέως ἀκούειν. ἐγὼ γὰρ οἶδα,
[1437] νομίζω δὲ καὶ ὑμᾶς, ὅτι νῦν μὲν ἀρέσκουσι μάλισθ᾽
ὑμῖν οἱ ταῦθ᾽ οἷς ὑμεῖς βούλεσθε λέγοντες· ἂν δέ
τι συμβῇ παρ᾽ ἃ νῦν οἴεσθ᾽, ὃ μὴ συμβαίη, τούτους
μὲν ἐξηπατηκέναι νομιεῖθ᾽ ὑμᾶς, ὧν δὲ νῦν οὐκ
ἀνέχεσθε τότ᾽ ὀρθῶς δόξουσι λέγειν. ἔστι δὲ τοῖς
μάλιστα πεπεικόσιν ὑμᾶς ταῦτ᾽ ἐφ᾽ ὧν νῦν ἐστε,
τούτοις καὶ μάλιστα συμφέρον τὸ λόγου τυχεῖν
3 τοὺς ἀντιλέγοντας. ἂν μὲν γὰρ διδάξαι δυνηθῶσιν
ὡς οὐκ ἔστ᾽ ἄρισθ᾽ ἃ τούτοις δοκεῖ, ὅτ᾽ οὐδὲν
ἡμάρτηταί πω, τοῦτο πράξαντες ἀθῴους τοὺς κινδύνους ποιήσουσιν αὐτοῖς· ἐὰν δὲ μὴ δυνηθῶσιν,
οὔκουν ὕστερόν γ᾽ ἐπιτιμᾶν ἕξουσιν, ἀλλ᾽ ὅσ᾽ ἀνθρώπων ἦν ἔργον, ἀκοῦσαι, τούτων τετυχηκότες,
ἂν ἡττῶνται, δικαίως στέρξουσι, καὶ μεθ᾽ ἁπάντων
τῶν ἀποβαινόντων, ὁποῖ᾽ ἄττ᾽ ἂν ᾖ, κοινωνήσουσιν.[a]

ΚΖ

Οἶμαι δεῖν, ὦ ἄνδρες Ἀθηναῖοι, περὶ τηλικούτων
βουλευομένους, διδόναι παρρησίαν ἑκάστῳ τῶν
συμβουλευόντων. ἐγὼ δ᾽ οὐδεπώποθ᾽ ἡγησάμην
χαλεπὸν τὸ διδάξαι τὰ βέλτισθ᾽ ὑμᾶς (ὡς γὰρ
ἁπλῶς εἰπεῖν, πάντες ὑπάρχειν ἐγνωκότες μοι
δοκεῖτε), ἀλλὰ τὸ πεῖσαι πράττειν ταῦτα· ἐπειδὰν
γάρ τι δόξῃ καὶ ψηφισθῇ, τότ᾽ ἴσον τοῦ πραχθῆναι

---

[a] They will be spared the anger of the Assembly : XIV,
conclusion.

ing what has been done.   I myself know, and I think 2
you do too, that just now those please you most who
express the same views that you yourselves wish to
hear ; but if something turns out contrary to what
you now expect—and may this not be the case !—that
you will believe that these men have deceived you,
while those whom you cannot now endure you will
then think to be right.   In reality, it is those who have
done most to persuade you of the wisdom of the
proposals which you are now considering who have
most to gain by the opposition securing an opportunity to speak.   For if it shall be able to show that 3
the proposals which seem best to these men are not
the best, when as yet no mistake has been made,
it will by so doing nullify their risks for them [a] ;   yet
if it fails to persuade, they will later, at any rate,
have no occasion to find fault, but, having obtained
all that it was the duty of men to give, a hearing,
they will rightly be content if defeated, and along
with all the rest share in the outcome, whatever that
may be.

27 [b]

I THINK it your duty, men of Athens, when deliberating about such important matters to allow freedom of
speech to every one of your counsellors.   For my
own part, I have never at any time considered it
difficult to make you understand what proposals are
best—for, to put it simply, I think you all have
decided that,—but only difficult to persuade you to
act on these proposals.   For when a measure has
been approved and confirmed by a vote, it is then as

[b] The beginning of XV is identical.

2 ἀπέχει, ὅσονπερ πρὶν δόξαι. ἔστι μὲν οὖν ὧν ἐγὼ
νομίζω χάριν ὑμᾶς τοῖς θεοῖς ὀφείλειν τὸ τοὺς
διὰ τὴν ἑαυτῶν ὕβριν ὑμῖν πολεμήσαντας οὐ πάλαι,
νῦν ἐν ὑμῖν μόνοις τῆς αὐτῶν σωτηρίας ἔχειν τὰς
ἐλπίδας, ἄξιον δ' ἡσθῆναι τῷ παρόντι καιρῷ·
συμβήσεται γάρ, ἂν ἃ χρὴ βουλεύσησθ' ὑπὲρ αὐτοῦ,
τὰς παρὰ τῶν διαβαλλόντων τὴν πόλιν ἡμῶν βλασ-
[1438] φημίας ἔργῳ μετὰ δόξης καλῆς ἀπολύσασθαι.

ΚΗ

Αἱ μὲν ἐλπίδες, ὦ ἄνδρες Ἀθηναῖοι, μεγάλαι
καὶ καλαὶ τῶν προειρημένων, πρὸς ἃς οἴομαι τοὺς
πολλοὺς ἄνευ λογισμοῦ τι πεπονθέναι. ἐγὼ δ'
οὐδεπώποτ' ἔγνων εἵνεκα τοῦ παραχρῆμ' ἀρέσαι
λέγειν τι πρὸς ὑμᾶς, ὅ τι ἂν μὴ καὶ μετὰ ταῦτα
συνοίσειν ἡγῶμαι. ἔστι μὲν οὖν τὸ κοινὸν ἔθος
τῶν πλείστων τοὺς μὲν συνεπαινοῦντας ἑαυτοῖς ὅ
τι ἂν πράττωσι φιλεῖν, πρὸς δὲ τοὺς ἐπιτιμῶντας
ἀηδῶς ἔχειν. οὐ μὴν ἀλλὰ δεῖ τὸν εὖ φρονοῦντα
τὸν λογισμὸν ἀεὶ τῶν ἐπιθυμιῶν κρείττω πειρᾶσθαι
2 ποιεῖν. ἐγὼ δ' ἡδέως ἂν ἑώρων ἃ καὶ συνοίσειν
ἤμελλε, ταῦτ' ἐν ἡδονῇ πράττειν ὄνθ' ὑμῖν, ἵνα καὶ
χαριζόμενος καὶ χρηστὰ λέγων ἐφαινόμην. ἐπειδὴ
δὲ τἀναντί' ὁρῶ τούτων ἐπιχειροῦντας ὑμᾶς, οἴομαι
δεῖν ἀντειπεῖν, εἰ καί τισι μέλλω ἀπεχθήσεσθαι·
ἂν μὲν οὖν μηδ' ὑπομείνητ' ἀκοῦσαι μηδὲ ἕν, οὐ τῷ

far from being put into effect as before it was approved. It certainly is something for which I think 2 you owe gratitude to the gods that those who, through their own arrogance, not long ago made war upon you now repose the hopes of their own deliverance in you alone, and you have good reason to be delighted at the present opportunity. For the effect will be, if you decide about it as you ought, to rid ourselves, by the language of deeds, of the slanders circulated by the traducers of our city, and also to maintain our good repute.

28

THE hopes aroused by what has been previously said, men of Athens, are great and glorious ; I fancy that most of you have been somewhat swayed by them without really thinking. As for myself, I have never been minded to tell you for the sake of your momentary gratification anything that I did not think would also subsequently prove to be of advantage. Naturally it is a trait common to most men to like those who join in applauding them, whatever they do, but to dislike those who find fault with them. Nevertheless, the sensible man should always strive to make reason the master of his feelings. I should have been glad, myself, to 2 see you happy at putting into effect the measures that were going to profit you, that I might have been found both meeting your wishes and giving good advice. But since I see you about to try the opposite measures, I think I ought to speak against them, even if I shall be hated for it by certain persons. So, if you will not endure to hear even one word from me, you will be thought to be preferring

δοκιμάζοντες διαμαρτεῖν, ἀλλὰ τῷ φύσει πονήρ'
ἐπιθυμεῖν πράττειν τοιαῦτα προαιρεῖσθαι δόξετε.
ἐὰν δ' ἀκούσητε, τυχὸν μὲν ἴσως κἂν μεταπει-
σθείητε, ὃ μάλιστ' ἐγὼ νομίζω συνενεγκεῖν ἂν
ὑμῖν· εἰ δὲ μή, οἱ μὲν ἀγνοεῖν τὸ συμφέρον, οἱ δ',
ὅ τι ἄν τις βούληται, τοῦτ' ἐρεῖ.

ΚΘ

Πρῶτον μὲν οὐδέν ἐστι καινόν, ὦ ἄνδρες Ἀθηναῖοι, τοῖς δόξασι παρ' ὑμῖν εἶναί τινας οἵτινες
ἀντεροῦσιν, ἐπειδὰν πράττειν τι δέη. εἰ μὲν οὖν
ἀποδόντων ὑμῶν λόγον αὐτοῖς ὅτ' ἐβουλεύεσθε,
τοῦτ' ἐποίουν, τούτων ἂν ἦν ἄξιον κατηγορεῖν, εἰ
[1439] περὶ ὧν ἥττηντ' ἐβιάζοντο πάλιν λέγειν· νῦν δὲ
τούτους μὲν οὐδέν ἐστ' ἄτοπον, εἰπεῖν βουληθῆναι
2 ταῦθ' ἃ τότ' οὐχ ὑπεμείνατ' ἀκοῦσαι, ὑμῖν δ' ἄν
τις εἰκότως ἐπιτιμήσειεν, ἄνδρες Ἀθηναῖοι, ὅτι
ὁπόταν περί του βουλεύησθε, οὐκ ἐᾶτε λέγειν ἕκαστον ἃ γιγνώσκει, ἀλλ' ἂν ἕτεροι τῷ λόγῳ προ-
λάβωσιν ὑμᾶς, οὐδενὸς ἂν τῶν ἑτέρων ἀκούσαιτε.
ἐκ δὲ τούτου συμβαίνει πρᾶγμ' ἀηδὲς ὑμῖν· οἷς γὰρ
πρὶν ἁμαρτεῖν ὑμῖν ἐξῆν συμβουλεύουσι πείθεσθαι,
3 τούτους ὕστερον κατηγοροῦντας ἐπαινεῖτε. τοῦτο
δὴ τοῦτό μοι πάλιν δοκεῖτε πείσεσθαι, εἰ μὴ παρασχόντες ἴσους ἀκροατὰς πάντων ὑμᾶς αὐτοὺς ἐν
τῷ παρόντι, καὶ τοῦτον τὸν πόνον ὑπομείναντες,
ἑλόμενοι τὰ κράτιστα τοὺς ὁτιοῦν τούτοις ἐπιτιμῶντας φαύλους νομιεῖτε.

---

[a] The Assembly could vote at any time to reopen the
debate. See 34.

such a course of action, not through an error of judgement, but through your natural propensity to do wrong. However, if you do listen, you may perhaps be won over to the other view, which I think would be most to your advantage. But if you refuse to listen, some will say that you mistook your own interest, while others—well, what a man likes to say he will say.

29

In the first place, it is nothing strange, men of Athens, that among you are found some who, when action has to be taken, will speak against measures already voted.[a] Now, if they were doing this after you had given them the floor while still deliberating, it would be the right thing to denounce them for insisting upon speaking a second time to questions on which they had been defeated ; as it is, there is nothing unreasonable in their desiring to express views which then you did not submit to hear, and it is you who 2 may well be criticized, men of Athens, because, when you deliberate about something, you do not allow each to say what he thinks, but, if the one side captures you first by their plea, you would hear no one from the other side. From this arises a situation embarrassing for you, because the men whose advice, before going wrong, you might have followed, you applaud later for denouncing your mistakes. This 3 very thing is about to happen to you again, it seems to me, unless on the present occasion, giving impartial audience to all, and submitting to this tedious duty, you shall choose the best proposals and judge those who find any fault with them to be no loyal citizens.

Ἐγὼ μὲν δὴ δίκαιον ὑπείληφα πρῶτον ἁπάντων
αὐτὸς εἰπεῖν τί μοι δοκεῖ περὶ ὧν σκοπεῖσθε, ἵν᾽, ἂν
μὲν ὑμῖν ἀρέσκῃ, καὶ τὰ λοιπὰ διδάσκω, εἰ δὲ μή,
μήθ᾽ ὑμῖν ἐνοχλῶ μήτ᾽ ἐμαυτὸν κόπτω.

Λ

Ἔδει μέν, ὦ ἄνδρες Ἀθηναῖοι, πρὸ τοῦ πολεμεῖν
ἐσκέφθαι τίς ὑπάρξει παρασκευὴ τῷ γενησομένῳ
πολέμῳ· εἰ δ᾽ ἄρα μὴ πρόδηλος ἦν, ὅτε πρῶτον
ἐβουλεύεσθ᾽ ὑπὲρ αὐτοῦ φανεροῦ γενομένου, τότε
καὶ περὶ τῆς παρασκευῆς ἐσκέφθαι. εἰ δὲ φήσετε
πολλὰς ἐγκεχειρικέναι δυνάμεις ἃς λελυμάνθαι
τοὺς ἐπιστάντας, οὐκ ἀποδέξεται τοῦθ᾽ ὑμῶν οὐ-
δείς· οὐ γάρ ἐστι τῶν αὐτῶν τούς τ᾽ ἐπὶ τῶν πραγμάτων ἀπολύειν καὶ λέγειν ὡς διὰ τούτους κακῶς
2 ταῦτ᾽ ἔχει. ἐπειδὴ δὲ τὰ μὲν παρεληλυθότ᾽ οὐκ
ἂν ἄλλως ἔχοι δεῖ δ᾽ ἐκ τῶν παρόντων ἐπαμῦναι
[1440] τοῖς πράγμασι, τοῦ μὲν κατηγορεῖν οὐδένα καιρὸν
ὁρῶ, πειράσομαι δ᾽ ἃ κράτιστα νομίζω συμβουλεῦσαι.

Πρῶτον μὲν οὖν ὑμᾶς ἐκεῖνο ἐγνωκέναι δεῖ, ὅτι
τὴν ἴσην ὑπερβολὴν τῆς σπουδῆς καὶ φιλονικίας
ἐπὶ τοῖς πράγμασι πάντ᾽ ἄνδρα παρασχέσθαι δεῖ
ὅσηνπερ ἐκ τῶν ἄνωθεν χρόνων ἀμελείας· μόλις
γὰρ οὕτως ἐλπὶς ἐκ πολλοῦ διώκοντας τὰ προειμέν᾽
3 ἑλεῖν δυνηθῆναι. ἔπειτ᾽ οὐκ ἀθυμητέον τοῖς γε-
γενημένοις· ὃ γάρ ἐστι τῶν παρεληλυθότων χείριστον, τοῦτο πρὸς τὰ μέλλοντα βέλτιστον ὑπάρχει.

ᵃ Possibly Chares and Charidemus, who failed to save
Olynthus in 348 B.C.
ᵇ This commonplace is found also in XVIII. 192 ; *Olynth.*
iii. 6.

Now I have thought it fair to tell you first of all my views about the questions you are considering, in order that, if these meet with your favour, I may also explain the rest of my ideas, but, if you disapprove, that I may neither bore you nor tire myself out.

30

It was your duty, men of Athens, before going to war to have considered what armament would be available for the coming campaign, but if, as a matter of fact, war was not foreseen, it was your duty to have considered also the question of armament on that occasion when you were deliberating for the first time about war after it had become certain. If you shall say that you have commissioned many armies which your commanders [a] have ruined, no one will accept this excuse of you. For the same people cannot both absolve those in charge of their operations and claim that through fault of these men these operations are not succeeding. Since, however, past 2 events cannot be altered [b] and it is necessary to safeguard our interests as present facilities permit, I see no fitting occasion for laying charges but shall try to offer what I think is the best counsel.

Now, first of all, you must admit this principle, that it is the duty of every man to apply to the task the same superabundance of eagerness and emulation that he displayed of indifference in times past; because thus there is a bare hope that we may be able, though far behind in the pursuit, to overtake what we have let slip. In the next place, there must be no dis- 3 couragement over what has happened, because what is worst in the past is the best hope for the future.

137

τί οὖν τοῦτ᾽ ἔστιν, ὦ ἄνδρες Ἀθηναῖοι; ὅτι οὐδὲν ὑμῶν τῶν δεόντων ποιούντων κακῶς ἔχει τὰ πράγματα· ἐπεὶ εἴ γε πάνθ᾽ ἃ προσῆκε πραττόντων οὕτως εἶχεν, οὐδ᾽ ἂν ἐλπὶς ἦν αὐτὰ γενέσθαι βελτίω.

ΛΑ

Οὐδέν ἐστιν, ὦ ἄνδρες Ἀθηναῖοι, χαλεπώτερον ἢ τοῖς αὐτοῖς ἔθεσιν ἐπιτιμᾶν τε καὶ χρῆσθαι τοὺς δημηγοροῦντας. τὸ γὰρ στασιάζειν πρὸς αὑτοὺς καὶ κατηγορεῖν ἀλλήλων ἄνευ κρίσεως οὐδείς ἐστιν οὕτως ἀγνώμων ὅστις οὐ φήσειεν ἂν βλάβην εἶναι τοῖς πράγμασιν. ἐγὼ δ᾽ οἶμαι τούτους μὲν ἂν εἶναι βελτίους, εἰ τὴν πρὸς αὑτοὺς φιλονικίαν ἐπὶ τοὺς τῆς πόλεως ἐχθροὺς τρέψαντες ἐδημηγόρουν· ὑμῖν δὲ παραινῶ μὴ συστασιάζειν μηδετέροις τούτων, μηδ᾽ ὅπως ἅτεροι κρατήσουσι σκοπεῖν, ἀλλ᾽ 2 ὅπως ὑμεῖς ἅπαντες τῶν ἐχθρῶν περιέσεσθε. εὔχομαι δὲ τοῖς θεοῖς τοὺς ἢ φιλονικίας ἢ ἐπηρείας ἤ τινος ἄλλης ἕνεκ᾽ αἰτίας ἄλλο τι, πλὴν ἅ ποθ᾽ ἡγοῦνται συμφέρειν, λέγοντας παύσασθαι· τὸ γὰρ [1441] καταρᾶσθαι συμβουλεύοντ᾽ ἴσως ἔστ᾽ ἄτοπον. αἰτιασαίμην μὲν οὖν ἔγωγ᾽ οὐδέν᾽, ὦ ἄνδρες Ἀθηναῖοι, τοῦ κακῶς τὰ πράγματ᾽ ἔχειν, ἀλλ᾽ ἢ πάντας τούτους· οἶμαι δὲ δεῖν παρὰ μὲν τούτων ἐφ᾽ ἡσυχίας λόγον ὑμᾶς λαβεῖν, νῦν δ᾽ ὑπὲρ τῶν παρόντων, ὅπως ἔσται βελτίω, σκοπεῖν.

---

[a] This is called a paradox in *Phil.* iii. 5 ; *cf. Phil.* i. 2.
[b] See 11 and note.

What, then, do I mean by this, men of Athens? That it is because you do nothing that you ought to do that your affairs are in a bad way; since if you were doing everything you should and your affairs were in this state, there would be not even a hope of improvement.[a]

31

NOTHING is more mischievous, men of Athens, than that those who address your Assembly should both censure and employ the same practices. For there is no man so unintelligent as to deny that to behave factiously among themselves and to accuse one another when no one is on trial [b] means damage to your interests. I think myself that these men would be better citizens if, when addressing the Assembly, they should turn the contentiousness they feel toward one another against the enemies of the State; and to you I recommend not to take sides with either of these factions or to consider how either one is to gain the mastery, but how you as a body are to prevail over your enemies. And I pray to the gods that those 2 who out of contentiousness or spite or any other motive express any other sentiments than those they believe to be advantageous may cease to do so; for to invoke a curse when speaking in council is perhaps unseemly. Therefore, while I should myself lay the blame for this bad state of affairs, men of Athens, upon no one except these men as a class, and although I think you ought to exact an accounting of them when you have the leisure, yet for the present I think you should consider only how the existing situation may be bettered.

DEMOSTHENES

ΛΒ

Ἠβουλόμην ἄν, ὦ ἄνδρες Ἀθηναῖοι, τὴν ἴσην
σπουδὴν ἐνίους τῶν λεγόντων ποιεῖσθαι ὅπως τὰ
βέλτιστ' ἐροῦσιν ὅσηνπερ ὅπως εὖ δόξουσι λέγειν,
ἵν' οὗτοι μὲν ἀντὶ τοῦ δεινοὶ λέγειν ἐπιεικεῖς ἐνο-
μίζοντ' εἶναι, τὰ δ' ὑμέτερ', ὥσπερ ἐστὶ προσῆκον,
βέλτιον εἶχε. νῦν δ' ἔνιοί μοι δοκοῦσι παντάπασι
τὴν ἀπὸ τοῦ λόγου δόξαν ἠγαπηκότες, τῶν μετὰ
2 ταῦτα συμβησομένων ὑμῖν μηδὲν φροντίζειν. καὶ
δῆτα θαυμάζω πότερόν ποθ' οἱ τοιοῦτοι λόγοι τὸν
λέγονθ' ὁμοίως πεφύκασιν ἐξαπατᾶν ὥσπερ πρὸς
οὓς ἂν λέγωνται, ἢ συνιέντες οὗτοι τἀναντία τοῖς
δοκοῦσιν ἑαυτοῖς εἶναι βελτίστοις δημηγοροῦσιν.
εἰ μὲν γὰρ ἀγνοοῦσ' ὅτι τὸν μέλλοντα πράξειν τὰ
δέοντα, οὐκ ἐπὶ τῶν λόγων θρασύν, ἀλλ' ἐπὶ τῆς
παρασκευῆς ἰσχυρὸν εἶναι δεῖ, οὐδ' ἐπὶ τῷ τοὺς
ἐχθροὺς μὴ δυνήσεσθαι θαρρεῖν, ἀλλ' ἐπὶ τῷ κἂν
δύνωνται κρατήσειν, τὰ τῶν λόγων ἀστεῖ' ὡς ἔοικε
τοῦ τὰ μέγιστ' αἰσθάνεσθαι κεκώλυκεν αὐτούς. εἰ
δὲ ταῦτα μὲν μηδ' ἂν φήσαιεν ἀγνοεῖν, πρόφασις δ'
ἄλλη τις ὕπεστι δι' ἣν ταῦτα προαιροῦνται, πῶς οὐ
χρὴ φαύλην ταύτην ὑπολαμβάνειν, ἥτις ποτ' ἐστίν;
3 Ἐγὼ δ' οὐκ ἀποτρέψομαι λέγειν ἃ δοκεῖ μοι,
καίπερ ὁρῶν ἠγμένους ὑμᾶς· καὶ γὰρ εὔηθες, λόγῳ
[1442] ψυχαγωγηθέντων ὑμῶν οὐκ ὀρθῶς, λόγον αὖ τὸν
μέλλοντα βελτίω λέγειν καὶ μᾶλλον συμφέρονθ'

---

[a] This meaning of the verb comes from magical practices ;
see Lexicon under ἀγώγιμον.

140

32

I sHOULD have wished, men of Athens, that some of the speakers had displayed as much eagerness to present the best proposals as they did to be thought good speakers, in order that these men might have been regarded as honest instead of clever at speaking and that your interests, just as is proper, might have been in better shape. As it now is, however, some seem to me to be entirely content with the reputation for speaking, but to be taking no thought for what will subsequently befall you. And certainly 2 I wonder whether speeches of this sort are capable of deceiving the speaker as much as those to whom they are addressed, or whether these men knowingly express before the Assembly opinions directly opposed to what they themselves think best. For if they are unaware that he who is going to do what requires to be done must not have audacity based upon words but power based upon armament, nor yet self-confidence based upon the assumption that our enemies will be weak, but confidence that we shall overmaster them even if they shall be strong, the elegance of their speeches has prevented them, as it seems, from apprehending the most vital facts. Yet if they should not even deny awareness of these facts, and some ulterior motive underlies their predilection for this conduct, how can one help assuming that this motive, whatever it may be, is base ?

As for me, I shall not be deterred from saying what 3 I think, although I see that you have been bewitched[a]; for it would be foolish, because you have wrongly yielded to the spell of oratory, for the man who in his turn is going to offer better proposals and much

ὑμῖν καταδεῖσαι. ἀξιῶ δὲ καὶ ὑμᾶς ὑπομεῖναι,
ἐνθυμηθέντας ὅτι οὐδὲ τὰ νῦν δοκοῦντ᾽ ἔδοξεν ἂν
ὑμῖν, εἰ μὴ τοὺς λόγους ἠκούσατ᾽ ἐξ ὧν ἐπείσθητε.
4 ὥσπερ ἂν τοίνυν εἰ νόμισμ᾽ ἐκρίνεθ᾽ ὁποῖόν τί ποτ᾽
ἐστί, δοκιμάσαι δεῖν ἂν ᾠήθητε, οὕτω καὶ τὸν λόγον
ἀξιῶ τὸν εἰρημένον ἐξ ὧν ἀντειπεῖν ἡμεῖς ἔχομεν
σκεψαμένους, ἐὰν μὲν συμφέρονθ᾽ εὕρητ᾽, ἀγαθῇ
τύχῃ πείθεσθαι, ἂν δ᾽ ἄρ᾽ ἕκαστα λογιζομένοις
ἀλλοιότερος φανῇ, πρὶν ἁμαρτεῖν μεταβουλευσα-
μένους, τοῖς ὀρθῶς ἔχουσι χρήσασθαι.

ΛΓ

Μάλιστα μέν, ὦ ἄνδρες Ἀθηναῖοι, βουλοίμην ἂν
ὑμᾶς ἃ μέλλω λέγειν πεισθῆναι· εἰ δ᾽ ἄρα τοῦτ᾽
ἄλλῃ πῃ συμβαίνοι, ἐμαυτῷ γ᾽ ἂν εἰρῆσθαι πρὸ
παντὸς αὐτὰ δεξαίμην.

Ἔστι δ᾽ οὐ μόνον, ὡς δοκεῖ, τὸ πρὸς ὑμᾶς εἰπεῖν
χαλεπὸν τὰ δέοντα, ἀλλὰ καὶ καθ᾽ αὑτὸν σκοπού-
μενον εὑρεῖν· γνοίη δ᾽ ἄν τις εἰ, μὴ τὸν λόγον
ὑμᾶς ἀλλὰ τὰ πράγματ᾽ ἐφ᾽ ὧν ἐστε σκέψεσθαι
νομίσαι, καὶ πλείω σπουδὴν τοῦ δοκεῖν ἐπιεικὴς
2 εἶναι ἢ τοῦ δεινὸς εἰπεῖν φανῆναι ποιοῖτο. ἐγὼ
γοῦν (οὕτω τί μοι γένοιτ᾽ ἀγαθόν) ἐπειδὴ περὶ τῶν
παρόντων ἐπῄει μοι σκοπεῖν, λόγοις μὲν καὶ μάλ᾽
ἀφθόνοις, οὓς οὐκ ἂν ἀηδῶς ἠκούεθ᾽ ὑμεῖς, ἐνετύγ-
χανον. καὶ γὰρ ὡς δικαιότατοι τῶν Ἑλλήνων ἐστέ,

more to your advantage, to give in to fear. And I ask of you to listen patiently, bearing in mind that you would not have formed your present opinions either unless you had listened to the speeches by which you have been persuaded. Accordingly, just 4 as you would have thought it necessary to test a coin if you were judging what its worth might be, so I ask of you to scrutinize in the light of what we have to say against it the speech that has been made, and if you find it to your advantage, agree with the speaker, and may good fortune attend you ; but if, after all, as you examine each detail, it shall seem alien to your interests, to change your plans before falling into error and to adopt the counsels that are right.

33

Most of all I should desire, men of Athens, that you be convinced by the words I am about to utter, but if after all it should turn out otherwise, I should prefer above all else that by me, at least, they had been spoken.

It is a difficult thing, as it seems, not only to explain to you what ought to be done, but even to discover it by solitary reflection. Anyone would observe this if he believed you would consider, not his speech, but the business upon which you are engaged, and set more value upon being thought an honest man than upon showing himself to be a clever speaker. I, at any 2 rate,—so help me Heaven—after it occurred to me to reflect upon our present problems, began to hit upon themes, and no end of them, to which you would have listened not without pleasure. For instance, on the theme " You are the most just of the Greeks," I

πόλλ' εἰπεῖν καὶ ἑώρων καὶ ὁρῶ, καὶ ὡς ἀρίστων
προγόνων, καὶ πολλὰ τοιαῦτα. ἀλλὰ ταῦτα μὲν
3 τὸν χρόνον ἡσθῆναι ποιήσανθ' ὅσον ἂν ῥηθῇ, μετὰ
[1443] ταῦτ' οἴχεται· δεῖ δὲ πράξεώς τινος τὸν λέγοντα
φανῆναι σύμβουλον δι' ἣν καὶ μετὰ ταῦτ' ἀγαθοῦ
τινος ὑμῖν ἔσται παρουσία. τοῦτο δ' ἤδη καὶ
σπάνιον καὶ χαλεπὸν πεπειραμένος οἶδα ὂν εὑρεῖν.
οὐδὲ γὰρ αὔταρκες τὸ ἰδεῖν ἐστι τὰ τοιαῦτα ἂν μὴ
καὶ πεῖσαί τις τοὺς συναρομένους ὑμᾶς δυνηθῇ.
οὐ μὴν ἀλλ' ἐμὸν μὲν ἔργον εἰπεῖν ἴσως ἃ πέπεικ'
ἐμαυτὸν συμφέρειν, ὑμέτερον δ' ἀκούσαντας κρῖναι,
κἂν ἀρέσκῃ, χρήσασθαι.

ΛΔ

Οὐκ ἄδηλον ἦν, ὦ ἄνδρες Ἀθηναῖοι, πρῴην ὅτε
τῶν ἀντιλέγειν βουλομένων οἷς ὁ δεῖν' ἔλεγ' οὐκ
ᾤεσθ' ἀκούειν χρῆναι, ὅτι συμβήσεται τοῦθ' ὃ νυνὶ
γίγνεται, ὅτι οἱ τότε κωλυθέντες ἐροῖεν εἰς ἑτέραν
ἐκκλησίαν. ἂν τοίνυν ταῦθ' ἅπερ πρότερον ποιήσητε, καὶ τῶν τοῖς τότε δόξασι συνειπεῖν βουλομένων μὴ θελήσητ' ἀκοῦσαι, πάλιν ταῦτ' εἰς τὴν
ἑτέραν ἐκκλησίαν οὗτοι λαβόντες τούτων κατηγο-
2 ρήσουσιν. οὐδαμῶς, ὦ ἄνδρες Ἀθηναῖοι, οὔτε τὰ
πράγματ' ἂν χείρω γένοιτο οὔθ' ὑμεῖς ἀτοπώτεροι
φανείητε, εἰ μήτε τῶν δοξάντων ὑμῖν πέρας μηδὲν

---

a These were stock topics of funeral speeches : see lx. and
the Introduction to the same.

b *Cf.* VIII. 73.

c It has been suggested that ὁ δεῖνα was a blank to be
filled in as occasion required, the *Exordia* being composed in
advance of use.

144

observed and now observe many changes to ring, and
again, " You are born of the noblest ancestors," and
many such topics.[a]   Yet these themes, though afford-
ing pleasure so long as they are being aired, after
that vanish away ; and it is the duty of the speaker 3
to show himself the adviser of some course of action
through which the gain of some real benefit shall also
afterwards accrue to you.[b]   Such a policy as this I
know by now from experience to be rare and hard
to discover.   Neither is it enough merely to get a
vision of such policies unless a man shall also be able
to convince you, who jointly are to assume the responsibility.   On the contrary, there is an obligation resting upon both alike, upon me to tell you
what I have convinced myself is advantageous, upon
you to listen, to judge and, if it is your pleasure,
to adopt.

34

It was not hard to see, men of Athens, the other day
when you thought there was no need to hear those
who desired to speak in opposition to the views of
a certain speaker,[c] that what is now coming to pass
would occur—that those who were then prevented
from speaking would do so before a subsequent
meeting of the Assembly.[d]   If, therefore, you shall
do the same as before, and refuse to listen to those
who wish to support the decisions then approved,
these men in turn will take the matter to the next
meeting and denounce these decisions.   In no way, 2
men of Athens, could your situation be made worse
nor could you show yourselves more absurd than if
none of your decisions should seem to be finally

[d] See 29 and note.

ἔχειν δοκοίη, μήτ᾽, ἀφέντες ἃ¹ συμφέρει, τῶν πρὸ
ὁδοῦ τι περαίνοιτε, εἴητε δ᾽ ὥσπερ τὰ θέατρα τῶν
προκαταλαμβανόντων. μηδαμῶς, ὦ ἄνδρες Ἀθηναῖοι, ἀλλὰ πονήσαντες τὸν πόνον τοῦτον, καὶ
παρασχόντες ἴσους ἀκροατὰς ἀμφοτέροις ὑμᾶς αὐτούς, πρῶτον μὲν ἕλεσθ᾽ ὅ τι καὶ ποιήσετε, ἔπειθ᾽
ὑπολαμβάνετ᾽, ἄν τις ἐναντιῶται τοῖς ἅπαξ οὕτω
3 δοκιμασθεῖσι, πονηρὸν καὶ κακόνουν ὑμῖν. τὸ μὲν
γὰρ λόγου μὴ τυχόντα πεπεῖσθαι βέλτιον τῶν ὑμῖν
δοκούντων αὐτὸν ἐντεθυμῆσθαι συγγνώμη· τὸ δ᾽
ἀκουσάντων ὑμῶν καὶ διακρινάντων ἔτ᾽ ἀναισχυν-
[1444] τεῖν, καὶ μὴ συγχωρεῖν ἐνδόντα τῇ τῶν πλειόνων
γνώμῃ, ἄλλην τιν᾽ ὑποψίαν οὐχὶ δικαίαν ἂν ἔχειν
φανείη. ἐγὼ μὲν δὴ σιωπᾶν ἂν ᾤμην δεῖν ἐν τῷ
παρόντι, εἰ μένοντας ὑμᾶς ἑώρων ἐφ᾽ ὧν ἔδοξεν·
εἰμὶ γὰρ τῶν ἐκεῖνα πεπεισμένων συμφέρειν ὑμῖν·
ἐπειδὴ δ᾽ ὑπὸ τῶν παρὰ τούτων λόγων μεταβεβλῆ-
σθαί μοί τινες δοκοῦσιν, ὡς οὔτ᾽ ἀληθῆ λέγουσιν
οὔθ᾽ ὑμῖν συμφέροντα ἴσως μὲν εἰδότας, οὐ μὴν
ἀλλ᾽ εἰ καὶ τυγχάνετ᾽ ἀγνοοῦντες, διδάξω.

ΛΕ

Ἔδει μέν, ὦ ἄνδρες Ἀθηναῖοι, καὶ δίκαιον ἦν
τότε πείθειν ὑμᾶς ὅ τι ἄριστον ἕκαστος ἡγεῖτο ὅτ᾽
ἐβουλεύεσθε τὸ πρῶτον περὶ τούτων, ἵνα μὴ συνέβαινεν ἃ δὴ δύο πάντων ἐστὶν ἀλυσιτελέστατα τῇ
πόλει, μήτε πέρας μηδὲν εἶχεν τῶν ὑμῖν δοξάντων,

¹ ἃ μὴ Blass, Rennie.

ᵃ In both Greek and Latin the word "theatre" often
denotes the spectators or audience. Seneca, *Epist.* 7. 11,
wrote : "for we two are audience (*theatrum*) enough for each
other."

settled and, disregarding the policies that pay, you should achieve no forward step, but, like the crowds at shows, side with those who captivate you first.[a] Do not let this happen, men of Athens, but performing this tedious duty and giving impartial audience to both sides, first choose a policy you will also carry out and then assume that whoever opposes measures thus once sanctioned is unprincipled and disloyal to you. For while it is pardonable that a man who has not 3 obtained a hearing should feel convinced that he has himself better plans thought out than those approved by you, yet to go on acting shamelessly after you have given a hearing and decided between alternatives, instead of giving in to the judgement of the majority and retiring, would plainly justify suspicion of some other motive by no means honourable. As for me, although I should have thought it proper to remain silent on this occasion had I observed you abiding by your previous decisions—for I am one of those who are convinced that these are to your advantage—yet, now that certain members seem to have changed their minds because of the speeches made by these men, even though you perhaps know that what they say is neither true nor for your good, I will nevertheless make this clear in case you are unaware of it.

35

It would have been just and proper, men of Athens, for each member then to try to convince you of what he believed to be best when you were considering these matters for the first time, in order that two evils might not be resulting which are above all others damaging to the city—that no decision of yours should

παράνοιάν θ' ὑμεῖς κατεγιγνώσκεθ' ὑμῶν αὐτῶν
μεταβουλευόμενοι. ἐπειδὴ δὲ σιωπήσαντες τότε
νῦν ἐπιτιμῶσί τινες, βούλομαι μικρὰ πρὸς αὐτοὺς
εἰπεῖν.

2 Ἐγὼ γὰρ θαυμάζω τὸν τρόπον τῆς πολιτείας τῆς
τούτων, μᾶλλον δ' ἡγοῦμαι φαῦλον. εἰ γὰρ ἐξὸν
παραινεῖν ὅταν σκοπῆτε, βεβουλευμένων κατηγορεῖν αἱροῦνται, συκοφαντῶν ἔργον, οὐχ, ὡς φασίν,
εὔνων ποιοῦσιν ἀνθρώπων. ἡδέως δ' ἂν ἐροίμην
αὐτούς (καὶ μηδεμιᾶς λοιδορίας ὃ μέλλω λέγειν
ἀρχὴ γενέσθω) τί δὴ τἀλλ' ἐπαινοῦντες Λακεδαι-
μονίους, ὃ μάλιστ' ἄξιόν ἐστι τῶν παρ' ἐκείνοις
ἄγασθαι, τοῦτ' οὐ μιμοῦνται, μᾶλλον δ' αὐτὸ τού-
3 ναντίον ποιοῦσιν; φασὶ γάρ, ὦ ἄνδρες Ἀθηναῖοι,
παρ' ἐκείνοις μέχρι μὲν τοῦ δόξαι γνώμην ἦν ἂν
[1445] ἕκαστος ἔχῃ λέγειν, ἐπειδὰν δ' ἐπικυρωθῇ, ταῦθ'
ἅπαντας ἐπαινεῖν καὶ συμπράττειν, καὶ τοὺς ἀντ-
ειπόντας. τοιγάρτοι πολλῶν μὲν ὄντες οὐ πολλοὶ
περιγίγνονται, λαμβάνουσι δ' ὅσ' ἂν μὴ τῷ πολέμῳ
δύνωνται τοῖς καιροῖς, οὐδεὶς δ' αὐτοὺς ἐκφεύγει
χρόνος οὐδὲ τρόπος τοῦ τὰ συμφέρονθ' ἑαυτοῖς
περαίνειν, οὐ μὰ Δί' οὐχ ὥσπερ ἡμεῖς καὶ διὰ
τούτους καὶ τοὺς ὁμοίους τούτοις, ἀλλήλων περι-
γιγνόμενοι, καὶ οὐχὶ τῶν ἐχθρῶν, πάντ' ἀνηλώκαμεν
4 τὸν χρόνον, ἂν μὲν εἰρήνην τις ἐκ πολέμου ποιήσῃ,
τοῦτον μισοῦντες, ἂν δ' ἐξ εἰρήνης πόλεμόν τις λέγῃ,
τούτῳ μαχόμενοι, ἂν δ' ἔχειν ἡσυχίαν τις παραινῇ
καὶ τὰ ἡμέτερ' αὐτῶν πράττειν, οὐδὲ τοῦτον ὀρθῶς
λέγειν φάσκοντες, ὅλως δ' αἰτιῶν καὶ κενῶν ἐλπίδων ὄντες πλήρεις.

---

[a] The meaning of " sycophant " is made clear in XVIII.
188-189.

148

be proving final and that you should be convicting yourselves of madness by changing your minds. Since, however, certain men who then kept silence are now finding fault, I wish to address a few words to them.

For I am amazed at the political procedure of these 2 men, or rather I consider it vile. For if, though free to recommend measures when you are considering questions, they choose instead to denounce decisions once made, they play the part of double-dealers,[a] not as they claim, of men of goodwill. I should like to ask them—and what I am about to say is not to become the signal for any tirade—just why, since they praise the Spartans in all other respects, they do not imitate the most admirable of all their practices, but rather do the very opposite. For they 3 say, men of Athens, that among them each man airs any opinion he may have until the question is put, but when the decision has been ratified, they all approve it and work together, even those who opposed it. Therefore, though few, they prevail over many and by actions well timed they get what they cannot get by war ; nor does any occasion or means of effecting what is to their own advantage escape them ; not, by Zeus, as we do who, thanks to these men and their like, in trying to get the better of one another instead of the enemy,[b] have wasted all our time, and if anyone is for making peace in time 4 of war, we hate him, and if anyone talks war in time of peace, we fight him, and if anyone advocates keeping quiet and minding our own business, we claim that he is wrong too, and in general we are overfull of recriminations and empty hopes.

[b] *Cf. Olynth.* ii. 25.

Τί οὖν, ἄν τις εἴποι, σὺ παραινεῖς, ἐπειδὴ ταῦτ᾽
ἐπιτιμᾷς; ἐγὼ νὴ Δί᾽ ἐρῶ.

Λϛ

Πρῶτον μέν, ὦ ἄνδρες Ἀθηναῖοι, οὐ πάνυ μοι
δοκεῖ τις ἂν εἰκότως περὶ ὑμῶν δεῖσαι μὴ παρὰ
τὸ τῶν συμβουλευόντων οὐκ ἐθέλειν ἀκούειν χεῖρον
βουλεύσησθε. πρῶτον μὲν γὰρ ἡ τύχη, καλῶς
ποιοῦσα, πολλὰ τῶν πραγμάτων ὑμῖν αὐτόμαθ᾽,
ὡς ἂν εὔξαισθε, παρίστησιν, ἐπεὶ τῇ γε τῶν προ-
εστηκότων προνοίᾳ βραχέ᾽ αὐτῶν εἶχεν ἂν καλῶς.
ἔπειθ᾽ ὑμεῖς οὐ μόνον τοὺς λόγους οὓς ἂν ἕκαστος
εἴποι πρόϊστε, ἀλλὰ καὶ ὧν ἕνεκ᾽ αὐτῶν ἕκαστος
δημηγορεῖ, εἰ δὲ μὴ φιλαπέχθημον ἦν, εἶπον ἂν καὶ
2 πόσου. τὸν δὴ τοῦ φενακίζεσθαι χρόνον ὡς εἰς
μικρότατον συνάγοντες σωφρονεῖν ἔμοιγε δοκεῖτε.
εἰ μὲν δή τι τῶν αὐτῶν ἔμελλον τοῖς ἄλλοις ἐρεῖν,
οὐκ ἂν ᾤμην δεῖν λέγων ἐνοχλεῖν. νῦν δὲ συμφέ-
[1446] ροντα μὲν ὑμῖν ἀκοῦσαι, παντάπασι δ᾽ ἀφεστηκότα
τῶν ὑπὸ τῶν πολλῶν προσδοκωμένων οἴομαι λέγειν ἔχειν. βραχὺς δ᾽ ἔσται χρόνος. σκέψασθε δ᾽
ἀκούσαντες, κἂν ὑμῖν ἀρέσκῃ, χρήσασθε.

ΛΖ

Καὶ βραχεῖαν, ὦ ἄνδρες Ἀθηναῖοι, καὶ δικαίαν
ποιήσομαι τὴν ἀρχὴν τοῦ λόγου· καὶ οὐδὲ τὰ πάντ᾽
ἐρῶ. ἡγοῦμαι γὰρ ἐξαπατᾶν μὲν εἶναι βουλομένου

" What then, Sir," someone may say, " what do you recommend, since you find fault with this conduct ? " By Zeus, I will tell you.

36

In the first place, men of Athens, I am not altogether sure that a man would reasonably fear on your account lest your deliberations would be the worse for your refusing to listen to your counsellors. For, to begin with, Fortune—to whom be thanks—arranges much of your business to take care of itself, so well that you would pray for nothing better, because little of it would be in good shape through such foresight as is exercised by those in authority. Next, you know in advance, not only what speeches each man will make, but also with what motives each one harangues you, and if it were not spiteful, I should also have said, for what price. I think you 2 are prudent in reducing to a minimum the time for being cheated. If I were intending to speak in the same vein as the rest, I should not have thought it necessary to bore you by speaking. As it is, I think I have something to say that will be worth your while to hear, and utterly different from what is expected by the majority. It will be short. Listen and examine it, and, if it pleases you, adopt it.

37

I shall make the beginning of my speech both short and reasonable, men of Athens, nor shall I deliver the whole of it. For I believe that, while it is the way of a man who intends deception to cast about for

σκοπεῖν ὄντιν' ὑμᾶς τρόπον τοὺς ἀκούοντας τὰ τοῦ
πράγματος δυσχερῆ τῷ λόγῳ συγκρύψεται, ἁπλῶς
δὲ πεπεικότος αὑτὸν ὑμῖν προσφέρεσθαι τοῦτο
πρῶτον εἶναι, εἰπεῖν πότερ' ἐγνωκὼς παρελήλυθεν,
2 ἵν' ἐὰν μὲν ἀκούσαντες τοῦτο τοὺς μετὰ ταῦτα
λόγους βούλησθ' ἀκούειν, καὶ διδάσκῃ καὶ φράζῃ
τὰ βέλτισθ' αὑτῷ δοκοῦντα, ἂν δ' ἀποδοκιμάσητ',
ἀπηλλαγμένος ᾖ καὶ μήθ' ὑμῖν ἐνοχλῇ μήθ' αὑτὸν
κόπτῃ.

Ἐγὼ δὴ τοῦτο πρῶτον ἐρῶ. ἐμοὶ δοκεῖ Μυτιλη-
ναίων ὁ δῆμος ἠδικῆσθαι, καὶ δίκην ὑμῖν ὑπὲρ
αὐτοῦ προσήκειν λαβεῖν. καὶ ὅπως λήψεσθ' ἔχω
λέγειν, ἐπειδὰν ὡς ἠδίκηνται καὶ ὑμῖν προσήκει
βοηθεῖν ἐπιδείξω.

ΛΗ

Πρῶτον μὲν οὐ πάνυ θαυμαστόν ἐστιν, ὦ ἄνδρες
Ἀθηναῖοι, τὸ μὴ ῥᾳδίους τοῖς συμβουλεύειν βουλομένοις εἶναι τοὺς λόγους· ὅταν γὰρ τὰ πράγματ'
ἔχῃ φαύλως περὶ ὧν δεῖ σκοπεῖν, δυσχερεῖς ἀνάγκη
περὶ αὐτῶν εἶναι καὶ τὰς συμβουλίας. εἰ μὲν οὖν
ἐκ τοῦ μὴ θέλειν ἀκούειν ἐλπὶς ταῦτα γενέσθαι
βελτίω, τοῦτο χρὴ πράττειν· εἰ δὲ χείρω μὲν
ἅπαντα βέλτιον δ' οὐδὲν ἐκ τούτου γενήσεται, τί
δεῖ, πρὸς τὸ φαυλότατον ἐλθεῖν ἐάσαντας, ἐκ πλείονος ἢ νῦν καὶ χαλεπωτέρως σῴζειν πειρᾶσθαι, ἐξὸν

ᵃ The democracy was overthrown in Mytilenê after the
Social War in 355 B.C.: XIII. 8 and XV. 19.

a plan whereby he may conceal from you, his hearers, by means of his words the disagreeable aspects of the situation, on the other hand, the first duty of a man who has resolved to deal candidly with you is to declare which side he has come forward to endorse, in order that, if after hearing this statement you are 2 willing to hear the sequel, he may enlighten you and explain what measures seem best to himself, but if you shall reject his views, that he may have done with the matter and neither annoy you nor tire himself out.

This, then, will be my first statement : It is my opinion that the democratic party in Mytilenê has been wronged and that it is your duty to obtain justice for them.[a] For obtaining this justice I have a plan to propose when once I have demonstrated that they have been wronged and that it is your duty to go to their aid.

38

FIRST of all, men of Athens, it is not altogether surprising that those who wish to tender you advice do not readily find the words, because, when the conditions that require consideration are bad, it is inevitable that the recommendations made concerning them should also be disagreeable. Of course, if by your refusing to listen there is hope of this situation becoming better, that is the thing to do, but if everything is going to get worse and nothing better by so doing, why should you, having allowed things to come to the worst, after a longer interval than has now elapsed, and with greater difficulty, try to save the situation, though, starting from present condi-

DEMOSTHENES

[1447] ἐκ τῶν παρόντων ἔτι καὶ νῦν ἐπανορθώσασθαι καὶ προαγαγεῖν ἐπὶ τὸ βέλτιον;

2 Τὸ μὲν οὖν ὀργίλως ὑμᾶς ἔχειν εἰκός ἐστι ταῦτα πάσχοντας· τὸ δὲ μὴ τοῖς αἰτίοις ἀλλὰ πᾶσιν ἐφεξῆς ὀργίζεσθαι, τοῦτ' οὐκέτ' εἰκὸς οὐδ' ὀρθῶς ἔχον ἐστίν. οἱ γὰρ μηδενὸς μὲν αἴτιοι τῶν παρεληλυθότων, τὰ δὲ λοιπὰ πῶς ἔσται βελτίω λέγειν ἔχοντες, χάριν, οὐκ ἀπέχθειαν, κομίσαιντ' ἂν δικαίως παρ' ὑμῶν· οὕς, ἐὰν ἀκαίρως δυσκολαίνητε, ὀκνεῖν 3 ἀνίστασθαι ποιήσετε. καίτοι ἔγωγ' οὐκ ἀγνοῶ, ὅτι πολλάκις οὐ τοῖς αἰτίοις, ἀλλὰ τοῖς ἐμποδὼν οὖσι τοῖς ὀργιζομένοις ἀηδές τι παθεῖν συνέβη. ὅμως δ' ἀνέστην συμβουλεύσων, πιστεύω γὰρ ἔγωγ', ὦ ἄνδρες Ἀθηναῖοι, φλαύρου μὲν μηδενὸς ὢν αἴτιος εὑρεθήσεσθαι, βελτίω δ' ἑτέρων ὑμῖν ἔχειν συμβουλεῦσαι.

ΛΘ

Τὰ μὲν γεγενημέν', ὦ ἄνδρες Ἀθηναῖοι, τοιαῦθ' οἷα πάντες ἀκηκόατε· δεῖ δ' ὑμᾶς μηδὲν ἐκπεπληγμένως διακεῖσθαι, λογιζομένους ὅτι πρὸς μὲν τὰ παρόντ' ἀθύμως ἔχειν οὔτε τοῖς πράγμασι συμφέρον οὔθ' ὑμῶν ἄξιόν ἐστι, τὸ δὲ ταῦτ' ἐπανορθοῦν αὐτοῖς ἡγεῖσθαι προσῆκον καὶ τῆς ὑμετέρας δόξης ἄξιον ἂν φανείη. χρὴ δὲ τοὺς ὄντας οἷοι φήσαιτ' ἂν ὑμεῖς εἶναι ἐν τοῖς δεινοῖς ἑτέρων διαφέροντας 2 φαίνεσθαι. ἐγὼ δ' οὐδαμῶς μὲν ἂν ἠβουλόμην

154

tions, it is still possible even now to set things to rights and effect a change for the better ?

Certainly it is reasonable for you to feel angry 2 after these unhappy experiences ; but to vent your anger, not upon the parties responsible, but upon everybody in turn, ceases to be either reasonable or right : because those who are in no way responsible for past events but can tell you how an improvement may be effected for the future would rightly meet with gratitude, not hostility, from you. If you treat these men with untimely irritation, you will make them hesitate to rise and speak. And yet I am 3 myself not unaware that often it is the lot, not of those who are guilty, but of persons who get in the way of those who are angry, to suffer unpleasant consequences. In spite of this I have risen to advise you, for I have confidence myself that I shall not be found to be the cause of any past misfortune, men of Athens, and have really better proposals to offer you than other speakers.

39

THE events that have occurred, men of Athens, are such as you have all heard, but you must not allow yourselves to be at all dismayed, reflecting that to be discouraged in the face of the present troubles is neither improving the situation nor worthy of yourselves. On the contrary, to consider it incumbent on yourselves to set these things to rights would manifestly be in keeping also with your reputation. Men such as you would profess to be should prove themselves superior to other breeds in times of stress. As for me, I should by no means have wished these 2

ταῦτα συμβῆναι τῇ πόλει οὐδ' ἀτυχεῖν ὑμᾶς οὐδέν·
εἰ δ' ἄρ' ἔδει γενέσθαι καί τι δαιμόνιον τοῦτ'
ἀπέκειτο, ὥσπερ πέπρακται τὰ γεγενημένα λυσι-
τελεῖν οἴομαι. τὰ μὲν γὰρ τῆς τύχης ὀξείας ἔχει
[1448] τὰς μεταβολὰς καὶ κοινὰς ἀμφοτέροις τὰς παρου-
σίας· ἃ δ' ἂν δι' ἀνδρῶν κακίαν πραχθῇ βεβαίους
3 ποιεῖ τὰς ἥττας. οἶμαι μὲν οὖν οὐδὲ τοὺς κε-
κρατηκότας ἀγνοεῖν, ὅτι βουληθέντων ὑμῶν καὶ
παροξυνθέντων τῷ γεγενημένῳ, οὐ πάνυ πω δῆλον
πότερ' εὐτύχημ' ἢ καὶ τοὐναντίον αὐτοῖς ἐστιν τὸ
πεπραγμένον· εἰ δ' ἄρ' ἐπῆρκε τὸ πρᾶγμ' αὐτοὺς
θρασύνεσθαι, κἂν τοῦτο πρὸς ὑμῶν ἤδη γίγνοιτο.
ὅσῳ γὰρ ἂν μᾶλλον καταφρονήσωσι, τοσούτῳ θᾶττον ἁμαρτήσονται.

M

Οὔ μοι δοκεῖτ', ὦ ἄνδρες Ἀθηναῖοι, περὶ ἧς
οἴεσθε νυνὶ μόνον βουλεύεσθαι πόλεως, ἀλλὰ πασῶν
τῶν συμμαχίδων. ὅπως γὰρ ἂν περὶ ταύτης γνῶτε,
πρὸς ταῦτ' εἰκὸς ἀποβλέποντας τοὺς ἄλλους καὐ-
τοὺς τῶν αὐτῶν τεύξεσθαι νομίζειν. ὥστε δεῖ καὶ
τοῦ βελτίστου καὶ τῆς ὑμετέρας αὐτῶν εἵνεκα
δόξης σπουδάσαι ὅπως ἅμα καὶ συμφέροντα καὶ
δίκαια φανήσεσθε βουλευόμενοι.
2 Ἡ μὲν οὖν ἀρχὴ τῶν τοιούτων πραγμάτων ἁπάντων ἐστὶ τῶν στρατηγῶν· ὧν οἱ πλεῖστοι τῶν παρ'

calamities to come upon the city nor yet for you to suffer misfortune, but if, after all, this had to happen and was in store as something predestined, I consider it to your profit that these events have occurred just as they have. For the dispensations of Fortune exhibit sharp reversals and impartial visitations to both sides, whereas the events that follow upon the villainy of men make for sure defeat. Now, while 3 I am of the opinion that even those who have gained the upper hand are not unaware that, should you form your resolve and be stung to action by what has happened, it is not yet quite clear whether what has been done is good fortune or the opposite for them, yet if it turns out that the exploit has inspired them to become over-confident, this would already be another point in your favour. For the more they look down upon you, the sooner will they blunder.

40

I DO not believe, men of Athens, that you are deliberating upon this occasion concerning only the city you have in mind, but concerning all the allied cities. For however you decide concerning the city in question, the other cities, looking to this decision, will probably expect to receive the same treatment themselves. Consequently you must, for the sake both of doing what is best and of guarding your own reputation, strive earnestly that you may be clearly seen to be devising measures which are alike expedient and just.

Now, the initiative in all such matters is in the 2 hands of the generals. Most of these men, though

ὑμῶν ἐκπλεόντων οὐ τοὺς ὑμετέρους φίλους, οὓς
διὰ παντὸς τοῦ χρόνου τῶν αὐτῶν κινδύνων μετ-
εσχηκότας παρειλήφασι, θεραπεύειν τούτους οἴονται
δεῖν, ἀλλ' ἰδίους φίλους ἕκαστος ἑαυτῷ κατα-
σκευάσας, ὑμᾶς ἀξιοῖ τοὺς αὐτῶν κόλακας καὶ
ὑμετέρους ἡγεῖσθαι φίλους· οὗ πᾶν ἐστι τοὐναν-
3 τίον. οὔτε γὰρ ἐχθροτέρους οὔτ' ἀναγκαίους μᾶλλον
ἐχθροὺς ἂν τούτων εὕροιτε. ὅσῳ γὰρ πλείω παρα-
κρουόμενοι πλεονεκτοῦσι, τοσούτῳ πλειόνων ὀφεί-
[1449] λειν ἡγοῦνται δίκην δοῦναι. οὐδεὶς δ' ἂν γένοιτ'
εὔνους τούτοις ὑφ' ὧν ἄν τι κακὸν πείσεσθαι προσ-
δοκᾷ. τοῦ μὲν οὖν κατηγορεῖν ἴσως οὐχ ὁ παρὼν
καιρός· ἃ δ' ἡγοῦμαι συμφέρειν ὑμῖν, ταῦτα συμ-
βουλεύσω.

ΜΑ

Οὐδέν', ὦ ἄνδρες Ἀθηναῖοι, τῶν πάντων ὑμῶν
οὕτως οἴομαι κακόνουν εἶναι τῇ πόλει ὥστε μὴ
χαλεπῶς φέρειν μηδὲ λυπεῖσθαι τοῖς γεγενημένοις.
εἰ μὲν τοίνυν ἀγανακτοῦντας ἦν ἄπρακτόν τι ποιῆσαι
τούτων, τοῦτ' ἂν ἔγωγε παρῄνουν ὑμῖν ἅπασιν·
ἐπειδὴ δὲ ταῦτα μὲν οὐκ ἂν ἄλλως ἔχοι δεῖ δ'
ὑπὲρ τῶν λοιπῶν προνοηθῆναι ὅπως μὴ ταῦτα
πείσεσθε, ὥσπερ, ὦ ἄνδρες Ἀθηναῖοι, νῦν γεγενημένων ἀγανακτεῖτε, οὕτω χρὴ σπουδάσαι ὑπὲρ τοῦ
μὴ πάλιν ταῦτα συμβῆναι, καὶ νομίζειν μηδέν'
ἔχειν λόγον εἰπεῖν τῶν συμβουλευόντων τοιοῦτον,
ὃς δυνήσεται σῶσαι τὰ παρόντα μηδενὸς ὑμῶν

they sail out under your orders, do not consider it
their duty to cultivate those who are friendly to you,
people whom they have taken over from their prede-
cessors as men who have shared the same dangers as
you throughout all our history, but each and all, having established their own private friendships, expect
you to regard their personal flatterers as your friends
also. But the facts are exactly the opposite. You 3
could find no more bitter or inevitable enemies than
these flatterers. For the more gains they make by
deception, the greater is the number of offences for
which they think they are due to be punished. And
no one could feel goodwill toward those at whose
hands he expects to suffer some harm. However, the
present is perhaps not the time to denounce them.
Instead, I shall give you the advice that I consider
in your interests.

41

I DO not suppose, men of Athens, that there is one of
all your number so disloyal to the city as not to feel
distressed and pained by these events. If, then, it
were possible by nursing indignation to render un-
done any of the things that have been done, this is
what I should be urging upon you all. But since the
facts are unalterable and you must take forethought
whereby you may escape the same misfortune in the
future, the keenness of your indignation, men of
Athens, over what has now taken place ought to set
the measure for your determination that the same
shall not occur again, nor should you think that any
of your advisers has such a wonderful plan to propose
as will be capable of redressing the present evils
without any of you shouldering a share of the burden.

DEMOSTHENES

μηδὲν συναραμένου· οὐ γὰρ ἂν λόγος, ἀλλὰ θεός τις ὁ τοιοῦτος εἴη.

2 Ἡ μὲν οὖν ἀρχὴ τοῦ ταῦθ' οὕτως ἔχειν ἐκεῖθεν ἤρτηται, ἐκ τοῦ τῆς παραχρῆμα πρὸς ὑμᾶς ἕνεκα χάριτος ἐνίους τῶν λεγόντων ἐνταυθοῖ δημηγορεῖν, ὡς οὔτ' εἰσφέρειν οὔτε στρατεύεσθαι δεῖ, πάντα δ' αὐτόματ' ἔσται. ἔδει μὲν οὖν ταῦθ' ὑπ' ἄλλου τινὸς ἐξελέγχεσθαι μετὰ τοῦ λυσιτελοῦντος ἐλέγχου τῇ πόλει· δοκεῖ δέ μοι τρόπον τινὰ καὶ νῦν ἀμείνων 3 ἡ τύχη περὶ ὑμᾶς τῶν ἐφεστηκότων εἶναι. τὸ μὲν γὰρ ἕκαστ' ἀπόλλυσθαι τῆς τῶν ἐπιμελουμένων κακίας σημεῖον προσήκει ποιεῖσθαι, τὸ δὲ μὴ πάλαι πάντ' ἀπολωλέναι τῆς ὑμετέρας τύχης εὐεργέτημ' ἔγωγε κρίνω. ἐν ᾧ τοίνυν ἡ τύχη διαλείπει καὶ τοὺς ἐχθροὺς ἀνέχει, τῶν λοιπῶν ἐπιμελήθητε. εἰ [1450] δὲ μή, σκοπεῖθ' ὅπως μὴ ἅμα τούς τ' ἐφεστῶτας ἑκάστοις ὑμεῖς κρινεῖτε, καὶ τὰ πράγμαθ' ὑμῶν, ὦ ἄνδρες Ἀθηναῖοι, κλινεῖ. οὐ γὰρ ἔσθ' ὅπως ταῦτ' ἄνευ μεγάλου τινὸς στήσεται, μηδενὸς ἀντιλαμβανομένου.

ΜΒ

Οὐδέν ἐστιν, ὦ ἄνδρες Ἀθηναῖοι, τοῦτ' ἄλογον, τοὺς ἀεὶ καὶ συνεχῶς ὑπὲρ τῶν ὀλιγαρχιῶν πολιτευομένους, καὶ νῦν ταῦτα ποιοῦντας ἐξελέγχεσθαι. ἀλλ' ἐκεῖνο μᾶλλον ἄν τις εἰκότως θαυμάσαι τὸ

---

[a] Cf. Olynth. iii. 35-36.

For no speech would be wonderful enough for that, only some divine intervention.

Now the origin of this present state of affairs 2 hinges upon this fact, that, for the sake of a momentary popularity with you, some of those who speak in this place declared to the Assembly : " There is no need to pay a special war-tax or to do military service, but everything will take care of itself." To be sure, the absurdity of this ought to have been exposed by some other speaker—the sort of exposure that profits the State : still, even as things now are, it seems to me that Fortune is somehow kinder to you than are those at the head of affairs. For while the occurrence 3 of one loss after another ought to be counted evidence of the villainy of those who are in charge, the fact that all your resources have not been destroyed long ago I, at least, judge to be a benefaction of the Fortune that attends you. In the interval, therefore, while Fortune allows a respite and is holding your foes in check, have a care for what lies in the future. Otherwise take heed lest at one and the same time you shall be bringing to justice those who have been appointed to the several posts, and your power, men of Athens, shall be declining ; for it is impossible that this shall continue to stand, barring some miracle, if not one of you puts his hand to the task.[a]

42

It is nothing out of the ordinary, men of Athens, that those public men who are always and unceasingly agitating on behalf of the oligarchies should be convicted of doing so upon this occasion also. On the contrary, one might much more reasonably be aston-

τοὺς εἰδότας ὑμᾶς ταῦτα πολλάκις ἥδιον τούτων
ἀκούειν ἢ τῶν ὑπὲρ ὑμῶν λεγόντων. ἴσως μὲν οὖν
ὥσπερ οὐδ' ἰδίᾳ ῥᾴδιόν ἐστιν ἅπαντ' ὀρθῶς πράττειν, οὕτως οὐδὲ κοινῇ· ἀλλ' οὐ δὴ τὰ μέγιστά γε
2 χρὴ παρορᾶν. τὰ μὲν οὖν ἄλλα πάντ' ἐστὶν ἐλάττω·
ὅταν δ' ὑπὲρ πολιτείας καὶ σφαγῶν καὶ δήμου
καταλύσεως εὐχερῶς ἀκούητε, πῶς οὐκ ἔξω χρὴ
τοῦ φρονεῖν ὑμᾶς αὐτοὺς[1] ἡγεῖσθαι; οἱ μὲν γὰρ
ἄλλοι πάντες ἄνθρωποι τοῖς ἑτέρων παραδείγμασι
χρώμενοι μᾶλλον εὐλαβεῖς αὐτοὶ γίγνονται· ὑμεῖς
δ' οὐδὲ τὰ τοῖς ἄλλοις συμβαίνοντ' ἀκούοντες
φοβηθῆναι δύνασθε, ἀλλ' ὃ τοὺς ἰδίᾳ περιμένοντας
ἀβελτέρους νομίζετε, τοῦτ' αὐτοὶ δημοσίᾳ μοι
δοκεῖτ' ἀναμένειν—παθόντες αἰσθέσθαι.

ΜΓ

Οὐδεὶς πώποτ' ἴσως ὑμῶν ἐζήτησεν, ὦ ἄνδρες
Ἀθηναῖοι, τί δήποθ' οἱ κακῶς πράττοντες ἄμεινον
περὶ τῶν πραγμάτων τῶν εὖ πραττόντων βουλεύον-
ται. ἔστι δ' οὐχ ἑτέρωθέν ποθεν τοῦτο γιγνόμενον,
ἀλλ' ὅτι συμβαίνει τοῖς μὲν μήτε φοβεῖσθαι μηδὲν
μήθ' ἅ τις ἂν λέγοι δεινὰ προσήκονθ' αὑτοῖς ἡγεῖ-
σθαι· τοὺς δὲ πλησίον ὄντας τῶν ἁμαρτημάτων οἷς
1451] ἂν εἰς τὸ κακῶς πράττειν ἀφίκωνται, σώφρονας
2 πρὸς τὰ λοιπὰ καὶ μετρίους παρέχει.[2] σπουδαίων

[1] αὐτοὺς bracketed by Blass.
[2] ὑπάρχειν (συμβαίνει) Rennie.

---

[a] There is an ironical touch in πολιτείας as if implying that
oligarchy was the ideal form of government to those whose
phrases he here quotes.

[b] Cf. XV. 16.

[c] Aeschylus, Agamemnon 176-178 " Zeus who sets mortals

ished that you, though aware of the truth, repeatedly prefer to listen to them rather than to those who speak in your own defence. It may very well be that it is difficult to act wisely in all public matters, just as it is in private matters, but certainly it is wrong to take a light view of things of the very greatest importance. Assuredly all other considera- 2 tions are of less consequence, and when you listen good-naturedly to speeches on behalf of government efficiency [a] and killings and the overthrow of demo- cracy, how can one help but consider that you too are out of your minds ? For all other men profit by the example of their fellows and are themselves rendered much more cautious thereby,[b] but you, even when you hear what is happening to the rest of the Greeks are incapable of taking alarm, but the very thing that you consider men to be witless for awaiting as individuals you seem to me to be calmly awaiting yourselves as a community—that is, to learn by bitter experience.

43

PERHAPS none of you has ever inquired, men of Athens, just why men in adversity deliberate more wisely over their affairs than do the prosperous. This comes about for no other reason than this, that it is not natural for the prosperous to feel any alarm or to believe that such dangers as someone may report concern themselves ; those, however, who are close in time to the mistakes through which they have come to adversity are rendered discreet with refer- ence to future actions and inclined to moderation.[c]

in the path of wisdom and hath enacted a law of learning by suffering."

τοίνυν ἐστὶν ἀνθρώπων, ὅταν βελτίστῃ τῇ παρούσῃ
τύχῃ χρῶνται, τότε πλείω[1] τὴν σπουδὴν πρὸς τὸ
σωφρονεῖν ἔχειν· οὐδὲν γὰρ οὔτε φυλαττομένοις
οὕτω δεινὸν ὥστ᾽ ἀφύλακτον εἶναι, οὔτ᾽ ὀλιγωροῦσιν
ἀπροσδόκητον παθεῖν. λέγω δὲ ταῦτ᾽ οὐχ ἵνα τὴν
ἄλλως ὑμᾶς δεδίττωμαι, ἀλλ᾽ ἵνα μὴ διὰ τὴν παρ-
οῦσαν εὐπραξίαν, ἃ γένοιτ᾽ ἄν, εἰ μὴ προνοήσεσθε
τῶν πραγμάτων, δεῖν᾽ ἀκούοντες καταφρονῆτε, ἀλλ᾽
ἄνευ τοῦ παθεῖν, ὥσπερ ἐστὶ προσῆκον φάσκοντάς
γε μηδένων ἀπολείπεσθαι τῷ σωφρονεῖν, φυλά-
ξησθε.

ΜΔ

Οὐχὶ τὸν αὐτὸν εἶναι καιρὸν ὑπείληφ᾽, ὦ ἄνδρες
Ἀθηναῖοι, τοῦ χαρίζεσθαι καὶ τοῦ τὰ δοκοῦντά μοι
βέλτιστα παραινεῖν. πολλάκις γὰρ ὁρῶ τὸ χαρίζε-
σθαί τι παρὰ γνώμην πλεῖον᾽ ἀπέχθειαν ἐνεγκὸν
τοῦ τὸ πρῶτον ἐναντιωθῆναι. εἰ μὲν οὖν ἅπαντες
ἐγιγνώσκετε ταῦτά, οὔτ᾽ ἄν, εἴ μοι τὰ δέοντ᾽ ἐδο-
κεῖτε προαιρεῖσθαι, παρῆλθον, περίεργον ἡγούμενος
τοῖς ἀφ᾽ αὑτῶν ἃ χρὴ ποιοῦσι λέγειν, οὔτ᾽ ἂν εἰ
τοὐναντίον· μᾶλλον γὰρ ἂν ἡγησάμην ἕν᾽ ὄντ᾽
ἐμαυτὸν ἀγνοεῖν τὰ κράτιστ᾽ ἢ πάντας ὑμᾶς.
2 ἐπειδὴ δ᾽ ὁρῶ τινὰς ὑμῶν ταυτὰ μὲν γιγνώσκοντας
ἐμοί, τἀναντία δ᾽ ἄλλοις, πειράσομαι μετὰ τούτων
τοὺς ἑτέρους πεῖσαι. εἰ μὲν οὖν οἰήσεσθε δεῖν μὴ

[1] πλείστην Blass.

[a] Cf. Phil. i. 3.

It therefore becomes serious-minded men at the 2
very time that they enjoy the presence of Fortune
at her best to show the greater eagerness to practise
discretion. For no danger is so formidable that
men who are on their guard cannot guard against
it,[a] and there is none that men who belittle it may
not expect to suffer. I say this, not to frighten
you needlessly, but in order that, when you hear
rumours of danger, you may not despise them because of your present prosperity—they may come
true unless you take forethought for your interests—
but rather in order that, without waiting to learn
by experience, you may forestall trouble, just as
becomes men who at least claim to be second to none
in point of discretion.

44

I ASSUME, men of Athens, that the time for humouring
you and the time for recommending the measures I
regard as best are not the same ; for often, I observe,
humouring you contrary to one's own judgement has
earned more hatred than opposing at the outset.
Now, if you all held the same opinions, I should not
have come forward if you seemed to me to prefer the
right course, considering it superfluous to speak
before people doing the right thing of their own
accord, nor again, if the contrary were true, for I
should have thought that a lone person like myself
was more likely to misapprehend the best measures
than all of you. But since I see some of you holding 2
the same views as myself and the opposite to those
held by others, I shall try with the support of these to
persuade those who differ. Now, if you shall think
it right to refuse to listen, you will make a mistake ;

θέλειν ἀκούειν οὐκ ὀρθῶς ποιήσετε· ἂν δ᾽ ἀκούσητε
σιωπῇ καὶ τοῦθ᾽ ὑπομείνητε, δυοῖν ἀγαθοῖν θάτερον
ὑμῖν ὑπάρξει· ἢ γὰρ πεισθήσεσθ᾽, ἄν τι δοκῶμεν
λέγειν συμφέρον, ἢ βεβαιότερον περὶ ὧν ἐγνώκατ᾽
[1452] ἔσεσθε πεπεισμένοι. ἂν γάρ, οἷς τι[1] διαμαρτάνειν
οἰόμεθ᾽ ἡμεῖς ὑμᾶς, ταῦτα μηδενὸς ἄξια φανῇ, μετ᾽
ἐλέγχου τὰ δεδογμένα νῦν ὑμεῖς ἔσεσθ᾽ ᾑρημένοι.

ΜΕ

Βουλοίμην ἄν, ὦ ἄνδρες Ἀθηναῖοι, περὶ ὧν
ηὐδοκίμηκεν λέγων παρ᾽ ὑμῖν ὁ δεῖνα, ἐπὶ τῶν
ἔργων καὶ τῶν πραττομένων ἴσον αὐτῷ τὸν ἔπαινον
γενέσθαι· οὔτε γὰρ τούτῳ κακόνους εἰμί, μὰ τοὺς
θεούς, ὑμῖν τ᾽ ἀγαθὸν βούλομαι ἂν γενέσθαι.[2] ἀλλ᾽
ὁρᾶτ᾽, ὦ ἄνδρες Ἀθηναῖοι, μὴ κεχωρισμένον ᾖ
λόγον εἰπεῖν εὖ, καὶ προελέσθαι πράγματα συμφέροντα, καὶ τὸ μὲν ῥήτορος ἔργον ᾖ, τὸ δὲ νοῦν
2 ἔχοντος ἀνθρώπου. ὑμεῖς τοίνυν οἱ πολλοί, καὶ
μάλισθ᾽ οἱ πρεσβύτατοι, λέγειν μὲν οὐκ ὀφείλεθ᾽
ὁμοίως δύνασθαι τοῖς δεινοτάτοις· τῶν γὰρ εἰθι-
σμένων τὸ πρᾶγμα τοῦτο· νοῦν δ᾽ ἔχειν ὀφείλεθ᾽
ὁμοίως καὶ μᾶλλον τούτων· αἱ γὰρ ἐμπειρίαι καὶ
τὸ πόλλ᾽ ἑορακέναι τοῦτ᾽ ἐμποιοῦσιν. μὴ τοίνυν,
ὦ ἄνδρες Ἀθηναῖοι, φανῆτ᾽ ἀγνοοῦντες ἐν τῷ
παρόντι νῦν, ὅτι αἱ διὰ τῶν λόγων ἀνδρεῖαι καὶ
θρασύτητες, ἐὰν μὴ μεθ᾽ ὑπαρχούσης ὦσι παρασκευῆς καὶ ῥώμης, ἀκοῦσαι μέν εἰσιν ἡδεῖαι, πράτ-
3 τειν δ᾽ ἐπικίνδυνοι. αὐτίκα γὰρ τὸ μὴ ᾽πιτρέπειν

---

[1] τι bracketed by Blass.
[2] ἄν τι γενέσθαι βουλοίμην, βουλοίμην ἂν γενέσθαι codd. alii ;
Blass brackets ἂν γενέσθαι.

but if you will listen in silence and bear with me
in this, one of two benefits will accrue to you :
for either you will be persuaded if we seem to advocate something advantageous, or you will be more
firmly convinced of the rightness of your own views ;
for if the grounds upon which we think you are going
somewhat astray shall be proved valueless, your
choice of the same measures as before will this time
be preceded by the test of argument.

45

I COULD wish, men of Athens, that a certain person,[a]
who has won your approval as a speaker on the
measures before you, might have deserved equal
praise for the feasiblity and workableness of his proposal. For I call the gods to witness that I bear
the man no ill will and wish that his plan had been
a good one for you. But do not forget, men of
Athens, that making a good speech and choosing
sound policies are miles apart, and that the one is the
part of an orator and the other of a man of sense.
Now, you, the multitude, and especially the oldest 2
among you, while not obliged to speak as well as the
cleverest, for this art is for the practised speakers, are
yet under obligation to have as much sense as they
and even more, for it is long experience and " having
seen much " [b] that begets this faculty in us. Do not
therefore, men of Athens, show yourselves unaware
in this crisis that valorous deeds and bold exploits
by word of mouth, unless backed by ready armament
and physical force, though pleasant to hear, are
hazardous in action. For example, " Do not leave 3

---

[a] See p. 144, note c.   [b] Homer, *Odyssey* i. 1-5.

τοῖς ἀδικοῦσιν, ὁρᾶθ' ὡς καλὸν τὸ ῥῆμα. ἀπο-
βλέψατε δὴ πρῶτον πρὸς τὸ ἔργον αὐτό. δεῖ
κρατῆσαι μαχομένους τῶν ἐχθρῶν τοὺς τὴν τοῦ ῥή-
ματος τούτου σεμνότητ' ἔργῳ ληψομένους. εἰπεῖν
μὲν γάρ, ὦ ἄνδρες Ἀθηναῖοι, πάντα πέφυκε ῥάδιον,
πρᾶξαι δ' οὐχ ἅπαντα. οὐ γὰρ ἴσος πόνος καὶ
ἱδρὼς πρό τε τοῦ λέγειν καὶ πρὸ τοῦ πράττειν ἐστίν.

4 ἐγὼ δ' οὐ χείρους ὑμᾶς ἡγοῦμαι φύσει Θηβαίων
[1453] (καὶ γὰρ ἂν μαινοίμην), ἀλλ' ἀπαρασκευοτέρους.
φημὶ δὴ δεῖν τοῦ παρασκευάζεσθαι νῦν ποιεῖσθαι
τὴν ἀρχήν, ἐπειδὴ τέως ἠμελεῖτε, οὐ τοῦ διαγωνί-
ζεσθαι. οὐ γὰρ ἀντιλέγω τὸ ὅλον, ἀλλ' ὑπὲρ τοῦ
τρόπου τῆς ἐγχειρήσεως ἐναντιοῦμαι.

Μς

Ὅσην μέν, ὦ ἄνδρες Ἀθηναῖοι, πεποίηνται σπουδὴν οἱ πρέσβεις κατηγορῆσαι τῆς πόλεως ἡμῶν,
ἅπαντες ἑωράκατε· πλὴν γὰρ οὐκ ἔχω τίνος εἴπω,
τἄλλα πάνθ' ὑμῖν ἀναθεῖναι πεπείρανται. εἰ μὲν
οὖν ἦσαν αὐτῶν ἀληθεῖς αἱ κατηγορίαι, χάριν γ'
εἴχετ' εἰκότως ἄν, εἰ πρὸς ὑμᾶς οὕτως ὑμῶν κατ-
2 ηγόρουν καὶ μὴ πρὸς ἄλλους. ἐπειδὴ δὲ διαστρέ-
ψαντες τἀληθῆ καὶ τὰ μὲν παραβαίνοντες ἀφ' ὧν
ἂν μεγάλους ἐπαίνους κομίσαισθε δικαίως, τὰ δ'
αἰτιασάμενοι ψευδῆ καὶ οὐ προσήκονθ' ὑμῖν, κέ-
χρηνται τῷ λόγῳ, πονηροὺς δίκαιον αὐτούς, ἐπειδὰν
ἐξελεγχθῶσι ταῦτα πεποιηκότες, νομίζειν. εἰ γὰρ
ῥήτορες δεινοὶ μᾶλλον εἶναι δοκεῖν ἢ μετ' ἀληθείας
ἐπιεικεῖς ἄνθρωποι νομίζεσθαι προείλοντο, οὐδ'

---

[a] Hesiod, *Works and Days* 289-290 " But in front of
virtue have the deathless gods set sweat."

168

a free hand to aggressors "; you see what a fine slogan that is ! Do not fail first to take a good look at the actual nature of the task. They must master the foe in battle who are really going to capture the majesty of this saying. For all things are easy to say, men of Athens, but not all are easy to do, for " not so much toil and sweat come before speech as before action." [a] I do not think you are naturally 4 inferior to the Thebans—I should be mad to say that —only less well prepared. What I do say is that now is the time to begin your preparation, since you have been negligent up to now, not the decisive struggle. For I am not speaking against the plan as a whole but I am opposed to your way of going about it.

46

You have all seen, men of Athens, with what zest the ambassadors [b] have denounced our city. For, apart from complaints against some unspecified offender, they have attempted to lay all offences at your doors. I admit, if their charges were true, you might reasonably be grateful that they were thus denouncing you to your faces instead of to others ; but since they have 2 used the privilege of speaking here to distort the truth, failing to mention some things from which you would justly derive great praise, and making charges that are false and inapplicable to you, it is right that you should consider them unprincipled, when once they have been proved guilty of such conduct as this. For if they prefer to be regarded as accomplished rhetoricians rather than truly fair-minded men,

[b] Probably the Chians, Byzantines and Rhodians : XV. 3.

αὐτοὶ καλοκἀγαθίας ἄν, ὡς ἔοικεν, ἀμφισβητοῖεν.
3 ἔστι μὲν οὖν χαλεπὸν τὸ παρ' ὑμῖν ὑπὲρ ὑμῶν
ἐροῦντ' ἀνεστηκέναι, ὥσπερ ῥᾴδιον τὸ καθ' ὑμῶν.
ἐγὼ γὰρ μὰ τὴν Ἀθηνᾶν οὐδένας ἂν τῶν ἄλλων
ἀνθρώπων οὕτως οἶμαι τὰ προσόνθ' αὐτοῖς ἀκοῦσαι
νουθετουμένους ὡς ὑμεῖς τὰ μὴ προσήκοντα κακῶς
ἀκούοντες. οὐ μὴν οὐδὲ τούτους θρασέως ἂν οὕτως
ἡγοῦμαι ψεύδεσθαι, εἰ μὴ συνῄδεσαν ταῦτα καὶ
πρόδηλον ἦν ὅτι δεινότατοι πάντων ὑμεῖς ἐστ'
ἀκούειν ὅ τι ἄν τις καθ' ὑμῶν λέγῃ.
[1454] Εἰ μὲν οὖν ταύτης τῆς εὐηθείας δίκην ὑμᾶς δεῖ
διδόναι, λόγους οὐ προσήκοντας κατὰ τῆς πόλεως
ἀκούειν τοῦτ' ἂν εἴη. εἰ δ' ὑπὲρ τῶν ἀληθῶν εἴ
τι δίκαιον ῥητέον, ἐπὶ τοῦτ' ἐγὼ παρελήλυθα,
πιστεύων οὐκ αὐτὸς ἀξίως τῶν ὑμῖν πεπραγμένων
5 εἰπεῖν δυνήσεσθαι, ἀλλὰ τὰ πράγμαθ', ὅπως ἄν τις
εἴπῃ, δίκαια φανεῖσθαι. βουλοίμην δ' ἂν ὑμᾶς, ὦ
ἄνδρες Ἀθηναῖοι, ἴσους ἀκροατὰς ὑπὲρ ὑμῶν αὐτῶν
γενέσθαι, καὶ μὴ τῷ προῆχθαι τοὺς λόγους ἐπαινέσαι τοὺς τούτων φιλονικεῖν. οὐ γὰρ ἂν ὑμετέραν
κακίαν οὐδεὶς ἔτι κρίναι, εἰ λέγοντός τινος εὖ
παρεκρούσθητε, ἀλλὰ τῶν ἐπὶ τούτῳ σπουδὴν ποι-
ησαμένων, ὅπως ὑμᾶς ἐξαπατήσουσιν.

MZ

Οἶμαι πάντας ἂν ὑμᾶς, ὦ ἄνδρες Ἀθηναῖοι,
φῆσαι, ἃ βέλτισθ' ἕκαστος ἡγεῖται τῇ πόλει, βούλε-

it is not likely that even they themselves would claim to be gentlemen. It is, of course, difficult to 3 rise up to speak before you in your own defence, just as it is easy to speak against you. For, by Athena, I do not think that there are any other people in the whole world who would listen so complacently when reminded of their real faults as you do when you are reviled for faults that are not yours. What is more, I do not believe that even these men would lie to you with such effrontery if they were not aware of this, and if it were not clear in advance that of all people you are the most addicted to listening to whatever anyone may say against you.

Now, if you must be punished for this fatuousness, 4 to listen to undeserved charges against the State would be that penalty ; but if something must, in all fairness, be said on behalf of the truth, it is for this purpose that I have come forward, confident, not that I shall unaided be able to speak with eloquence worthy of your past actions, but that these actions, however one may speak, will be seen to be just. It 5 would be my wish, men of Athens, that you become equally willing listeners when you are being defended, and not, through having been beguiled, become all too eager to praise the speeches of these men. For no one would go on judging it vice on your part if you have been led astray by some clever speaker, but it would be thought vice on the part of those who devoted their energies to deceiving you.

47

I suppose, men of Athens, you would all say you wish to have put into effect what each one considers best

σθαι ταῦτα πραχθῆναι. συμβαίνει δέ γε μὴ κατὰ
ταὐτὸ κεκρίσθαι παρὰ πᾶσι τὸ βέλτιστον· οὐ γὰρ
ἂν ὑμῶν οἱ μὲν λέγειν, οἱ δὲ μὴ λέγειν ἐκέλευον.
πρὸς μὲν τοίνυν τοὺς ὑπειληφότας ταὐτὰ[1] συμφέρειν
οὐδενὸς δεῖ λόγου τῷ μέλλοντι λέγειν· πεπεισμένοι
γὰρ ὑπάρχουσι· πρὸς δὲ τοὺς τἀναντία συμφέρειν
2 ἡγουμένους βραχέ' εἰπεῖν βούλομαι. μὴ θέλουσι
μὲν οὖν ἀκούειν οὐκ ἔνι δήπου μαθεῖν, οὐδὲν μᾶλλον
ἢ σιωπῶσι μηδενὸς λέγοντος· ἀκούσασιν δὲ δυοῖν
ἀγαθοῖν οὐκ ἔνι θατέρου διαμαρτεῖν. ἢ γὰρ πεισθέντες πάντες καὶ ταῦτ' ἐγνωκότες κοινότερον
βουλεύσεσθε, οὗ μεῖζον εἰς τὰ παρόντ' οὐδὲν ἂν
γένοιτ' ἀγαθόν· ἢ μὴ δυνηθέντος τοῦ λέγοντος
διδάξαι βεβαιότερον τοῖς ἐγνωσμένοις πιστεύσετε.
3 χωρὶς δὲ τούτων οὐδὲ καλὴν ὑποψίαν ἔχει ἥκειν
μὲν εἰς τὴν ἐκκλησίαν ὡς ἐκ τῶν ῥηθησομένων τὸ
[1455] κράτιστον ἑλέσθαι δέον, φανῆναι δέ, πρὶν ἐκ τῶν
λόγων δοκιμάσαι, παρ' ὑμῖν αὐτοῖς τι πεπεισμένους,
καὶ τοῦθ' οὕτως ἰσχυρὸν ὥστε μηδ' ἐθέλειν παρὰ
ταῦτ' ἀκούειν.

ΜΗ

Ἴσως ὀχληρός, ὦ ἄνδρες Ἀθηναῖοι, τισὶν ὑμῶν
εἶναι δοκῶ, πολλάκις λέγων περὶ τῶν αὐτῶν ἀεί.
ἀλλ' ἐὰν ὀρθῶς σκοπῆτε, οὐκ ἐγὼ φανήσομαι τούτου δίκαιος ὢν ἔχειν τὴν αἰτίαν, ἀλλ' οἱ μὴ πειθό-

---

[1] ταῦτα edd.

[a] This commonplace appears also in 3, 4 and 5.

for the city. Quite so, but it happens that the same plan has not been judged the best by all of you ; otherwise some of you would not be bidding the speaker " Go on " and others " Sit down." Now, to those who hold the same measures to be expedient as does the one who is about to speak there is no need of a single word, for they are already convinced ; but to those who think that the opposite course is for the best, I wish to speak briefly. Unless 2 you will listen, it is, of course, absolutely impossible to learn anything,[a] any more than if you keep quiet when no one is speaking. But if you do listen it is impossible to miss one or the other of two benefits : for either, being all persuaded and of the same mind, you will be more unanimous in your decision—and nothing better than this could happen for the present emergency—or else, if the speaker be unable to make his point, you will have more confidence in the decisions already reached. Apart from these two possi- 3 bilities, there is a suspicion, and by no means to your credit, that, although you have come to the assembly under obligation to choose the best plan on the basis of what shall be said, instead, you will be found, before reaching a judgement on the basis of the speeches, to have been convinced of something in your own minds, and this so strongly that you are not even willing to hear anything to the contrary.

48

PERHAPS some of you, men of Athens, regard me as a nuisance, speaking on the same subjects time after time. But if you scan things rightly, it is not I who shall justly bear the blame for this, but rather those

μένοι τοῖς ὑμετέροις ψηφίσμασιν. εἰ γὰρ ἐκεῖνοι
τὸ πρῶτον ἐποίησαν ἃ ὑμεῖς προσετάξατε, οὐδὲν
ἂν τὸ δεύτερον ἡμᾶς ἔδει λέγειν, οὐδ' εἰ τὸ δεύτερον, αὖθις. νῦν δ' ὅσῳ πλεονάκις τὰ προσήκονθ'
ὑμῖν ὑμεῖς ἐψηφίσασθε, τοσούτῳ μοι δοκοῦσιν
2 ἧττον ἐκεῖνοι παρεσκευάσθαι ποιεῖν. πρότερον μὲν
οὖν ἔγωγε μὰ τοὺς θεοὺς οὐκ ᾔδειν, πρὸς τί ποτ'
εἴη τοῦτ' εἰρημένον "ἀρχὴ ἄνδρα δείκνυσι"· νῦν
δὲ κἂν ἄλλον μοι δοκῶ διδάξαι. οἱ γὰρ ἄρχοντες
ἤ τινες αὐτῶν, ἵνα μὴ πάντας λέγω, τῶν μὲν
ὑμετέρων ψηφισμάτων ἀλλ' οὐδὲ τὸ μικρότατον
φροντίζουσιν, ὅπως δὲ λήψονται. εἰ μὲν οὖν ἐνῆν
δοῦναι, δικαίως ἂν αὐτὸ τοῦτό μοί τις ἐπέπληξεν,
εἰ διὰ μικρὸν ἀνάλωμ' ἐνοχλεῖν ὑμῖν ᾑρούμην· νῦν
3 δ' οὐκ ἔνι, καθάπερ οὐδὲ τούτους λέληθεν. εἰ δ'
ὑπὲρ ὧν ὑμῖν λῃτουργεῖν δεῖ, προσθήσειν αὐτοῖς
οἴονταί με, ληροῦσι. καὶ ταῦτ' ἴσως καὶ βούλονται
καὶ προσδοκῶσιν· ἐγὼ δ' οὐ ποιήσω ταῦτα, ἀλλ'
ἐὰν μὲν ἔωσι, καθέλξω τὴν ναῦν καὶ τὰ προσήκοντα
ποιήσω, εἰ δὲ μή, τοὺς αἰτίους ὑμῖν ἀποφανῶ.

ΜΘ

Οὐδέν' ἂν εὖ φρονοῦντ' ἀντειπεῖν, ὦ ἄνδρες Ἀθηναῖοι, νομίζω, ὡς οὐχ ἁπάντων ἄριστόν ἐστι τῇ

---

[a] On this topic Demosthenes quotes Sophocles, *Antigonê*
175-190 in XIX. 247.

[b] Public services required of wealthy citizens at their own
expense were called λῃτουργίαι; these are to be distinguished
from services to which salaries were attached, ὑπηρεσίαι:
see 52 and note.

[c] Demosthenes, as member of a group (συντέλεια) responsible for equipping a trireme under the system of Navy-
Boards, protests against being assessed more than his equi-

who do not obey your decrees. For if those men had done at the outset what you enjoined, it would not have been necessary for us to speak a second time or, if they had complied on the second occasion, a third time. As it is, the more often you have voted what your duty demanded, the less those men, it seems to me, have been prepared to act upon it. Previously, 2 I confess by the gods, I did not know what was the point of the saying : " Responsibility reveals the man." [a] But now I think I could even tell another what it means. For the officials, or some of them— to avoid saying all—feel not even the slightest regard for your decrees but consider how they shall make some gain. Certainly, if it had been feasible for me to make a payment, I might have been justly rebuked for this very reason, if I chose to annoy you through balking at a paltry expenditure. But as things are, it is not feasible, as these men themselves have not failed to observe. What is more, if, in the 3 case of a service [b] due to you they think I am going to leave it to themselves to decide, they are fools. And, perhaps, they both wish and expect it ; this I will not do, but if they will allow me, I shall launch the ship and do my duty ; otherwise, I shall reveal to you the names of those responsible. [c]

49

In my opinion, men of Athens, no intelligent citizen would deny that it is best of all for the city, prefer-

table share. Apparently, the expenditures were specified in the decrees of the Assembly but the officials were making demands in excess of the specifications. For abuses of the system see XVIII. 104 and XXI. 155. Demosthenes may have been chairman of a Navy-Board at the time : XXI. 157.

[1456] πόλει, μάλιστα μὲν ἐξ ἀρχῆς μηδὲν ἀσύμφορον
πράττειν, εἰ δὲ μή, παρεῖναι εὐθὺς τοὺς ἐναντιωσο-
μένους. δεῖ μέντοι τούτῳ προσεῖναι θέλοντας
ἀκούειν ὑμᾶς καὶ διδάσκεσθαι· οὐδὲν γὰρ πλέον
εἶναι τὸν ἐροῦντα τὰ βέλτιστα ἂν μὴ τοὺς ἀκουσο-
2 μένους ἔχῃ. οὐ μὴν οὐδ' ἐκεῖνο ἀλυσιτελὲς μετὰ
ταῦτ' ἂν φανείη, ὅσ' ἄν τις ὑμᾶς ἢ διὰ καιρὸν ἢ
δι' ὥραν ἡμέρας ἢ δι' ἄλλην τιν' αἰτίαν παρα-
κρούσηται, ταῦθ' ὅταν ποτὲ βούλησθ' ὑμῶν αὐτῶν
ὄντες ἀκούειν, εἶναι τὸν ἐξετάσοντα πάλιν, ἵν' ἐὰν
μὲν οἷά φασιν οἱ τότε πείσαντες φανῇ, προθυμότερον πράττηθ' ὡς ἔλεγχον δεδωκότα, ἐὰν δ' ἄρα
μὴ τοιαῦθ' εὑρεθῇ, πρὶν πορρωτέρω προελθεῖν ἐπί-
σχητε. καὶ γὰρ ἂν δεινὸν εἴη, εἰ τοῖς τοῦ κρατί-
στου διαμαρτοῦσι τὸ χείριστον ἀνάγκη πράττειν
εἴη, καὶ μὴ τὸ δεύτερον ἐκ τῶν λοιπῶν ἐξείη
3 μεταβουλεύσασθαι. τοὺς μὲν οὖν ἄλλους ἅπαντας
ἔγωγ' ὁρῶ τὴν ἀειλογίαν προτεινομένους, ὅταν τι
πιστεύωσι δικαίως αὐτοῖς πεπρᾶχθαι· οὗτοι δ' αὖ[1]
τοὐναντίον ἐγκαλοῦσιν εἰ περὶ ὧν ἡμάρτετε νῦν
ἀναθέσθαι βούλεσθε, τὴν ἀπάτην κυριωτέραν οἰό-
μενοι δεῖν εἶναι τῆς μετὰ τοῦ χρόνου βασάνου. τὴν
μὲν οὖν τούτων σπουδὴν οὐδ' ὑμῶν ἴσως ἀγνοοῦσιν
οἱ πολλοί· δεῖ δ' ὑπὲρ τῶν πραγμάτων, ἐπειδήπερ

---

[1] αὐτὸ Blass.

---

a Demosthenes in *Epistle* ii. 14 claimed to have been condemned, καιρῷ τινὶ ληφθείς, because his name appeared first
on the list of those accused of complicity in the affair of
Harpalus.

ably at the outset not to do anything inexpedient, but otherwise, that those should be on hand who will object at once. To this must be added, however, that you shall be willing to listen and learn ; for nothing is gained by having a man who will give the best counsel unless he shall have people who will listen to him. Neither would the following sugges- 2 tion prove unprofitable as the next step, that whatever deceptions anyone shall practise upon you through some well-timed manœuvre,[a] or the late hour of the day or by any other opening, that there should be someone who will scrutinize the measures a second time, when you, being arbiters of your own conduct, are willing to listen, so that of the measures should prove to be such as those assert who then persuaded you, you may put them into effect more wholeheartedly as having passed the test : but if, after all, they are found to be otherwise, that you may halt before going farther. For it would be a shocking thing that those who had failed to choose the best plan should be forced to put the worst into effect, and not have a chance to reconsider and choose from among other alternatives the plan that had stood second. Now while all other men, I observe, 3 stand ready to submit to an accounting at any time, whenever they are confident that some measure of theirs has been honestly put through,[b] yet these men, on the contrary, resent it if you desire now to reverse your action in matters wherein you have made a mistake, thinking their deception ought to prevail rather than spend time on an inquiry. So, even if the majority of you are perhaps not unaware of pressure on the part of these men, it is still one's duty, once

[b] This principle was invoked against Aeschines : XIX. 2.

γέγονεν λόγου τυχεῖν, ἅ τις ἡγεῖται κράτιστα λέγειν.

N

῟Ο τι μὲν μέλλει συνοίσειν πάσῃ τῇ πόλει, τοῦτο καὶ λέγειν εὔχομαι πάντας, ὦ ἄνδρες ᾿Αθηναῖοι, καὶ ὑμᾶς ἑλέσθαι. ἐγὼ δ᾿ οὖν, ἃ πεπεικὼς ἐμαυτὸν [1457] τυγχάνω μάλιστα συμφέρειν ὑμῖν, ταῦτ᾿ ἐρῶ, δεηθεὶς ὑμῶν τοσοῦτον, μήτε τοὺς ἐξιέναι κελεύοντας ὑμᾶς διὰ τοῦτο νομίζειν ἀνδρείους, μήτε τοὺς ἀντιλέγειν ἐπιχειροῦντας διὰ τοῦτο κακούς. οὐ γὰρ ὁ αὐτὸς ἔλεγχος, ὦ ἄνδρες ᾿Αθηναῖοι, τῶν τε λόγων καὶ τῶν πραγμάτων ἐστίν, ἀλλὰ δεῖ νῦν μὲν εὖ βεβουλευμένους ἡμᾶς φανῆναι, τότε δ᾿, ἂν ἄρα
2 ταῦτα δοκῇ, τὰ τῆς ἀνδρείας ἀποδείξασθαι. ἡ μὲν οὖν ὑμετέρα προθυμία παντὸς ἀξία καὶ τοιαύτη πάρεστιν οἵαν ἄν τις εὔξαιτ᾿ εὔνους ὢν τῇ πόλει· νῦν δ᾿ ὅσῳ τυγχάνει σπουδαιοτέρα, τοσούτῳ δεῖ μᾶλλον προϊδεῖν ὅπως εἰς δέον καταχρήσεσθ᾿ αὐτῇ. οὐδενὸς γὰρ εὐδοκιμεῖ πράγματος ἡ προαίρεσις ἂν μὴ καὶ τὸ τέλος συμφέρον καὶ καλὸν λάβῃ. ἐγὼ δ᾿ οἶδά ποτ᾿, ὦ ἄνδρες ᾿Αθηναῖοι, παρ᾿ ὑμῖν ἀκούσας ἀνδρὸς οὔτ᾿ ἀνοήτου δοκοῦντος εἶναι οὔτ᾿ ἀπείρου
3 πολέμου, ᾿Ιφικράτους λέγω, ὃς ἔφη δεῖν οὕτω προαιρεῖσθαι κινδυνεύειν τὸν στρατηγόν, ὅπως μὴ τὰ ἢ τὰ γενήσεται, ἀλλ᾿ ὅπως τά· οὕτω γὰρ εἶπε τῷ ῥήματι. ἦν δὴ τοῦτο γνώριμον, ὅτι ὅπως καλῶς ἀγωνιεῖται ἔλεγεν. ἐπειδὰν μὲν τοίνυν ἐξέλθητε,

---

ᵃ Iphicrates died in 353 B.C. when Demosthenes was about

178

he has been given the floor, to declare what action he thinks best under the circumstances.

50

WHATEVER measure is going to benefit the whole State, men of Athens, I pray that all speakers will propose and you will adopt. I, at any rate, shall say what I have persuaded myself is most to your advantage, asking only this of you—that you neither consider those who urge you to take the field to be for this reason brave, nor those who undertake to oppose them to be for this reason cowards; for the test of speech and the test of action, men of Athens, are not the same; rather we must now show ourselves to have been wise in counsel and later, if in the end this proposal is adopted, display the deeds of courage. Your enthusiasm, I allow, is worthy of all 2 praise and such as a man of goodwill toward the State might pray for; but the more intense your enthusiasm the more foresighted you should now be to employ it as you ought. For you know that no choice of a course of action justifies itself unless the end it achieves be beneficial and honourable. I am sure I once heard here in your presence, men of Athens, a man who was thought to be lacking neither in sense nor in experience of war. I refer to Iphicrates,[a] who 3 said, "A general must so choose to risk a battle, that not this or that may result but just this," for such were his exact words. The meaning of this was obvious, for he meant "that he might come off victorious." So, when you take the field, whoever is

thirty years of age. The orator's admiration is revealed in XXI. 62-63 and XXIII. 129-131.

ὃς ἂν ἡγῆται κύριος ὑμῶν ἐστι· νῦν δ' ἕκαστος
ὑμῶν αὐτῶν[1] στρατηγεῖ. δεῖ δὴ τοιαῦτα φανῆναι
βεβουλευμένους δι' ὧν πανταχῶς συνοίσει τῇ πόλει,
καὶ μὴ μελλουσῶν ἕνεκ' ἐλπίδων τῆς παρούσης
εὐδαιμονίας χεῖρόν τι ποιήσετε.

NA

Οὐδέν' ἂν ᾠόμην, ὦ ἄνδρες Ἀθηναῖοι, πιστεύ-
οντα τοῖς πεπραγμένοις ἐγκαλέσαι τοῖς καθιστᾶσιν
εἰς λόγον ταῦτα· ὅσῳ γὰρ ἂν πλεονάκις ἐξετάζῃ τις
[1458] αὐτά, ἀνάγκη τοὺς τούτων αἰτίους εὐδοκιμεῖν. οὐ
μὴν ἀλλά μοι δοκοῦσιν αὐτοὶ φανερὸν καθιστάναι,
οὐκ ἐπὶ τῶν τῇ πόλει συμφερόντων πράξαντες.
ὡς γοῦν ἐξελέγχεσθαι μέλλοντες, ἂν πάλιν εἰς λόγον
ἔλθωσι, φεύγουσι καὶ δεινὰ ποιεῖν ἡμᾶς φασιν.
καίτοι ὅταν τοὺς ἐξελέγχειν βουλομένους δεινὰ
ποιεῖν αἰτιᾶσθε, τί ἡμεῖς τοὺς ἡμᾶς αὐτοὺς ἐξηπα-
τηκότας τηνικαῦτα λέγωμεν;

NB

Ἦν μὲν δίκαιον, ὦ ἄνδρες Ἀθηναῖοι, τὴν ἴσην
ὑπάρχειν παρ' ὑμῶν ὀργὴν τοῖς ἐπιχειροῦσιν ὅσηνπερ τοῖς δυνηθεῖσιν ἐξαπατῆσαι. ὃ μὲν γὰρ ἦν ἐπὶ
τούτοις πεποίηται, καὶ προήγαγον ὑμᾶς· τοῦ δὲ
μηδὲν τέλος ταῦτ' ἔχειν ἡ τύχη, καὶ τὸ βέλτιον νῦν

---

[1] αὐτὸς Blass.

leader is master of you, but now each one of yourselves is a general. Thus it is your duty to show yourselves to have made such decisions as will inevitably be good for the State and that you shall not, for the sake of mere hopes of future goods, bring about something not so good as the prosperity you at present enjoy.

51

I should have thought, men of Athens, that no one who has a clean conscience about the measures taken would prefer a complaint against those who move to bring these matters to an accounting ; for the more often one examines into them, the more the authors of them are bound to grow in esteem. These men themselves, however, seem to me to render it manifest that they have not acted with the State's interests in view. At any rate, just as if they were bound to be found guilty if they should come again to an accounting, they assume the defensive and say we are acting outrageously. And yet when you accuse of outrageous conduct those who wish to investigate, what are we citizens to say of those who in that very transaction have perpetrated a fraud against our own selves ?

52

It would be the righteous thing, men of Athens, for you to feel the same anger toward those who attempt to deceive you as toward those who have been able to do so. For what it was in the power of these men to do has been done, and they led you along. That these designs have fallen short of success, credit

ὑμᾶς φρονεῖν ἢ ὅτ' ἐξήχθητ' ὑπὸ τούτων, γέγον'
αἴτια. οὐ μὴν ἀλλ' ἔγωγ' οὕτω πόρρω νομίζω τὴν
πόλιν εἶναι τοῦ δίκην παρὰ τῶν ἀδικούντων λαμβάνειν ὥστ' ἀγαπητὸν εἶναί μοι δοκεῖ ἂν ὅπως
μὴ πείσεσθε κακῶς δύνησθε φυλάττεσθαι· τοσαῦται
τέχναι καὶ γοητεῖαι καὶ ὅλως ὑπηρεσίαι τινές εἰσιν
ἐφ' ὑμᾶς κατεσκευασμέναι. τῆς μὲν οὖν τούτων
κακίας οὐκ ἂν ἐν τῷ παρόντι τις ἐν δέοντι μάλιστα
κατηγορήσειε· βούλομαι δ' ὑπὲρ ὧν ἀνέστην, ἃ
νομίζω συμφέροντ', εἰπεῖν.

ΝΓ

Ἡ μὲν εἰωθυῖα πάντα τὸν χρόνον βλάπτειν, ὦ
ἄνδρες Ἀθηναῖοι, τὴν πόλιν λοιδορία καὶ ταραχή,
καὶ νυνὶ γέγονεν παρὰ τῶν αὐτῶν ὦνπερ ἀεί. ἄξιον
δ' οὐχ οὕτω τούτοις ἐπιτιμῆσαι (ἴσως γὰρ ὀργῇ καὶ
φιλονικίᾳ ταῦτα πράττουσι καί, τὸ μέγιστον ἁπάντων, ὅτι συμφέρει ταῦτα ποιεῖν αὐτοῖς) ἀλλ' ὑμῖν,
[1459] εἰ περὶ κοινῶν, ὦ ἄνδρες Ἀθηναῖοι, πραγμάτων
καὶ μεγάλων συνειλεγμένοι, τὰς ἰδίας λοιδορίας
ἀκροώμενοι κάθησθε, καὶ οὐ δύνασθε πρὸς ὑμᾶς
αὐτοὺς λογίσασθαι τοῦθ', ὅτι αἱ τῶν ῥητόρων ἁπάντων ἄνευ κρίσεως πρὸς ἀλλήλους λοιδορίαι, ὧν ἂν
ἀλλήλους ἐξελέγξωσιν ὑμᾶς τὰς εὐθύνας διδόναι
2 ποιοῦσι. πλὴν γὰρ ἴσως ὀλίγων, ἵνα μὴ πάντας
εἴπω, οὐδεὶς αὐτῶν ἅτερος θατέρῳ λοιδορεῖται ἵνα

---

a The word ὑπηρεσίαι denotes services to which pay was
attached ; in all such the people took an avid interest, leaving
unpaid offices to the wealthy : see 55. 3 and the Pseudo-

is due to Fortune and to the fact that you are now wiser than when you were misled by these men. Yet the State, I believe, is so far from being able to exact justice of the wrongdoers, that it seems to me you must content yourselves if you shall be able to avoid sustaining loss ; so formidable are the trickeries and chicaneries and, not to particularize, certain salaried public services *a* that have been organized against you. To denounce the villainy of these men, however, would not at this juncture be most opportune : but I do wish to say what I deem advantageous with reference to the matters I have risen to discuss.

53

THE bickering and disorder, men of Athens, that are accustomed to injure the State all the time, have proceeded on this occasion from the same men as always. But the thing to do is not so much to blame these men—for perhaps they do it out of spite and quarrelsomeness and, what is the chief reason, because it pays them to do so—as to blame yourselves, men o Athens, if, after assembling on matters of common interest and prime importance, you sit and listen to private bickerings and cannot figure out for yourselves that the tirades directed against one another by all the speakers, when no one is on trial, cause you to pay the penalties for the offences of which they convict one another. For outside of a few perhaps, 2 to avoid saying all, not one of them abuses another

Xenophon, *Athen. Const.* 3. These could readily be made channels of financial corruption.

For λητουργίαι, services for which the performer himself paid, see 48 and *Epistle* ii. 12, and notes.

βέλτιόν τι τῶν ὑμετέρων γίγνηται· πολλοῦ γε
καὶ δεῖ· ἀλλ' ἵν', ἃ τὸν δεινά φησι ποιοῦντ' ἄν[1]
δεινότατ' ἀνθρώπων ποιεῖν, ταῦτ' αὐτὸς μετὰ
3 πλείονος ἡσυχίας διαπράττηται. ὅτι δ' οὕτω ταῦτ'
ἔχει, μὴ ἐμοὶ πιστεύσητε, ἀλλ' ἐν βραχεῖ λογίσασθε.
ἔστιν ὅπου τις ἀναστὰς εἶπε παρ' ὑμῖν πώποτε
" βουλόμενός τι λαβεῖν τῶν ὑμετέρων παρελήλυθ',
ὦ ἄνδρες Ἀθηναῖοι, οὐχ ὑπὲρ ὑμῶν ''; οὐδεὶς
δήπου, ἀλλ' ὑπὲρ ὑμῶν καὶ δι' ὑμᾶς, καὶ ταύτας
τὰς προφάσεις λέγουσι.

Φέρε δὴ σκέψασθε, τί δή ποτ', ὦ ἄνδρες Ἀθηναῖοι, ὑπὲρ ὧν ἅπαντες λέγουσιν, οὐδὲν βέλτιον
τοῖς ὅλοις νῦν ἢ πρότερον πράττετε, οὗτοι δ' οἱ
πάνθ' ὑπὲρ ὑμῶν, ὑπὲρ αὑτῶν δ' οὐδεὶς οὐδὲν
πώποτ' εἰρηκώς, ἐκ πτωχῶν πλούσιοι γεγόνασιν;
ὅτι φασὶ μέν, ὦ ἄνδρες Ἀθηναῖοι, φιλεῖν ὑμᾶς,
4 φιλοῦσι δ' οὐχ ὑμᾶς, ἀλλ' αὑτούς. καὶ γελάσαι καὶ
θορυβῆσαι καί ποτ' ἐλπίσαι μετέδωκαν ὑμῖν, λαβεῖν
δ' ἢ κτήσασθαι τῇ πόλει κυρίως ἀγαθὸν οὐδὲν ἂν
βούλοιντο. ᾗ γὰρ ἂν ἡμέρα τῆς λίαν ἀρρωστίας
ἀπαλλαγῆτε, ταύτῃ τούτους οὐδ' ὁρῶντες ἀνέξεσθε.
νῦν δὲ δραχμῇ καὶ χοῖ καὶ τέτταρσιν ὀβολοῖς ὥσπερ
[1460] ἀσθενοῦντα τὸν δῆμον διάγουσιν, ὁμοιότατ', ὦ ἄνδρες Ἀθηναῖοι, τοῖς παρὰ τῶν ἰατρῶν σιτίοις δι-

---

[1] ἂν δέῃ codd.; δέῃ del. Post.

---

[a] On the wealth of politicians see XIII. 20, XXI. 158 and
Olynth. iii. 29.
[b] The drachma was the fee for attending the Assembly ;
the four obols is the juror's fee, which had long been three
obols. The χοῦς is the measure for a largess of grain. Its
content is more accurately known than formerly from a
specimen found on the side of the Acropolis in 1937, which

that any of your interests may be forwarded ; very far from it, but in order that he may himself with the greater immunity succeed in doing what he says, if so-and-so did it, would be the most outrageous conduct imaginable. Do not take my word for it that 3 this is so but consider for a little. Has anyone ever stood up before you and said, " I have come forward, men of Athens, desiring to get my hands on something of yours, not for your sakes " ? Certainly not a single one. Instead, they say " for your sakes " and " on your account " and cite these plausible motives.

Come now, men of Athens, consider why in the world you, " for whose sakes " they all speak, are on the whole no better off now than before, while these, who all say " for your sakes," without a single one having ever said " for our own sakes," have turned from beggars into rich men.[a] It is because, though they say they love you, men of Athens, they love not you but themselves. The portion they allow you is 4 to have a laugh and to raise a hubbub and now and then to have a hope, but they would not want you to get or acquire for the State any benefit in the proper sense of the word. Yes, and on the day when you are freed of this lamentable weakness you will be unable to endure even the sight of them. At present with their drachma and gallon measure and four obols [b] they regulate the populace like a sick man, giving you, men of Athens, doles very similar

measures 3.2 litres or 2.816 imperial qts. or 3.379 U.S. qts. This find was confirmed by the discovery of a clepsydra in the Agora marked two χόες and measuring 6.4 litres. The χοῦς was one-twelfth of a medimnus, the portion doled out to each citizen according to XXXIV. 37. *Cf. Hesperia*, viii. 1939, 278 ff.

δόντες ὑμῖν. καὶ γὰρ ἐκεῖν οὔτ' ἰσχὺν ἐντίθησιν
οὔτε ἀποθνήσκειν ἐᾷ· καὶ ταῦτ' οὔτ' ἀπογνόντας
ἄλλο τι μεῖζον πράττειν ἐᾷ, οὔτ' αὖτ' ἐξαρκεῖν
δύναται.

ΝΔ

Καὶ δίκαιον, ὦ ἄνδρες 'Αθηναῖοι, καὶ καλὸν καὶ
σπουδαῖον, ὅπερ ὑμεῖς εἰώθατε, καὶ ἡμᾶς προνοεῖν,
ὅπως τὰ πρὸς τοὺς θεοὺς εὐσεβῶς ἕξει. ἡ μὲν οὖν
ἡμετέρα γέγον' ἐπιμέλει' ὑμῖν εἰς δέον· καὶ γὰρ
ἐθύσαμεν τῷ Διὶ τῷ σωτῆρι καὶ τῇ 'Αθηνᾷ καὶ τῇ
Νίκῃ, καὶ γέγονεν καλὰ καὶ σωτήρια ταῦθ' ὑμῖν τὰ
ἱερά. ἐθύσαμεν δὲ καὶ τῇ Πειθοῖ καὶ τῇ Μητρὶ
τῶν θεῶν καὶ τῷ 'Απόλλωνι καὶ ἐκαλλιερούμεν καὶ
ταῦτα. ἦν δ' ὑμῖν καὶ τὰ τοῖς ἄλλοις θεοῖς τυθένθ'
ἱέρ' ἀσφαλῆ καὶ βέβαια καὶ καλὰ καὶ σωτήρια.
δέχεσθ' οὖν παρὰ τῶν θεῶν διδόντων τἀγαθά.

ΝΕ

῏Ην τις, ὡς ἔοικε, χρόνος παρ' ὑμῖν, ὦ ἄνδρες
'Αθηναῖοι, ὅτ' ἐπηνάγκαζεν ὁ δῆμος ὃν ἄνθρωπον
ἴδοι σώφρονα καὶ χρηστὸν πράττειν τὰ κοινὰ καὶ
ἄρχειν, οὐ σπάνει τῶν τοῦτο βουλομένων ποιεῖν
(πάντα γὰρ τἄλλ' εὐτυχῆ τὴν πόλιν κρίνων, ἐν
οὐδέποτ' εὐτυχῆσαι τοῦτο νομίζω, ἐπιλείπειν αὐτὴν
τοὺς τὰ κοινὰ καρποῦσθαι βουλομένους), ἀλλ' ὅραμα

---

[a] This passage is found with variations in *Olynth.* iii. 33.

[b] Demosthenes makes an official report upon the execution of a commission to perform certain sacrifices. Meidias
was chosen to perform similar functions: XXI. 171. *Cf.* Theo-
phrastus, *Char.* xxi. (vii. Jebb-Sandys). This is not a true
exordium but included by some error.

to the diets of the physicians.   For these diets neither
put strength into the patient nor allow him to die,
and these doles neither allow you to cry quits and
engage in some different and better business, nor can
they alone suffice.[a]

54

It is just and right and important, men of Athens,
that we too should exercise care, as you are accustomed, that our relations with the gods shall be
piously maintained.[b]   Therefore our commission has
been duly discharged for you, for we have sacrificed
to Zeus the Saviour and to Athena and to Victory,
and these sacrifices have been auspicious and salutary
for you.   We have also sacrificed to Persuasion and to
the Mother of the Gods and to Apollo, and here also
we had favourable omens.   And the sacrifices made
to the other gods portended for you security and
stability and prosperity and safety.   Do you, therefore, accept the blessings which the gods bestow.

55

There was, as it seems, a time in your history, men
of Athens, when the democracy compelled any man
whom it observed to be prudent and honest to perform public service and to hold office, not through
lack of those who wished to do so—for, while deeming
the city to be fortunate in all other respects, in this
one particular I consider it has never been fortunate,
that the supply of those who wish to reap a harvest
from the public business never fails it—but the

τοῦτ᾽ ἐποιεῖθ᾽ ὁ δῆμος αὐτοῦ, καλόν, ὦ ἄνδρες
2 Ἀθηναῖοι, καὶ λυσιτελὲς τῇ πόλει. οἵ τε γὰρ
[1461] συνεχεῖς οἶδε παραζευγνυμένων¹ σφίσιν ἐξ ἰδίων²
σπουδαίων καὶ δικαίων ἀνδρῶν, εὐλαβεστέρους αὑτοὺς παρεῖχον· οἵ τε χρηστοὶ μὲν ὑμῶν καὶ δικαίως³
ἄρχοντες, μὴ πάνυ δ᾽ οἷοί τ᾽ ἐνοχλεῖν καὶ παραγγέλ-
λειν, οὐκ ἀπηλαύνοντο τῶν τιμῶν. νῦν δὲ παντάπασι τὸν αὐτὸν τρόπον, ὦ ἄνδρες Ἀθηναῖοι, ὅνπερ
τοὺς ἱερεῖς, οὕτως καθίστατε καὶ τοὺς ἄρχοντας.
εἶτα θαυμάζετε, ἐπειδὰν ὁ δεῖν᾽ εὐδαίμων καὶ ὁ
δεῖν᾽ ὑμῖν ᾖ συνεχῶς πολλὰ λαμβάνων, οἱ δ᾽ ἄλλοι
3 περιίητε τὰ τούτων ἀγαθὰ ζηλοῦντες. δεινότατοι
γάρ ἐστ᾽ ἀφελέσθαι μὲν ὅσ᾽ ὑμῖν ὑπάρχει, καὶ
νόμους περὶ τούτων θεῖναι, ἄν τις ἀστυνομήσῃ δὶς
ἢ τὰ τοιαῦτα, στρατηγεῖν δ᾽ ἀεὶ τοὺς αὐτοὺς
ἐᾶν. καὶ τὸ μὲν τοὺς ἐπὶ τῶν πράξεων ὄντας
ἴσως ἔχει πρόφασιν· τὸ δὲ τοὺς ἄλλους, οἳ ποιοῦσι
μὲν οὐδέν, χώραν δ᾽ ἀτέλεστον ἔχουσιν αὐτοὶ τετελε-
σμένοι, μωρία. ἀλλὰ καὶ ὑμῶν αὐτῶν, εἰσὶ δ᾽ οὐκ
ὀλίγοι, προσάγειν χρή. ἂν γὰρ ὥσπερ εἰ ζυγὸν

---

¹ παραζευγνύμενοι codd.   ² ἰδιωτῶν Schaefer, edd.
³ δικαίως ἂν Dobree.

ᵃ While some priesthoods were subject to choice by lot,
LIX. 106, the majority of them were perhaps hereditary, *ibid.*
104, and the reference is to these.   For a similar complaint
see 13.

ᵇ These ἀστυνόμοι were ten in number, five each for
Athens and the Peiraeus ; they were responsible for the
streets but not for the markets.   *Cf.* Aristotle, *Athen. Const.*
50. 2.

democracy used to make out of this a fine showing for itself, creditable and profitable to the State, men of Athens. For on the one hand, these men, the kind who hold office year after year, when earnest and upright men from a different class were given them as yokemates, used to show themselves more circumspect ; and on the other hand, the kind of men among you who are honest and upright in office, but not at all of the sort to push their way and appeal for support, were not shut out of the posts of trust. But now, men of Athens, you appoint your magistrates in exactly the same manner as you appoint your priests.ᵃ Then you are amazed when this one is prosperous and that one, to your dismay, is year after year taking a rich spoil, while the rest of you go around envying these men their blessings ! For you are the worst people for taking away the offices that fall to your class, and for enacting laws about them if someone serves twice as commissioner of police ᵇ or something of the sort, but you allow the same men to be generals all the time.ᶜ There is perhaps some excuse for allowing those engaged in the active services to continue, but to allow the others, who, though doing nothing, have an endless tenure of office and are themselves endlessly benefited is folly.ᵈ Instead, you ought to bring in some of your own number, and there are not a few of you. For if you set up a standard, as it were, anyone who

ᶜ The last statement is confirmed by Aristotle, *ibid.* 62.3.

ᵈ There is a touch of tragedy and the mysteries in the diction. Perhaps better : " hold an unserviceable post to the service of which they have themselves been consecrated." For similar irony *cf.* XIII. 19 τελεσθῆναι στρατηγός, " to be consecrated general."

ἱστῆτε, πρόσεισ᾽ ὃς ἂν ἄξιος ᾖ του μετὰ ταῦτ᾽
αὐτός.

Nϛ

Τὸ μέν, ὦ ἄνδρες Ἀθηναῖοι, πεπεικόθ᾽ ἑαυτὸν
ἔχειν τι συμφέρον εἰπεῖν ἀνίστασθαι, καὶ καλὸν καὶ
προσῆκον εἶναί μοι δοκεῖ, τὸ δὲ μὴ βουλομένους
ἀκούειν βιάζεσθαι παντελῶς ἔγωγ᾽ αἰσχρὸν ἡγοῦμαι εἶναι. οἶμαι δ᾽, ἐὰν ἐθελήσητέ μοι πείθεσθαι
τήμερον, καὶ τὰ βέλτιστα μᾶλλον ὑμᾶς ἑλέσθαι
δυνήσεσθαι καὶ τοὺς τῶν ἀναβαινόντων λόγους
2 βραχεῖς ποιήσειν. τί οὖν συμβουλεύω; πρῶτον
μέν, ὦ ἄνδρες Ἀθηναῖοι, περὶ αὐτῶν ὧν σκοπεῖτε
τὸν παριόντα λέγειν ἀξιοῦν. πολλὰ γὰρ ἄλλα τις
[1462] ἂν περιέλθοι τῷ λόγῳ καὶ πόλλ᾽ ἂν ἀστεῖ᾽ εἴποι,
ἄλλως τε καὶ ὥσπερ τούτων ἔνιοι δεινῶν ὄντων.
ἀλλ᾽ εἰ μὲν ῥημάτων ἥκετ᾽ ἀκουσόμενοι, ταῦτα
λέγειν καὶ ἀκούειν χρή· εἰ δ᾽ ὑπὲρ πραγμάτων
αἱρέσεως βουλευσόμενοι, αὐτὰ καθ᾽ αὑτὰ παραινῶ
τὰ πράγμαθ᾽ ὡς μάλιστα κρίνειν, ἀφελόντας ὅσοι
3 λόγοι πεφύκασιν ἐξαπατᾶν. ἐν μὲν οὖν τοῦτο λέγω,
δεύτερον δ᾽, ὅ τισιν παράδοξον ἴσως ἔσται πρὸς τὸ
τοὺς λόγους ἐλάττους εἶναι, σιωπῶντας ἀκούειν.
περὶ μὲν γὰρ τοῦ ταῦτ᾽ ἢ κεῖνα συμφέρειν, καὶ
πότερ᾽ ἂν δικαιότερον προέλοιθ᾽ ἡ πόλις, οὔτ᾽ εἰσὶ
λόγοι πολλοὶ μὴ βουλομένοις μάτην ἀδολεσχεῖν,
οὔτε πάλιν τις ἂν αὐτοὺς εἰπεῖν ἔχοι· ὡς δὲ καὶ
δίκαιον ἀκούειν καὶ πρὸς τὸν θόρυβον[1] ἀποκρίνα-

[1] θορυβοῦντ᾽ Blass.

190

is worth anything will thereafter come forward of his own accord.

56

It seems to me a fine and seemly thing, men of Athens, for a man who has convinced himself he has something profitable to say to take the floor, but I consider it altogether shameful to force people to listen against their will. And I think, if you will but take my advice to-day, you will be better able both to choose the best measures and to shorten the speeches of those who come to the platform. What, then, do 2 I advise? First of all, men of Athens, to require the man who comes forward to confine himself to the matters you are considering. For otherwise someone may embrace many other topics in his speech and say many witty things, especially those who are smart at it, as some of these are. Well, if you have come here to listen to fine phrases, the thing to do is to make them and listen to them, but if you have come to deliberate about a choice of measures, I urge you to judge the measures strictly by themselves, eliminating all passages of a nature to mislead. This, then, 3 is my first point. My second, which to some of you will perhaps be inconsistent with cutting the speeches shorter, is that you listen in silence. For on the question whether this or that is expedient and which choice the State might more rightly prefer, there are few arguments to be presented, unless by such persons as wish to prattle aimlessly, nor would anyone have occasion to state them a second time. As for the claim that it is only fair to listen to the heckling,[a]

[a] This seems to refer to genuine heckling and not to organized interruption as in XIII. 20 and *Olynth.* ii. 29.

σθαι καὶ λόγον ἐκ λόγου λέγειν, οὐδεὶς ὅστις οὐχὶ δύναιτ' ἄν. ἐκ δὴ τοῦ θορυβεῖν οὐκ ἀπαλλάττεσθε λόγων, ἀλλὰ καὶ περὶ τῶν οὐδὲν εἰς χρείαν ἐπαναγκάζεσθ' ἀκούειν. ἡ μὲν οὖν ἐμὴ γνώμη περὶ ὧν βουλεύεσθ' ἥδ' ἐστίν.

and to give an answer and to make speech after speech, there is no one who could not do that. Thus by heckling you do not get rid of speeches ; instead you are forced in addition to hear speeches that are totally irrelevant. Accordingly my judgement concerning the matter before you now begins.

LETTERS

INTRODUCTION

LETTERS of Demosthenes are mentioned by Plutarch, *Vita* xx., by Quintilian x. 1. 107, and by Cicero, *Brutus* 121 and *Orator* 15. When Quintilian states in the passage mentioned above that " naturally there is no comparison," he probably means that Greek letters were rather what we call epistles, messages of public interest even when addressed to individuals. In this class fall the letters of Plato, Isocrates, Epicurus, Dionysius of Halicarnassus and Plutarch, to which may be added the epistles of the New Testament and the churchmen. Letters of purely private concern, such as many of those of Cicero, are more rare. Even in Italy it was the Greek, and not the Ciceronian, tradition that was perpetuated by Seneca and Symmachus.

The genuineness of these six letters ascribed to Demosthenes has been emphatically denied. For this scepticism, which applies to most other collections, there is a general and a special reason : letters are more easily forged than speeches or other literary works and it is known that the rhetorical schools busied themselves with this branch of fiction ; scholars remember also the humiliation suffered by an English scholar when Richard Bentley in 1697 proved the letters of Phalaris to be forgeries. Blass, however, was not deterred from declaring the second and third

196

to be authentic; the first he judged to be an unfinished draft, the fifth to be surely false and probably the fourth; about the sixth he was undecided.

Even sceptical critics are unable to point to anachronisms, and their condemnation is based upon such points of style as verbosity and rhythm, which are debatable. The drift of ideas in the first three letters harmonizes admirably with that of the speeches; one sentence in the third letter, section 42, is cited for its excellence eight times in the *Rhetores Graeci*. Harpocration cites the second and third letters. These citations will be found in the footnotes. All the letters except the fifth fall in the years 324–322 B.C., the last two of the orator's life, immediately preceding and following the death of Alexander. The first and last portions of this period were spent in exile; the letters are presumed to have been written during the first exile.

The reader may consult Blass, iii. pp. 439-455. Condensed information is found in Dindorf's *Demosthenes* vii. pp. 1443-1458. *Classical Texts from Papyri in the British Museum*, cxxxiii., of the first century B.C., include *Epist.* iii. 1-38.

ΕΠΙΣΤΟΛΑΙ

Α

ΠΕΡΙ ΤΗΣ ΟΜΟΝΟΙΑΣ

Παντὸς ἀρχομένῳ σπουδαίου καὶ λόγου καὶ ἔργου, ἀπὸ τῶν θεῶν ὑπολαμβάνω προσήκειν πρῶτον ἄρχεσθαι. εὔχομαι δὴ τοῖς θεοῖς πᾶσι καὶ πάσαις, [1463] ὅ τι τῷ δήμῳ τῷ ᾿Αθηναίων ἄριστόν ἐστι καὶ τοῖς εὐνοοῦσι τῷ δήμῳ καὶ νῦν καὶ ἐς τὸν ἔπειτα χρόνον, τοῦτ᾿ ἐμοὶ μὲν ἐλθεῖν ἐπὶ νοῦν γράψαι τοῖς δ᾿ ἐκκλησιάσασιν ᾿Αθηναίων ἑλέσθαι. εὐξάμενος δὲ ταῦτα, τῆς ἀγαθῆς ἐπινοίας ἐλπίδ᾿ ἔχων παρὰ τῶν θεῶν, τάδ᾿ ἐπιστέλλω.

ΔΗΜΟΣΘΕΝΗΣ ΤΗΙ ΒΟΥΛΗΙ ΚΑΙ ΤΩΙ ΔΗΜΩΙ ΧΑΙΡΕΙΝ

2 Περὶ μὲν τῆς ἐμῆς οἴκαδ᾿ ἀφίξεως ἀεὶ νομίζω πᾶσιν ὑμῖν ἔσεσθαι βουλεύσασθαι, διόπερ νῦν οὐδὲν περὶ αὐτῆς γέγραφα· τὸν δὲ παρόντα καιρὸν ὁρῶν ἑλομένων μὲν ὑμῶν τὰ δέοντα ἅμα δόξαν καὶ σωτηρίαν καὶ ἐλευθερίαν δυνάμενον κτήσασθαι, οὐ

---

[a] Citations from §§ 6 and 12 of this letter are found in Bekker's *Anecdota*, Antiatticista pp. 111. 31. and 110. 5, a lexicographical work. This is evidence for authenticity.

[b] Demosthenes is writing from exile on the island of Calauria south of Aegina, 323 B.C.

198

LETTERS

I

ON POLITICAL HARMONY [a]

For one who is about to take any serious step, whether in speech or action, I assume that the proper course is to take his beginning from the gods. Accordingly I entreat all the gods and goddesses that what is best for the democracy of the Athenians and for those who bear goodwill toward the democracy, both now and for time to come, I may myself be moved to write and the members of the Assembly to adopt. With this prayer, having hopes of good inspiration from the gods, I address this message.

Demosthenes to the Council and the Assembly sends greeting.

Concerning the question of my return [b] to my native land I believe that you as a body will always be able to authorize it ; consequently I am writing nothing about it at the present moment. Observing, however, that the present occasion, if you but choose the right course, is capable of securing for you at one stroke glory and safety and freedom, not for your-

μόνον ὑμῖν, ἀλλὰ καὶ τοῖς ἄλλοις ἅπασιν Ἕλλησιν,
ἀγνοησάντων δ᾽ ἢ παρακρουσθέντων οὐ ῥᾴδιον
αὖθις τὸν αὐτὸν ἀναλαβεῖν, ᾠήθην χρῆναι τὴν
ἐμαυτοῦ γνώμην ὡς ἔχω περὶ τούτων εἰς μέσον
3 θεῖναι. ἔστιν μὲν οὖν ἔργον ἐξ ἐπιστολῆς ἐμμεῖναι
συμβουλῇ· πολλοῖς γὰρ εἰώθατ᾽ ἀπαντᾶν ὑμεῖς πρὸ
τοῦ περιμεῖναι μαθεῖν. λέγοντι μὲν οὖν ἔστιν
αἰσθέσθαι τί βούλεσθε καὶ διορθώσασθαι τἀγνοού-
μενα ῥᾴδιον· τὸ δὲ βιβλίον οὐδεμίαν βοήθειαν ἔχει
τοιαύτην πρὸς τοὺς θορυβοῦντας. οὐ μὴν ἀλλ᾽
ἐὰν ἐθελήσητ᾽ ἀκοῦσαι σιγῇ καὶ περιμείνητε πάντα
μαθεῖν, οἴομαι, σὺν θεοῖς εἰρῆσθαι, καίπερ βραχέων
τῶν γεγραμμένων ὄντων, αὐτός τε φανήσεσθαι μετὰ
πάσης εὐνοίας τὰ δέονθ᾽ ὑπὲρ ὑμῶν πράττων καὶ
4 τὰ συμφέρονθ᾽ ὑμῖν ἐμφανῆ δείξειν. οὐχ ὡς ἀπο-
ρούντων δ᾽ ὑμῶν ῥητόρων οὐδὲ τῶν ἄνευ λογισμοῦ
ῥᾳδίως ὅ τι ἂν τύχωσιν ἐρούντων, ἔδοξέ μοι τὴν
ἐπιστολὴν πέμπειν· ἀλλ᾽ ὅσα τυγχάνω δι᾽ ἐμπειρίαν
καὶ τὸ παρηκολουθηκέναι τοῖς πράγμασιν εἰδώς,
[1464] ταῦτ᾽ ἐβουλήθην τοῖς μὲν προαιρουμένοις λέγειν
ἐμφανῆ ποιήσας, ἀφθόνους ἀφορμὰς ὧν ὑπολαμβάνω συμφέρειν ὑμῖν δοῦναι, τοῖς δὲ πολλοῖς ῥᾳδίαν
τὴν τῶν βελτίστων αἵρεσιν καταστῆσαι. ὧν μὲν
οὖν εἵνεκ᾽ ἐπῆλθέ μοι τὴν ἐπιστολὴν γράφειν,
ταῦτ᾽ ἐστί.
5 Δεῖ δ᾽ ὑμᾶς, ὦ ἄνδρες Ἀθηναῖοι, πρῶτον μὲν

selves alone but for all the rest of the Greeks as well, but that, if you act in ignorance or be led astray, it would not be easy to secure the same opportunity again, I thought I ought to place before the public the state of my opinion on these questions. It is a difficult thing, I know, for advice conveyed by 3 letter to hold its ground,[a] because you Athenians have a way of opposing many suggestions without waiting to understand them. In the case of a speaker, of course, it is possible to perceive what you want and easy to correct your misapprehensions; but the written page possesses no such aid against those who raise a clamour. In spite of this fact, if you will but consent to listen in silence and have the patience to learn all that I have to say, I think that,—to speak in the hope of divine favour—brief though the writing is, I shall myself be found to be doing my duty by you with all goodwill and that I shall demonstrate clearly where your interests lie. Not as supposing 4 you were running short of speakers, or of those, either, who will say glibly and without real thought what happens to occur to them, did I decide to send the letter; but I desired, after putting plainly before those who like to make speeches all that I happen to know through experience and long association with public business, first, to furnish them with ample means of arriving at what I deem to be your interests, and second, to render easy for the people the choice of the best procedures. Such, then, were the considerations that prompted me to write the letter.

First of all, men of Athens, it is necessary that you 5

---

[a] Isocrates enlarges upon this difficulty, *Epist.* i. 2-3 and *Philip* 25-26.

ἁπάντων πρὸς ὑμᾶς αὐτοὺς ὁμόνοιαν εἰς τὸ κοινῇ
συμφέρον τῇ πόλει παρασχέσθαι, καὶ τὰς ἐκ τῶν
προτέρων ἐκκλησιῶν ἀμφισβητήσεις ἐᾶσαι, δεύτερον δὲ πάντας ἐκ μιᾶς γνώμης τοῖς δόξασι προθύμως συναγωνίζεσθαι· ὡς τὸ μήθ' ἓν μήθ' ἁπλῶς
πράττειν οὐ μόνον ἐστὶν ἀνάξιον ὑμῶν καὶ ἀγεννές,
6 ἀλλὰ καὶ τοὺς μεγίστους κινδύνους ἔχει. δεῖ δὲ
μηδὲ ταῦτα λαθεῖν ὑμᾶς, ἃ καθ' αὑτὰ μὲν οὐκ ἔστιν
αὐτάρκη κατασχεῖν τὰ πράγματα, προστεθέντα δὲ
ταῖς δυνάμεσιν πολλῷ πάντ' εὐκατεργαστότερ' ὑμῖν
ποιήσει. τίν' οὖν ἐστι ταῦτα; μήτε πόλει μηδεμιᾷ
μήτε τῶν ἐν ἑκάστῃ τῶν πόλεων συνηγωνισμένων
τοῖς καθεστηκόσι μηδενὶ μήτε πικραίνεσθαι μήτε
7 μνησικακεῖν. ὁ γὰρ τοιοῦτος φόβος τοὺς συνειδότας
αὑτοῖς, ὡς ἀναγκαίοις τοῖς καθεστηκόσι καὶ κίνδυνον ἔχουσι πρόδηλον προθύμους συναγωνιστὰς
ποιεῖ· ἀφεθέντες δὲ τοῦ δέους τούτου πάντες ἠπιώ-
τεροι γενήσονται. τοῦτο δ' οὐ μικρὰν ὠφέλειαν ἔχει.
κατὰ μὲν δὴ πόλεις τὰ τοιαῦτ' εὔηθες προλέγειν,
μᾶλλον δ' οὐδ' ἐν δυνατῷ· ὡς δ' ἂν ὑμῖν αὐτοῖς
ὀφθῆτε χρώμενοι, τοιαύτην καὶ κατὰ τῶν ἄλλων
8 προσδοκίαν παραστήσεθ' ἑκάστοις. φημὶ δὴ χρῆναι
μήτε στρατηγῷ μήτε ῥήτορι μήτ' ἰδιώτῃ μηδενὶ
[1465] τῶν τὰ πρὸ τοῦ γε δοκούντων συνηγωνίσθαι τοῖς

---

[a] Cicero saturated his mind with the writings of Demosthenes. " Political harmony " will be recognized as his political ideal : *Ad Atticum* i. 14. 4 ; his friend Demetrius of Magnesia wrote on the subject : *ibid.* viii. 11. 7. The Romans deified this abstraction under the name Concordia.
[b] The cities of Greece were forced to set up pro-Macedonian governments after the battle of Chaeronea in 338 B.C. A
202

bring about harmony ^{a} among yourselves for the common good of the State and drop all the contentions inherited from previous assemblies and, in the second place, that you all with one mind vigorously support your decisions, since the failure to follow either a uniform policy or to act consistently is not only unworthy of you and ignoble but, in addition, involves the greatest risks. Those things must not 6 escape your attention either, which, though by themselves they are not sufficient to effect your purpose, yet when added to your military forces, will render all your aims much easier of accomplishment. To what, then, do I refer? Toward no city and toward none of the citizens in this or that city who have supported the existing order ^{b} must you harbour any bitterness ^{c} or bear a grudge. Because the fear of 7 such animosity causes those who are conscious of guilt in their own hearts to be zealous supporters of the existing order as essential and in manifest danger, but relieved of this fear they will all become more amenable, and this is of no slight usefulness. Now, to proclaim such intentions in the various cities would be foolish, or rather quite impossible, but in whatever spirit you shall be seen treating your own fellow-citizens, such will be the expectation you will create in the minds of each group concerning your feeling toward the rest also. Accordingly I 8 say that in general you must not cast any blame or censure whatsoever upon any general or orator or private individual of the groups that are believed,

Macedonian garrison was stationed in Thebes. Athens was less harshly treated but outspoken advocates of freedom were out of favour.

^{c} The verb πικραίνεσθαι is cited as used by Demosthenes, Bekker, i. p. 111. 31.

καθεστηκόσι μήτε μέμφεσθαι μήτ' ἐπιτιμᾶν μηδένα
μηδὲν ὅλως, ἀλλὰ συγχωρῆσαι πᾶσι τοῖς ἐν τῇ
πόλει πεπολιτεῦσθαι τὰ δέοντα, ἐπειδήπερ οἱ θεοί,
καλῶς ποιοῦντες, σώσαντες τὴν πόλιν, ἀποδεδώ-
κασιν ὑμῖν ὅ τι ἂν βούλησθ' ἐξ ἀρχῆς βουλεύσασθαι,
καὶ νομίζειν, ὥσπερ ἂν ἐν πλοίῳ τῶν μὲν ἱστίῳ,
τῶν δὲ κώπαις ἀποφαινομένων κομίζεσθαι, λέγεσθαι μὲν ὑπ' ἀμφοτέρων ἅπαντ' ἐπὶ σωτηρίᾳ, γεγενῆσθαι δὲ τὴν χρείαν πρὸς τὰ συμβάντ' ἀπὸ τῶν
9 θεῶν. ἐὰν τοῦτον τὸν τρόπον περὶ τῶν παρεληλυθότων ἐγνωκότες ἦτε, καὶ πιστοὶ πᾶσι γενήσεσθε,
καὶ καλῶν κἀγαθῶν ἀνδρῶν ἔργα πράξετε, καὶ τὰ
πράγματ' ὠφελήσετ' οὐ μικρά, καὶ τοὺς ἐναντιω-
θέντας ἐν ταῖς πόλεσιν ἢ μεταγνῶναι ποιήσετε
πάντας, ἢ ὀλίγους κομιδῇ τινας αὐτοὺς τοὺς αἰτίους
καταλειφθῆναι. μεγαλοψύχως τοίνυν καὶ πολιτι-
κῶς τὰ κοινῇ συμφέροντα πράττετε, καὶ¹ τῶν ἰδίων
μέμνησθε.

10 Παρακαλῶ δ' εἰς ταῦτ', οὐ τυχὼν αὐτὸς τῆς
τοιαύτης φιλανθρωπίας παρ' ἐνίων, ἀλλ' ἀδίκως
καὶ στασιαστικῶς εἰς τὴν ἑτέρων χάριν προποθείς.
ἀλλ' οὔτε τὴν ἰδίαν ὀργὴν ἀναπληρῶν τὸ κοινῇ
συμφέρον οἶμαι δεῖν βλάπτειν, οὔτε μείγνυμι τῆς
ἰδίας ἔχθρας εἰς τὰ κοινῇ συμφέροντ' οὐδέν, ἀλλ'
ἐφ' ἃ τοὺς ἄλλους παρακαλῶ, ταῦτ' αὐτὸς οἶμαι
δεῖν πρῶτος ποιεῖν.

¹ καὶ μη Schaefer.

---

[a] The implication is that the interests of the Athenians
coincide with the good of all, but the editors add μὴ : " Do
not think of your own interests."

[b] The odd metaphor derives from the reckless giving of

at least previously, to have supported the existing order, but rather concede to all parties in the city that they have done their duty as public men, inasmuch as the gods, to whom be thanks, by saving the city have bestowed upon you the privilege of deciding afresh what course you wish to take, and you must be of the opinion that, just as on board a ship, when some declare themselves for making good their escape by the sail and others by the oars, although all proposals of both parties aim at salvation, yet the chance to use either means to meet the crisis derives from the gods. If you have made up your minds to 9 regard past events in this way, you will gain the confidence of all and play the part of good and honourable men; you will also further your own interests not a little and will cause your opponents in the various cities either to change their minds, all of them, or will cause only a certain very small number of them, the ringleaders themselves, to be left. Acquit yourselves, therefore, with magnanimity and statesmanship in the general interest of Greece and bear in mind your own interests as Athenians.[a]

I urge you to this line of conduct, though I have 10 not myself met with such generosity from certain persons but have been unjustly and in a spirit of faction tossed off [b] for the gratification of others. I do not think, however, that I have the right while satisfying my private resentment to hurt the public interest, nor do I at all mix my private enmity with the general good. On the contrary, the conduct I urge upon the rest of men I think I ought to be myself the first to practise.

presents in connexion with the drinking of toasts at banquets. Lexicon under προπίνω.

11 Αἱ μὲν οὖν παρασκευαὶ καὶ ἃ δεῖ φυλάξασθαι, καὶ
ἃ πράττων τις ἂν κατ' ἀνθρώπινον λογισμὸν μάλιστα κατορθοίη, σχεδὸν εἴρηταί μοι· τοῖς δὲ καθ'
ἡμέραν ἐπιστατῆσαι, καὶ τοῖς ἐκ τοῦ παραχρῆμα
12 συμβαίνουσιν ὀρθῶς χρῆσθαι, καὶ γνῶναι τὸν
[1466] ἑκάστου καιρόν, καὶ κρῖναι τί τῶν πραγμάτων ἐξ
ὁμιλίας[a] δυνατὸν προσαγαγέσθαι καὶ βίας προσδεῖται, τῶν ἐφεστηκότων στρατηγῶν ἔργον ἐστί. διὸ
καὶ χαλεπωτάτην τάξιν ἔχει τὸ συμβουλεύειν· τὰ
γὰρ ὀρθῶς βουλευθέντα καὶ δοκιμασθέντα σὺν πολλῇ σπουδῇ καὶ πόνῳ πολλάκις τῷ τοὺς ἐπιστάντας
13 ἄλλως χρήσασθαι διελυμάνθη. νῦν μέντοι πάνθ'
ἕξειν καλῶς ἐλπίζω. καὶ γὰρ εἴ τις ὑπείληφεν εὐτυχῆ τὸν Ἀλέξανδρον τῷ πάντα κατορθοῦν, ἐκεῖνο
λογισάσθω, ὅτι πράττων καὶ πονῶν καὶ τολμῶν,
οὐχὶ καθήμενος ηὐτύχει. νῦν τοίνυν τεθνεῶτος
ἐκείνου ζητεῖ τινας ἡ τύχη μεθ' ὧν ἔσται, τού-
14 τους δ' ὑμᾶς δεῖ γενέσθαι. τούς θ' ἡγεμόνας, δι'
ὧν ἀνάγκη τὰ πράγματα πράττεσθαι, ὡς εὐνου-
στάτους ἐπὶ τὰς δυνάμεις ἐφίστατε· καὶ ὅ τι ποιεῖν
αὐτὸς ἕκαστος ὑμῶν δυνήσεται καὶ βουλήσεται,
τοῦτο πρὸς αὑτὸν εἰπάτω καὶ ὑποσχέσθω. καὶ
τοῦθ' ὅπως μὴ ψεύσεται, μηδ' ἐξηπατῆσθαι μηδὲ
15 πεισθῆναι παρακρουσθεὶς φήσας ἀναδύσεται, ὡς
τὴν ἔκδειαν ὧν ἂν ἐλλίπηθ' ὑμεῖς, οὐχ εὑρήσετε
τοὺς ἀναπληρώσοντας· οὐδὲ τὸν αὐτὸν ἔχει κίνδυνον,

---

[a] Under the word ὁμιλία this passage is cited by Bekker,
i. p. 110. 4-6.
[b] Plutarch wrote an essay entitled " Whether the success
of Alexander was due to luck or ability."

Now, the steps to be taken by way of preparation 11 and the mistakes to be guarded against, and the measures by which one might, as human calculations go, most likely succeed, have been, for practical purposes, stated by me ; but how to oversee our business from day to day and how to deal rightly with situations that arise unexpectedly, how to know the right 12 moment for each action and to judge which of our objectives it is possible to attain through negotiation ^a and which requires force in addition, these are the responsibility of the generals in charge. Therefore to give advice is to be in a very difficult position, because decisions that have been rightly taken and weighed with great care and pains are often spoiled through faulty execution on the part of those in authority. Yet I hope that all will be well this time ; 13 for if any man has assumed that Alexander was fortunate because he always succeeded,^b let him reflect upon the fact that it was by doing and toiling and daring, not by sitting still, that he continued to be fortunate. Now, therefore, since Alexander is dead, Fortune is seeking some people with whom to co-operate, and you ought to become her choice. As 14 for your leaders, through whom your interests must necessarily be handled, place at the head of your forces men whose loyalty is the greatest available, and as for yourselves, let every man of you repeat to himself a solemn promise to perform whatever he in particular shall be able and shall elect to do. And see to it that he does not break this pledge or shirk his responsibility, saying that he was deceived or misled and overpersuaded, because you will never find 15 others to make good the lack of those qualities in which you yourselves shall fall short ; neither does

περὶ ὧν ἐφ᾽ ὑμῖν ἐστιν ὅπως ἂν βούλησθε πρᾶξαι
μεταβουλεύεσθαι πολλάκις, καὶ περὶ ὧν ἂν ἐνστῇ
πόλεμος· ἀλλ᾽ ἡ περὶ τούτων μετάγνωσις ἧττα τῆς
προαιρέσεως γίγνεται. μὴ δὴ ποιήσητε τοιοῦτο
μηδέν, ἀλλ᾽ ὅ τι πράξετε γενναίως καὶ ἑτοίμως ταῖς
16 ψυχαῖς, τοῦτο χειροτονεῖτε, κἂν ἅπαξ ψηφίσησθε,
τὸν Δία τὸν Δωδωναῖον καὶ τοὺς ἄλλους θεούς, οἳ
πολλὰς καὶ καλὰς κἀγαθὰς καὶ ἀληθεῖς ὑμῖν
[1467] μαντείας ἀνῃρήκασιν, ἡγεμόνας ποιησάμενοι καὶ
παρακαλέσαντες, καὶ κατὰ τῶν νικητηρίων ἅπασιν
αὐτοῖς εὐξάμενοι, μετὰ τῆς ἀγαθῆς τύχης ἐλευθε-
ροῦτε τοὺς Ἕλληνας. εὐτυχεῖτε.

Β

ΠΕΡΙ ΤΗΣ ΙΔΙΑΣ ΚΑΘΟΔΟΥ

ΔΗΜΟΣΘΕΝΗΣ ΤΗΙ ΒΟΥΛΗΙ ΚΑΙ ΤΩΙ ΔΗΜΩΙ ΧΑΙΡΕΙΝ

Ἐνόμιζον μὲν ἀφ᾽ ὧν ἐπολιτευόμην, οὐχ ὅπως
μηδὲν ὑμᾶς ἀδικῶν τοιαῦτα πείσεσθαι, ἀλλὰ κἂν
μέτρι᾽ ἐξαμαρτὼν συγγνώμης τεύξεσθαι. ἐπειδὴ
δ᾽ οὕτω γέγονεν, ἕως μὲν ἑώρων ὑμᾶς, οὐδεμιᾶς
ἀποδείξεως φανερᾶς οὐδ᾽ ἐλέγχου γιγνομένου παρὰ

ᵃ Cf. Plutarch, *Marius* 26 εὔξατο τοῖς θεοῖς κατὰ ἑκατόμβης,
" He prayed to the gods for victory, taking a vow to sacrifice
a hecatomb."
ᵇ Three citations of this letter may be found in Walz's
Rhetores Graeci, which will be mentioned in the footnotes.
Harpocration refers to § 20 under the name *Calauria*.

it involve the same danger to change your minds
often about matters wherein it will be in your power
to do as you please as it does about matters over
which war will arise ; but in the case of the latter a
change of mind means defeat of your purpose.   So
do nothing of this kind, but whatever you intend to
execute honestly and promptly with your whole souls,
vote for that, and once you have passed a decree, 16
adopt as your leaders Zeus of Dodona and the rest
of the gods, who have uttered in your interest many
splendid, encouraging and true oracles, and summon
them to your aid and after you have prayed to all
of them for success with a vow of the fruits of victory,[a]
with good fortune attending you, proceed to liberate
the Greeks.   Farewell.

II

CONCERNING HIS OWN RESTORATION [b]

*Demosthenes to the Council and the Assembly
sends greeting*

I USED to believe, because of my conduct in public
life, that, as one who was guilty of no wrong toward
you, I should not only never meet with such treatment as this [c] but, even if I should have committed
some slight offence, that I might meet with forgive-
ness.   Since, however, it has turned out as it has, so
long as I observed you, without any manifest proof
or even a scrutiny of evidence on the part of the

[c] The opening sentence down to this point is cited by
Hermogenes, *Rhetores Graeci* 3, p. 349.

DEMOSTHENES

τῆς βουλῆς πρὸς τὰ ταύτης ἀπόρρητα καταψηφιζο-
μένους ἁπάντων, οὐδὲν ἐλαττόνων παραχωρεῖν ὑμᾶς
ἡγούμενος ἢ ἐμαυτὸν ἀποστερεῖσθαι, στέργειν ἡρού-
μην· τὸ γὰρ οἷς ἂν ἡ βουλὴ φήσῃ τοὺς ὀμωμοκότας
δικαστὰς προστίθεσθαι μηδεμιᾶς ἀποδείξεως ῥη-
2 θείσης, τῆς πολιτείας παραχωρεῖν ἦν. ἐπειδὴ δὲ
καλῶς ποιοῦντες ᾔσθησθε τὴν δυναστείαν ἥν τινες
τῶν ἐν τῇ βουλῇ κατεσκευάζονθ' ἑαυτοῖς καὶ πρὸς
τὰς ἀποδείξεις τοὺς ἀγῶνας κρίνετε τὰ δ' ἀπόρρητα τούτων ἐπιτιμήσεως ἄξι' εὑρήκατε, οἶμαι
δεῖν, ἐὰν καὶ ὑμῖν βουλομένοις ᾖ, τῆς ὁμοίας τυχεῖν
σωτηρίας τοῖς τῶν ὁμοίων αἰτιῶν τετυχηκόσι, καὶ
μὴ μόνος δι' αἰτίαν ψευδῆ τῆς πατρίδος καὶ τῶν
ὄντων καὶ τῆς τῶν οἰκειοτάτων συνηθείας ἀπο-
στερηθῆναι.

3 Εἰκότως δ' ἂν ὑμῖν, ὦ ἄνδρες Ἀθηναῖοι, μέλοι τῆς
[1468] ἐμῆς σωτηρίας, οὐ μόνον κατὰ τοῦθ' ὅτι οὐδὲν ὑμᾶς
ἀδικῶν δεινὰ πέπονθα, ἀλλὰ καὶ τῆς παρὰ τοῖς
ἄλλοις ἀνθρώποις ἕνεκ' εὐδοξίας. μὴ γάρ, εἰ μηδεὶς
ὑμᾶς ἀναμιμνήσκει τοὺς χρόνους μηδὲ τοὺς καιροὺς
4 ἐν οἷς τὰ μέγιστ' ἐγὼ χρήσιμος ἦν τῇ πόλει, τοὺς
ἄλλους Ἕλληνας ἀγνοεῖν νομίζετε, μηδ' ἐπιλελῆ-
σθαι τῶν ἐμοὶ πεπραγμένων ὑπὲρ ὑμῶν, ἃ ἐγὼ
δυοῖν εἵνεκα νῦν ὀκνῶ γράφειν καθ' ἕκαστον, ἑνὸς
μέν, τὸν φθόνον δεδιώς, πρὸς ὃν οὐδέν ἐστι προὔργου
τἀληθῆ λέγειν, ἑτέρου δ', ὅτι πολλὰ κἀνάξια
ἐκείνων διὰ τὴν τῶν ἄλλων Ἑλλήνων κακίαν νῦν

---

[a] In his *Life of Demosthenes* 26 Plutarch informs us that
the trial took place before the Areopagus. This was in the
spring of 324 B.C. The exile lasted a year.
210

Council,ᵃ condemning all the accused on the strength
of the unrevealed information of that body, I chose
to make the best of it, thinking that you were sur-
rendering rights no less valuable than those of which
I was being deprived. Because, for the jurors under
oath to assent to whatever the Council should declare, without any proof having been cited, that was
a surrender of a constitutional right. Since, however, 2
you have happily become aware of the undue ascen-
dancy which certain members of the Council were
contriving for themselves and since you are now
deciding the cases in the light of the proofs and have
found the secretiveness of these men deserving of
censure, I think it is my right, with your consent, to
enjoy the same acquittal as those who have incurred
the like accusations, and not to be the only one to be
deprived on a false charge of his fatherland, his
property, and the company of those who are nearest
and dearest to him.

And you would have good reason, men of Athens, 3
to be concerned about my deliverance, not only for
the reason that I have been outrageously treated,
though guilty of doing you no wrong, but also for the
sake of your good name abroad. For you must not
imagine, just because no one reminds you of those
times and occasions upon which I was of the greatest
service to the city, that the rest of the Greeks are 4
not aware of them or have forgotten what I have
accomplished in your behalf. At the present
moment I hesitate to write of these services in detail
for two reasons ; one reason is that I am afraid of
jealousy, in the face of which it is useless to speak
the truth ; the second is this, that because of the
cowardice of the rest of Greece we are now compelled

5 πράττειν ἀναγκαζόμεθα. ἐν κεφαλαίῳ δὲ τοιαῦτ᾽
ἔστ᾽ ἐφ᾽ οἷς ἐξηταζόμην ὑπὲρ ὑμῶν ἐγὼ ὥσθ᾽
ὑμᾶς μὲν ἐπ᾽ αὐτοῖς ὑπὸ πάντων ζηλοῦσθαι, ἐμοὶ
δ᾽ ἐλπίδα τῶν μεγίστων δωρειῶν προσδοκᾶσθαι
παρ᾽ ὑμῶν. τῆς δ᾽ ἀναγκαίας μέν, ἀγνώμονος δὲ
τύχης οὐχ ὡς δίκαιον ἦν, ἀλλ᾽ ὡς ἐβούλετο, κρι-
νάσης τὸν ὑπὲρ τῆς τῶν Ἑλλήνων ἐλευθερίας
6 ἀγῶνα, ὃν ὑμεῖς ἠγωνίσασθε, οὐδ᾽ ἐν τοῖς μετὰ
ταῦτα χρόνοις ἀπέστην τῆς εἰς ὑμᾶς εὐνοίας, οὐδ᾽
ἀντηλλαξάμην ἀντὶ ταύτης οὐδέν, οὐ χάριν, οὐκ
ἐλπίδας, οὐ πλοῦτον, οὐ δυναστείαν, οὐκ ἀσφάλειαν.
καίτοι πάντα ταῦθ᾽ ἑώρων ὑπάρχοντα τοῖς καθ᾽
ὑμῶν βουλομένοις πολιτεύεσθαι.

7 Ὁ δέ, πολλῶν ὄντων καὶ μεγάλων ἐφ᾽ οἷς εἰκότως ἐπέρχεταί μοι παρρησιάζεσθαι, μέγιστον
ἡγοῦμαι, οὐκ ὀκνήσω γράψαι πρὸς ὑμᾶς, ὅτι ἐν
παντὶ τῷ αἰῶνι τῶν μνημονευομένων ἀνθρώπων
δεινοτάτου γεγενημένου Φιλίππου, καὶ δι᾽ ὁμιλίας
πεῖσαι προσέχειν αὐτῷ τὸν νοῦν ὡς βούλοιτο, καὶ
διαφθεῖραι χρήμασι τοὺς ἐν ἑκάστῃ τῶν Ἑλληνί-
8 δων πόλεων γνωρίμους, ἐγὼ μόνος οὐδετέρου τού-
[1469] των ἡττήθην, ὃ κοινὴν ὑμῖν φιλοτιμίαν φέρει, πολλὰ
μὲν ἐντυχὼν Φιλίππῳ καὶ διαλεχθεὶς ἐφ᾽ οἷς ὑμεῖς
ἐπέμπετε πρεσβεύοντά με, πολλῶν δ᾽ ἀποσχόμενος
χρημάτων διδόντος ἐκείνου, ἃ τῶν συνειδότων ἔτι
πολλοὶ ζῶσιν. οὓς τίνα γνώμην ἔχειν περὶ ὑμῶν
εἰκὸς λογίσασθε· τὸ γὰρ τῷ τοιούτῳ τοῦτον κεχρῆ-
σθαι τὸν τρόπον, ἐμοὶ μὲν ἂν εὖ οἶδ᾽ ὅτι συμφορὰ

---

[a] The reference is to the battle of Chaeronea, 338 B.C.

[b] Demosthenes was one of ten envoys who negotiated with
Philip the Peace of Philocrates in 346 B.C. and was several
times sent on similar missions afterwards.

to do many things that are below the standard of
those services of mine.   In brief, however, the record 5
upon which I passed scrutiny as your servant was of
such a kind as to make you envied by all because
of it and myself confident of the greatest rewards
from you.   And when Fortune, as irresistible as she
was unkind, decided as she pleased, and not according
to justice, the struggle *a* for the liberty of Greece in
which you engaged, not even in the times that 6
followed did I retreat from my loyalty toward you,
nor did I bargain for anything in place of it, no man's
favour, no hopes of preferment, nor wealth, nor
power, nor personal safety.   Yet I observed that all
these prizes were accruing to those who chose to play
the game of politics to your detriment.

Now one fact which is especially significant— 7
although there are many significant facts which, it
occurs to me, would justify me in speaking frankly—I
shall not refrain from writing to you :   although of
men who are mentioned in history in all time, Philip
had the most uncanny ability of all, whether through
personal contact to persuade men to pay heed to
his wishes or to corrupt with bribes the notable
men in every one of the Greek cities, I was the 8
only man who did not fall a victim to either of these
methods, a fact that brings to you also cause for
pride, and although I met Philip often and parleyed
with him on those matters on which you sent me as
envoy,*b* yet I kept my hands off the substantial sums
he offered me, as many men are aware who still live.
Just ponder what opinion these men may reasonably
entertain of you, for to have dealt this treatment
to such a man, while for myself I am sure it would
seem a misfortune, though no conviction of vice, yet

φανείη, κακία δ' οὐδεμία, ὑμετέρα δ' ἀγνωμοσύνη·
ἦν τῷ μεταγνῶναι λύσατε.[1]

9 Πάντα τοίνυν τὰ προειρημέν' ἐλάττω νομίζω τῆς
συνεχοῦς καὶ καθ' ἡμέραν πολιτείας, ἐν ᾗ παρεῖχον
ἐμαυτὸν ἐγὼ πολιτευόμενον, οὐδεμιᾶς ὀργῆς οὐδὲ
δυσμενείας οὐδ' ἀδίκου πλεονεξίας οὔτε κοινῆς οὔτ'
ἰδίας προϊστάμενος, οὐδὲ συκοφαντήσας οὐδένα πώποτ' οὔτε πολίτην οὔτε ξένον, οὐδὲ καθ' ὑμῶν ἰδίᾳ
δεινὸς ὤν, ἀλλ' ὑπὲρ ὑμῶν, εἴ τι δεήσειεν, ἐξετα-
10 ζόμενος δημοσίᾳ. εἰδεῖεν δ' ἂν οἱ πρεσβύτεροι,
καὶ λέγειν τοῖς νεωτέροις ἐστὲ δίκαιοι, τὴν πρὸς
Πύθωνα τὸν Βυζάντιον ἐκκλησίαν, ὅτε τοὺς ἀπὸ
τῶν Ἑλλήνων ἦλθε πρέσβεις ἔχων, ὡς ἀδικοῦσαν
δείξων τὴν πόλιν, ἀπῆλθε δὲ τἀναντία τούτων
παθών, μόνου τῶν τότε ῥητόρων ἐξετάσαντος ἐμοῦ
τὰ ὑπὲρ ὑμῶν δίκαια. καὶ ἐῶ πρεσβείας ὅσας
ὑπὲρ ὑμῶν ἐπρέσβευσα, ἐν αἷς οὐδὲν ἠλαττώθητε
11 πώποτ' οὐδὲ καθ' ἕν. ἐπολιτευόμην γάρ, ὦ ἄνδρες
Ἀθηναῖοι, οὐχ ὅπως ἀλλήλων ὑμεῖς περιγενήσεσθε
σκοπῶν οὐδ' ἐφ' ἑαυτὴν ἀκονῶν τὴν πόλιν, ἀλλ'
ἀφ' ὧν δόξαν καὶ μεγαλοψυχίαν ὑμῖν ὑπάρξειν
[1470] ἐνόμιζον. ἐφ' οἷς ἅπασι μέν, μάλιστα δὲ τοῖς
νέοις, ἄγασθαι προσήκει, καὶ σκοπεῖν μὴ μόνον τὸν
διακονήσοντα πρὸς χάριν πάντ' ἐν τῇ πολιτείᾳ

---

[1] λύσαιτε Hermogenes.

^a This sentence is cited by Hermogenes, *Rhetores Graeci* 3,
p. 235 and by Maximus Planudes, *ibid.* 5, p. 495.
^b Python, pupil of Isocrates and a presumptuous orator,
headed a deputation of all the allies of Philip when they came
to Athens in 343 B.C. to accuse the people of unjust conduct.
See VII. 20-23, XVIII. 136, Plutarch, *Life of Dem.* 9, and
Lucian, *Encomium* 32.

on your part it would seem defiance of justice.[a] I beg of you to change your verdict and cancel this imputation.

All the considerations which I have mentioned 9 above, however, I consider of less importance than my conduct from first to last and every day in public life, in which I showed myself in action to be a statesman, never encouraging any nursing of a grudge or a feud or the grasping for unfair advantage, whether shared or for myself, never preferring false charges against either citizen or alien, never being over-clever to work in secret against your interests but always working for them, if occasion should arise, and aboveboard, subject to public approval. The older men 10 would know—and in all fairness you ought to inform the younger ones—of the hearing granted Python [b] of Byzantium before the Assembly when he arrived with the envoys from the Greeks, expecting to show that the city was acting unjustly, but went away with the tables turned against him after I, alone of those who spoke on that occasion, had brought out the rights of the matter in your defence. I forbear to mention all the embassies upon which I served in support of your interests, in which you were never worsted even in a single instance ; for I shaped my 11 policy, men of Athens, not with an eye to helping you get the better of one another, nor whetting the State against itself, but furthering measures from which I thought a reputation for magnanimity would redound to you. With such aspirations you should all be delighted, and especially the younger men, not looking for someone who will always play the lackey to win your favour in his public conduct—for of this

(τούτου μὲν γὰρ οὐδέποτ' ἔστ' ἀπορῆσαι), ἀλλὰ καὶ
τὸν ἐπ' εὐνοίᾳ περὶ ὧν ἂν ἀγνοῇτ' ἐπιτιμήσοντα.

12 Ἔτι τοίνυν παραλείπω πολλὰ ἐφ' οἷς ἕτερος καὶ
μηδὲν ἄλλο χρήσιμος γεγονὼς δικαίως ἂν ἠξίου
τυγχάνειν σωτηρίας, χορηγίας καὶ τριηραρχίας καὶ
χρημάτων ἐπιδόσεις ἐν πᾶσι τοῖς καιροῖς· ἐν οἷς
ἐγὼ φανήσομαι οὐ μόνον αὐτὸς ἐξητασμένος πρῶτος, ἀλλὰ καὶ τοὺς ἄλλους παρακεκληκώς. ὧν
ἕκαστον, ὦ ἄνδρες Ἀθηναῖοι, λογίσασθε, ὡς ἀνάξιόν
ἐστι τῆς περιεστηκυίας νῦν ἐμοὶ συμφορᾶς.

13 Ἀφθόνων δ' ὄντων, ἀπορῶ τί πρῶτον ὀδύρωμαι
τῶν παρόντων κακῶν. πότερον τὴν ἡλικίαν ἐν ᾗ
φυγῆς ἐπικινδύνου πειρᾶσθαι παρ' ἔθος καὶ παρὰ
τὴν ἀξίαν ἀναγκάζομαι; ἢ τὴν αἰσχύνην ἐφ' ᾗ κατ'
οὐδέν' ἔλεγχον οὐδ' ἀπόδειξιν ἁλοὺς ἀπόλωλα; ἢ
τὰς ἐλπίδας ὧν διαμαρτών, ὧν ἑτέροις προσῆκε

14 κεκληρονόμηκα κακῶν, οὔτ' ἐφ' οἷς ἐπολιτεύθην
πρότερον δίκην ὀφείλων δοῦναι, οὔτε τῶν ἐφ' οἷς
ἐκρινόμην ἐξελεγχθέντων; οὔτε γὰρ ἔγωγε τῶν
Ἁρπάλου φίλων φανήσομαι γεγονώς, τῶν τε γρα-
φέντων περὶ Ἁρπάλου μόνα τἀμοὶ πεπραγμέν'
ἀνέγκλητον πεποίηκε τὴν πόλιν. ἐξ ὧν πάντων
δῆλόν ἐσθ' ὅτι καιρῷ τινι ληφθεὶς καὶ οὐκ ἀδική-

---

[a] Prosperous citizens of Athens were required from time to
time to contribute money for the equipment of triremes,
dramatic choruses, and religious deputations to various
shrines. These were the λῃτουργίαι in contrast to the ὑπηρεσίαι mentioned in *Exordium 52.*

[b] His age was sixty. Cicero was only a year older when
he wrote his essay *On Old Age.*

[c] Harpalus was an absconding treasurer of Alexander who
sought refuge in Attica. Part of his illicit funds disappeared
from the Acropolis, where they had been sequestered by the
Athenians. Demosthenes was accused and convicted of

type there will never be a dearth—but for one who, actuated by loyalty, will even rebuke you for your errors of judgement.

Now I pass over many other considerations, on the 12 strength of which a different kind of a man and with no other service to his credit would justly demand to obtain acquittal ; I mean the equipping of choruses and triremes and the contributing of money on all occasions.[a] In these duties I shall be found, not only to have been the first to do my own part, but also to have urged the rest to do theirs. Reviewing these services one by one, men of Athens, consider how undeserved is the calamity that has now befallen me.

Since my present troubles are so abundant I am 13 at a loss to know what I shall bemoan first. Will it be my advanced age,[b] at which, for the first time and contrary to my deserts, I am compelled to experience the hazards of a perilous exile ? Or will it be the disgrace of having been convicted and ruined without any investigation or proof of guilt ? Or will it be in disappointment of my hopes in place of which I have fallen heir to evils that rightfully belonged to others, since neither because of my previous political record 14 was I deserving punishment nor had the charges been proved upon which I was being tried. For I shall never be shown to have been one of the friends of Harpalus,[c] and among the decrees that were passed concerning him only those proposed by me have afforded the State a clean record. From all these facts it is clear that I was caught in an un-

accepting twenty talents. Few historians believe that he was guilty ; some suggest that he may have spent part of the money in the cause of liberty.

DEMOSTHENES

ματι, τῇ πρὸς ἅπαντας τοὺς ἐν ταῖς αἰτίαις ὀργῇ
15 περιπέπτωκ' ἀδίκως τῷ πρῶτος εἰσιέναι. ἐπεὶ τί
τῶν δικαίων οὐκ εἶπον ἐγὼ τῶν σεσωκότων τοὺς
ὕστερον κρινομένους; ἢ τίν' ἔλεγχον εἶπεν ἡ βουλὴ
[1471] κατ' ἐμοῦ; ἢ τίνα νῦν ἂν εἰπεῖν ἔχοι; οὐ γὰρ
ἔστιν οὐδείς· τὰ γὰρ μὴ γενόμεν' οὐκ ἔστι ποιῆσαι
γεγενῆσθαι. ἀλλ' ὑπὲρ μὲν τούτων παύομαι, πολλὰ[1] γράφειν ἔχων· τὸ γὰρ μηδὲν ἐμαυτῷ συνειδέ-
ναι πεῖράν μοι δέδωκεν, εἰς μὲν ὠφέλειαν ἀσθενὲς
ὄν, εἰς τὸ μᾶλλον λυπεῖσθαι πάντων ὀδυνηρότατον.
16 ἐπειδὴ δὲ καλῶς ποιοῦντες πᾶσι τοῖς ἐν ταῖς αἰτίαις
διήλλαχθε, κἀμοὶ διαλλάγητ', ὦ ἄνδρες 'Αθηναῖοι·
οὔτε γὰρ ἠδίκηχ' ὑμᾶς οὐδέν, ὡς ἴστωσαν οἱ θεοὶ
καὶ ἥρωες· μαρτυρεῖ δέ μοι πᾶς ὁ πρόσθεν παρ-
εληλυθὼς χρόνος, ὃς δικαιότερον ἂν πιστεύοιθ' ὑφ'
ὑμῶν τῆς ἀνελέγκτου νῦν ἐπενεχθείσης αἰτίας· οὔτ'
ἐγὼ χείριστος οὐδ' ἀπιστότατος φανήσομαι τῶν
διαβληθέντων.
17 Καὶ μὴν τό γ' ἀπελθεῖν οὐκ ἂν εἰκότως ὀργὴν
πρός με ποιήσειεν· οὐ γὰρ ἀπεγνωκὼς ὑμᾶς οὐδ'
ἑτέρωσε βλέπων οὐδαμοῖ μετέστην, ἀλλὰ πρῶτον
μὲν τοὔνειδος τῆς εἱρκτῆς χαλεπῶς τῷ λογισμῷ
φέρων, εἶτα διὰ τὴν ἡλικίαν οὐκ ἂν οἷός τ' ὢν τῷ
σώματι τὴν κακοπάθιαν ὑπενεγκεῖν. ἔτι δ' οὐδ'

---

[1] πόλλ' ἂν Blass.

[a] Demigods or semi-divine ancestors of noble families.
[b] The suggestion is that another man might have offered
his services to the Macedonians.

218

fortunate conjuncture, not taken in wrongdoing, and that through coming first on the list into court I unjustly fell foul of the public rage against all those involved in those charges. Because, which of the 15 just pleas that have saved those subsequently tried did not I myself advance ? Or what proof did the Council allege against me ? Or what proof could it now allege ? There is none ; for it is impossible to make facts out of what never happened. I refrain, however, from enlarging upon these topics, though there is plenty to write, for the consciousness of innocence has afforded me proof through experience that, while a feeble help in time of trouble, it is the most excruciating of all means of enhancing one's suffering. So, since, quite rightly, you have 16 become reconciled with all others involved in these charges, be reconciled with me also, men of Athens ; for I have done no wrong against you, as I call upon the gods and heroes [a] to bear testimony. My witness is the whole extent of time that has gone by, which has a juster claim upon your credence than the unsupported charge which has now been brought against me ; nor shall I be found to be the worst or the least trustworthy of those who have been falsely accused.

And surely my departure from Athens would not 17 afford you just grounds for resentment against me, for it was not because I had renounced allegiance to you nor because I was looking to another quarter for comfort [b] that I changed my residence to another country, but because, in the first place, I was pained at contemplating the disgrace of imprisonment, and in the second, on account of my age I was in no condition to endure the bodily discomforts. Besides,

ὑμᾶς ἐνόμιζον ἀβουλεῖν ἔξω με προπηλακισμοῦ
γενέσθαι, ὃς οὐδὲν ὑμᾶς ὠφελῶν ἔμ' ἀπώλλυεν.
18 ἐπεὶ ὅτι γ' ὑμῖν προσεῖχον τὸν νοῦν καὶ οὐδέσιν
ἄλλοις πόλλ' ἂν ἴδοιτε σημεῖα. εἴς τε γὰρ πόλιν
ἦλθον, οὐκ ἐν ᾗ μέγιστα πράξειν αὐτὸς ἔμελλον,
ἀλλ' εἰς ἣν καὶ τοὺς προγόνους ἐλθόντας ᾔδειν ὅθ'
ὁ πρὸς τὸν Πέρσην κατελάμβανεν αὐτοὺς κίνδυνος,
καὶ παρ' ᾗ πλείστην εὔνοιαν ὑπάρχουσαν ὑμῖν ἠπι-
19 στάμην. ἔστι δ' ἡ Τροζηνίων αὕτη, ᾗ μάλιστα μὲν
οἱ θεοὶ καὶ τῆς πρὸς ὑμᾶς εὐνοίας εἴνεκα καὶ τῆς
[1472] εἰς ἔμ' εὐεργεσίας εὖνοι πάντες εἴησαν, εἶτα κἀγὼ
σωθεὶς ὑφ' ὑμῶν δυνηθείην ἀποδοῦναι χάριτας. ἔν
τε ταύτῃ τινῶν, ὡς ἐμοὶ χαριζομένων, ἐπιτιμᾶν
ὑμῖν τι πειρωμένων τῇ κατ' ἔμ' ἀγνοίᾳ, ἐγὼ πᾶσαν
εὐφημίαν, ὥσπερ ἐμοὶ προσῆκε, παρειχόμην· ἐξ
ὧν καὶ μάλιστα νομίζω πάντας ἀγασθέντας μου
δημοσίᾳ τιμῆσαι.
20 Ὁρῶν δὲ τὴν μὲν εὔνοιαν τῶν ἀνδρῶν μεγάλην,
τὴν δ' εἰς τὸ παρὸν δύναμιν καταδεεστέραν, μετ-
ελθὼν εἰς τὸ τοῦ Ποσειδῶνος ἱερὸν ἐν Καλαυρείᾳ
κάθημαι, οὐ μόνον τῆς ἀσφαλείας ἔνεκα, ἣν διὰ τὸν
θεὸν ἐλπίζω μοι ὑπάρχειν (οὐ γὰρ εὖ οἶδά γε· ἃ
γὰρ ἐφ' ἑτέροις ἐστὶν ὡς ἂν βούλωνται πρᾶξαι
λεπτὴν καὶ ἄδηλον ἔχει τῷ κινδυνεύοντι τὴν ἀσφάλειαν), ἀλλ' ὅτι καὶ τὴν πατρίδ' ἐντεῦθεν ἑκάστης

---

[a] He hints that he might have gone to some other city
friendly to the Macedonians, where a welcome would have
awaited him if he had renounced his allegiance to Athens.

[b] The Athenians abandoned the city before the battle of
Salamis in 480 B.C.

[c] Calauria is situated south of Aegina in the Saronic Gulf.
Harpocration cites the letter under the name Calauria, an
evidence of its authenticity.

I did not think that you, either, were averse to my getting beyond the reach of revilement which, without benefiting you, was breaking me down. For, as indications that it was on you my thoughts were centred and on no others, you may note many items of evidence ; for instance, I did not go to a city in which I was likely to play an outstanding rôle myself,[a] but to one where I knew our ancestors had gone when the Persian danger overtook them,[b] and where I knew too there existed abundant goodwill toward yourselves. I refer to the city of Troezen, to which it is my chief prayer that all the gods may be propitious, both because of its goodwill to you and because of its kindness to me, and my second prayer is that, having been delivered from this exile by you, I may be enabled to make repayment for kindnesses. In this city, when certain persons, thinking to make themselves agreeable to me, ventured to censure you for your arbitrary action in my regard, I preserved all reticence, as was my duty, which I believe was the chief reason for their being moved to admiration of me and honouring me in the name of the city.

Observing, however, that though the goodwill of the men there was strong, yet the power of the city was insufficient for the present need, I changed my residence and now have my quarters in the sanctuary of Poseidon in Calauria,[c] not only for the sake of my personal safety, which through the protection of the god I hope is assured—because I am not quite certain ; for the fact that it is in the power of unfriendly people to deal with matters as they choose renders frail and unpredictable the safety of a man in danger—but also because from here I look across

ἡμέρας ἀφορῶ, εἰς ἣν τοσαύτην εὔνοιαν ἐμαυτῷ
σύνοιδα, ὅσης παρ' ὑμῶν εὔχομαι τυχεῖν.

21 "Οπως οὖν, ὦ ἄνδρες 'Αθηναῖοι, μηκέτι πλείω
χρόνον τοῖς παροῦσι κακοῖς συνέχωμαι, ψηφίσασθέ
μοι ταῦθ' ἃ καὶ ἄλλοις τισὶν ἤδη, ἵνα μήτ' ἀνάξιον
ὑμῶν μηδέν μοι συμβῇ, μήθ' ἱκέτης ἑτέρων ἀναγ-
κασθῶ γενέσθαι· οὐδὲ γὰρ ὑμῖν τοῦτο γένοιτ' ἂν
καλόν. ἐπεὶ εἴ γέ μοι τὰ πρὸς ὑμᾶς ἀδιάλλακτα
22 ὑπάρχει, τεθνάναι μοι κρεῖττον ἦν. εἰκότως δ' ἄν
μοι πιστεύοιτε ταύτην τὴν διάνοιαν ἔχειν καὶ μὴ
νῦν μάτην θρασύνεσθαι· καὶ γὰρ ἐμαυτοῦ κυρίους
ὑμᾶς ἐποίησα, καὶ οὐκ ἔφυγον τὸν ἀγῶνα ἵνα μήτε
[1473] προδῶ τὴν ἀλήθειαν μήτ' ἄκυρος ὑμῶν ἐμοῦ μηδεὶς γένηται, ἀλλ' ὅ τι βούλοισθε, τοῦτο χρήσαισθε·
παρ' ὧν γὰρ ἁπάντων καλῶν κἀγαθῶν ἔτυχον, τούτους ᾠόμην δεῖν ἔχειν καὶ ἁμαρτεῖν, εἰ βούλοιντ',
23 εἰς ἐμέ. ἐπειδὴ δὲ καλῶς ποιοῦσ' ἡ δικαία τύχη
τῆς ἀδίκου κρατήσασα, δὶς περὶ τῶν αὐτῶν ἀπέδωκεν ὑμῖν βουλεύσασθαι, τῷ μηδὲν ἀνήκεστον
ἐψηφίσθαι περὶ ἐμοῦ, σώσατέ μ', ὦ ἄνδρες 'Αθηναῖοι, καὶ ψηφίσασθε καὶ ὑμῶν αὐτῶν ἄξια κἀμοῦ.
24 ἐπ' οὐδενὶ γὰρ τῶν πεπραγμένων ἠδικηκότα μ'
εὑρήσετε, οὐδ' ἐπιτήδειον ἄτιμον εἶναι οὐδ' ἀπολωλέναι, ἀλλὰ καὶ εὔνουν τῷ πλήθει τῷ ὑμετέρῳ
τοῖς μάλισθ' ὁμοίως, ἵνα μηδὲν ἐπίφθονον γράψω,

ᵃ Demosthenes terminated his second exile by taking
poison rather than submit to capture by the soldiers of Antipater, 322 B.C. From this passage it seems that he had been
prepared to do so the year before in the same Calauria.

the sea every day to my native land, toward which I am conscious in my heart of feeling an attachment as strong as I pray that I may enjoy on your part.

In order, therefore, men of Athens, that I may no 21 longer be held in the grip of these present miseries, enact for me those measures you have already voted for the benefit of certain others, so that neither shall anything unworthy of you become my lot nor I be compelled to become the suppliant of rival powers ; for that would not be an honourable thing for you either. Because, if the differences between you and me remain irreconcilable, it were better for me to be dead. With good reason you may have confidence 22 that I entertain this thought and that I am not now indulging in idle bluff.[a] I placed my fate in your hands, and I faced the trial in order that I might neither be a traitor to the truth nor place myself beyond the reach of any one of you, but that you might deal with me as you pleased ; for I thought that those from whom I had received all my blessings ought to possess the privilege even of erring against me if they chose. Since, however, a just Fortune—thanks be to 23 her—prevailing over the unjust, has bestowed upon you the opportunity of deliberating twice on the same questions, no irremediable decree concerning my case having been passed, save me, men of Athens, and vote a verdict worthy both of your own selves and of me. You will not find me to have done wrong 24 on the score of any of my measures, or a fit person to be deprived of my civic rights or destroyed, but a man who is as much devoted to your democracy as the best patriots—not to say anything invidious[b]—

[b] To claim that he was more loyal would be invidious.

καὶ πλεῖστα πεπραγματευμένον τῶν νυνὶ ζώντων
ὑπὲρ ὑμῶν, καὶ μέγισθ᾽ ὑπάρχοντά μοι τῶν κατ᾽
ἐμαυτὸν σύμβολ᾽ εὐνοίας πρὸς ὑμᾶς.

25 Μηδεὶς δ᾽ ὑμῶν ἡγείσθω μ᾽, ὦ ἄνδρες Ἀθηναῖοι,
μήτ᾽ ἀνανδρίᾳ μήτ᾽ ἄλλῃ προφάσει φαύλῃ μηδεμιᾷ
παρ᾽ ὅλην τὴν ἐπιστολὴν ὀδύρεσθαι. ἀλλὰ τοῖς
παροῦσιν ἕκαστος ἀφθόνως χρῆται, ἐμοὶ δὲ ταῦτα
νῦν πάρεστιν, ὡς μήποτ᾽ ὤφελε, λῦπαι καὶ δάκρυα,
καὶ τῆς πατρίδος καὶ ὑμῶν πόθος καὶ ὧν πέπονθα
λογισμός, ἃ πάντα ποιεῖ μ᾽ ὀδύρεσθαι· ἃ ἐπι-
σκοποῦντες δικαίως, ἐν οὐδενὶ τῶν πεπολιτευμένων
ὑπὲρ ὑμῶν οὔτε μαλακίαν οὔτ᾽ ἀνανδρίαν προσοῦσαν
εὑρήσετέ μοι.

26 Πρὸς μὲν δὴ πάντας ὑμᾶς τοσαῦτα· ἰδίᾳ δὲ τοῖς
ἐμοὶ προσκρούουσιν ἐναντίον ὑμῶν βούλομαι διαλεχθῆναι. ὅσα μὲν γὰρ τοῖς ὑφ᾽ ὑμῶν ἀγνοηθεῖσιν
ὑπηρετοῦντες ἐποίουν, ἔστω δι᾽ ὑμᾶς αὐτοῖς πεπρᾶ-
[1474] χθαι, καὶ οὐδὲν ἐγκαλῶ. ἐπειδὴ δ᾽ ἐγνώκαθ᾽ ὑμεῖς
οἷα ταῦτ᾽ ἐστίν, ἐὰν μέν, ὥσπερ ὑπὲρ τῶν λοιπῶν
ἐῶσι, καὶ ἐμοὶ συγχωρήσωσι, καλῶς ποιήσουσιν·
ἐὰν δ᾽ ἐπηρεάζειν ἐγχειρῶσιν, ὑμᾶς ἀξιῶ μοι βοηθεῖν ἅπαντας, καὶ μὴ κυριωτέραν τὴν τούτων ἔχθραν
τῆς παρ᾽ ὑμῶν χάριτός μοι γενέσθαι. εὐτυχεῖτε.

who of all men now living has accomplished most in your behalf and of all men of my time has available the most signal tokens of devotion to you.

Let not one of you think, men of Athens, that through lack of manhood or from any other base motive I give way to my grief from the beginning to the end of this letter. Not so, but every man is ungrudgingly indulgent to the feelings of the moment, and those that now beset me—if only this had never come to pass !—are sorrows and tears, longing both for my country and for you, and pondering over the wrongs I have suffered, all of which cause me to grieve. If you but scan this record fairly, in none of the political actions taken by me in your behalf will you find softness or lack of manhood attaching to me.

Now thus far I am appealing to you all, but for those in particular who are attacking me in your presence I wish to say a word : so far as concerns all that they were doing in pursuance of the decrees passed by you in disregard of the truth, let it be allowed that these actions have been taken by them as your agents, and I lodge no complaint. Since, however, you have yourselves come to recognize these decrees for what they are, if they will yield in my case, just as they are allowing the prosecution to be dropped in the case of the other defendants, they shall have my thanks ; but if they attempt to continue malicious, I appeal to you all to rally to my aid and not allow the enmity of these men to prevail over the gratitude due to me from you. Farewell.

DEMOSTHENES

Γ

ΠΕΡΙ ΤΩΝ ΛΥΚΟΥΡΓΟΥ ΠΑΙΔΩΝ

ΔΗΜΟΣΘΕΝΗΣ ΤΗΙ ΒΟΥΛΗΙ ΚΑΙ ΤΩΙ ΔΗΜΩΙ ΧΑΙΡΕΙΝ

Περὶ μὲν τῶν κατ' ἐμαυτόν, ἅ μοι παρ' ὑμῶν
ἐνόμιζον δίκαιον εἶναι γενέσθαι, τὴν προτέραν
ἔπεμψα πρὸς ὑμᾶς· ὑπὲρ ὧν ὅταν ὑμῖν δοκῇ, τότε
συγχωρήσετε. περὶ δ' ὧν νῦν ἐπέσταλκα, βουλοίμην ἂν ὑμᾶς μὴ παριδεῖν, μηδὲ πρὸς φιλονικίαν,
ἀλλὰ πρὸς τὸ δίκαιον ἀκοῦσαι. συμβαίνει γάρ μοι,
καίπερ ἐκποδὼν διατρίβοντι, πολλῶν ἀκούειν ἐπι-
τιμώντων ὑμῖν τοῖς περὶ τοὺς Λυκούργου παῖδας
2 γιγνομένοις.[1] ἐπέστειλα μὲν οὖν ἂν τὴν ἐπιστολὴν
καὶ τῶν ἐκείνῳ ζῶντι πεπραγμένων ἕνεκα, ὧν
ὁμοίως ἐμοὶ πάντες ἂν αὐτῷ δικαίως ἔχοιτε χάριν,
εἰ τὰ προσήκοντα βούλοισθε ποιεῖν. ἐκεῖνος γὰρ
αὐτὸν ἐν τῷ περὶ τὴν διοίκησιν μέρει τάξας τῆς
πολιτείας τὸ κατ' ἀρχάς, καὶ περὶ τῶν Ἑλληνικῶν

---

[1] γεγενημένοις Blass.

---

[a] Eight citations of this letter by Hermogenes, Aristeides
and others may be found in Walz's *Rhetores Graeci*. It is
cited also by Harpocration and by Antiatticista in Bekker's
Anecdota. It seems to have been known also to Photius and
to the author of the *Etymologicum Magnum*. References to
all of these will be found in the footnotes. In spite of these
evidences of authenticity the majority of editors reject the
letter. By Blass it is defended and of all six letters it certainly has the strongest case.

[b] Lycurgus managed the finances of Athens efficiently for

III

CONCERNING THE SONS OF LYCURGUS [a]

Demosthenes to the Council and the Assembly sends greeting.

I sent you the previous letter about matters that concern myself, stating what steps I thought in justice ought to be taken by you ; in regard to these you will take favourable action when it seems good to you. The message I now address to you I should not like you to overlook or to hear it in a spirit of contentiousness, but with due regard to the justness of it. For it happens that, although sojourning in an out-of-the-way place, I hear many people censuring you for your treatment of the sons of Lycurgus. Now I should have sent you the letter merely out 2 of regard for those services that Lycurgus performed during his lifetime, for which you would all, like myself, be in justice grateful if you would but do your duty. For Lycurgus, having taken a post in the financial department of the government [b] at the outset of his career and not being at all accustomed to draft documents pertaining to the general affairs of

twelve years (338–326), for one legal term of four years as treasurer and for two terms through others. During this period the income of the State was doubled and a large building programme was carried through. In politics Lycurgus was associated with Demosthenes. Though he ranked as one of the ten Attic orators, his style was rather forceful than polished. One speech, *Against Leocrates*, is extant and his Life in Ps. Plut. *Vit. X Orat.*, whose author seems to have made extensive use of the decree in his honour, *I.G.* ii². 457. *Cf.* also *I.G.* ii². 333, 1493–1496.

καὶ συμμαχικῶν οὐδὲν εἰωθὼς γράφειν, ὅτε καὶ
τῶν δημοτικῶν εἶναι προσποιουμένων οἱ πολλοὶ
κατέλειπον ὑμᾶς, τότε ταῖς τοῦ δήμου προαιρέσεσιν
[1475] 3 προσένειμεν ἑαυτόν, οὐχ ὅτι δωρεὰς καὶ προσόδους
ἐκ τούτων ὑπῆρχε λαμβάνειν· ἀπὸ γὰρ τῶν ἐναντίων πάντα τὰ τοιαῦτ' ἐγίγνετο· οὐδ' ὅτι ταύτην
ἀσφαλεστέραν τὴν προαίρεσιν οὖσαν ἑώρα· πολλοὺς
γὰρ καὶ προδήλους εἶχε κινδύνους, οὓς ἀναγκαῖον
ἦν ὑπομεῖναι τὸν ὑπὲρ τοῦ δήμου λέγειν προαιρού-
μενον· ἀλλ' ὅτι δημοτικὸς καὶ φύσει χρηστὸς ἀνὴρ
4 ἦν. καίτοι παρὼν ἑώρα τοὺς μὲν βοηθήσαντας ἂν
τῷ δήμῳ, ἀσθενεῖς ἐπὶ τοῖς συμβεβηκόσιν ὄντας,
τοὺς δὲ τἀναντία πράττοντας κατὰ πάντ' ἐρρω-
μένους. ἀλλ' ὅμως οὐδὲν ἧττον ἐκεῖνος εἴχετο τούτων ἃ συμφέρειν ἡγεῖτο τῷ δήμῳ, καὶ μετὰ ταῦτ'
ἀόκνως καὶ λέγων καὶ πράττων ἃ προσῆκ' ἦν
φανερός, ἐφ' οἷς εὐθὺς ἐξητεῖθ', ὡς ἅπαντες ἴσασιν.
5 Ἐπέστειλα μὲν οὖν ἄν, ὥσπερ εἶπον ἐν ἀρχῇ, καὶ
διὰ τὴν ἐκείνου χάριν· οὐ μὴν ἀλλὰ καὶ ὑμῖν νομίζων συμφέρειν τὰς παρὰ τοῖς ἔξω γιγνομένας
ἐπιτιμήσεις εἰδέναι, πολλῷ προθυμότερον πρὸς τὸ
πέμψαι τὴν ἐπιστολὴν ἔσχον. παραιτοῦμαι δὲ τοὺς
ἰδίᾳ πρὸς ἐκεῖνον ἔχοντας δυσκόλως, ὑπομεῖναι
τἀληθῆ καὶ τὰ δίκαι' ἀκούειν ὑπὲρ αὐτοῦ. εὖ γὰρ
ἴστ', ὦ ἄνδρες Ἀθηναῖοι, ὅτι νῦν ἐκ τῶν περὶ τοὺς
παῖδας αὐτοῦ γεγενημένων φαύλην δόξαν ἡ πόλις

---

[a] The Macedonians.
[b] The surrender of Lycurgus, along with that of Demosthenes and others, was demanded after the fall of Thebesin
228

the Greeks and their relations with their allies, only when the majority of those who pretended to be the friends of democracy were deserting you, began to devote himself to the principles of the popular party, not because from this quarter opportunity was offer- 3 ing to secure gifts and emoluments, since all such prizes were coming from the opposite party,[a] nor yet because he observed this policy to be the safer one, since there were many manifest dangers which a man was bound to incur who chose to speak on behalf of the people, but because he was truly democratic and by nature an honest man. And yet before his very 4 eyes he observed those who might have assisted the cause of the people growing weak with the drift of events and their adversaries gaining strength in every way. None the less for all that, this brave man continued to adhere to such measures as he thought were in the people's interest and subsequently he continued to perform his duty unfalteringly in word and deed, as was clear to see. As a consequence his surrender was straightway demanded,[b] as all men are aware.

Now I would have written this letter, as I said at the 5 outset, for the sake of Lycurgus alone, but over and above that, believing it to be to your interest to know the criticisms that are current beyond the borders of Athens, I became all the more eager to dispatch the letter. I beg of those who for private reasons were at odds with Lycurgus to endure to hear what in truth and justice may be said in his behalf ; for be well assured, men of Athens, that, as things now are, the city is acquiring an evil reputation because of the

335 B.C. Alexander was persuaded by the Athenian orator Demades to relent.

6 λαμβάνει. οὐδεὶς γὰρ τῶν Ἑλλήνων ἀγνοεῖ ὅτι
ζῶντα Λυκοῦργον ἐτιμᾶθ᾽ ὑμεῖς εἰς ὑπερβολήν, καὶ
πολλῶν αἰτιῶν ἐπενεχθεισῶν ὑπὸ τῶν φθονούντων
αὐτῷ, οὐδεμίαν πώποθ᾽ εὕρετ᾽ ἀληθῆ, οὕτω δ᾽
ἐπιστεύετ᾽ αὐτῷ καὶ δημοτικὸν παρὰ πάντας ἡγεῖ-
[1476] σθε ὥστε πολλὰ τῶν δικαίων ἐν τῷ φῆσαι Λυκοῦργον ἐκρίνετε καὶ τοῦθ᾽ ὑμῖν ἐξήρκει· οὐ γὰρ
7 ἦν ἂν¹ τοιοῦτον μὴ δοκοῦν ὑμῖν. νῦν τοίνυν ἅπαντες
ἀκούοντες τοὺς υἱεῖς αὐτοῦ δεδέσθαι, τὸν μὲν τε-
θνεῶτ᾽ ἐλεοῦσι, τοῖς παισὶ δ᾽ ὡς ἀνάξια πάσχουσι
συνάχθονται, ὑμῖν δ᾽ ἐπιτιμῶσι πικρῶς, ὡς οὐκ ἂν
τολμήσαιμι γράφειν ἐγώ· ἃ γὰρ ἄχθομαι τοῖς λέγουσι καὶ ἀντιλέγω καθ᾽ ὅσον δύναμαι βοηθῶν
ὑμῖν, ταῦτ᾽ ἄχρι μὲν τοῦ δῆλον ὑμῖν ποιῆσαι ὅτι
πολλοὶ μέμφονται, συμφέρειν ὑμῖν νομίζων εἰδέναι,
γέγραφα, ἀκριβῶς δὲ διεξιέναι δυσχερὲς κρίνω.
8 ὅσα μέντοι λοιδορίας χωρίς ἐστιν ὧν λέγουσί τινες,
καὶ ἀκηκοέναι συμφέρειν ἡγοῦμαι, ταῦτα δηλώσω.
οὐδεὶς γὰρ ὑπείληφεν ὡς ἄρ᾽ ἠγνοήκατε καὶ δι-
εψεύσθητε τῆς ἀληθείας περὶ αὐτοῦ Λυκούργου. τό
τε γὰρ τοῦ χρόνου πλῆθος, ὃν ἐξεταζόμενος, οὐδὲν
πώποθ᾽ εὑρέθη περὶ ὑμᾶς οὔτε φρονῶν οὔτε ποιῶν
ἄδικον, καὶ τὸ μηδέν᾽ ἀνθρώπων εἰς μηδὲν τῶν

---

¹ Dindorf and Blass assumed a lacuna after ἂν; the
papyrus does not confirm this.

ᵃ In addition to offices of trust Lycurgus several times
received the honour of a crown and of statues at the public
expense.

ᵇ There was a board of thirty men at Athens who acted as
accountants and auditors. Ten of the thirty were called
εὔθυνοι: any official who handled public money could be
charged before them with bribery or misappropriation of

way his sons have been treated. For none of the 6
Greeks is ignorant that during the lifetime of Lycurgus you honoured him extraordinarily,[a] and,
though many charges were brought against him by
those who were envious of him, you never found a
single charge to be true, and you so trusted him and
believed him to be truly democratic beyond all others
that you decided many points of justice on the ground
that " Lycurgus said so," and that sufficed for you.
It would not have been possible for any such thing
not to meet with your approval and consent. To-day, 7
therefore, all men, upon hearing that his sons are in
prison, while pitying the dead man, sympathize with
the children as innocent sufferers, and reproach you
bitterly after a manner that I, for one, should not
dare to write down ; for, touching the reports which
make me vexed at those who utter them, and which I
contradict as best I can, trying to come to your
defence, I have written these only to the extent of
making it clear to you that many people are blaming
you, since I believe it to be to your interest to know
this, though to quote their words verbatim I judge
would be offensive. Apart from mere abuse, how- 8
ever, I shall reveal all that certain people say and
which I believe it to your advantage to have heard.
For, after all, no one has supposed that you laboured
under a misunderstanding and deception concerning
the truth so far as Lycurgus himself is concerned, for
the length of time during which, where subject to
scrutiny,[b] he never was found guilty of any wrong
toward you in either thought or deed and the fact
that no human being could ever have accused you of

funds. All accounts were subject to their inspection. *Cf.*
Aristotle, *Athen. Const.* 48. 3-4 ; 53. 2.

ἄλλων ἀναισθησίαν ἂν ὑμῶν καταγνῶναι, εἰκότως
ἀναιρεῖ τὴν ὑπὲρ τῆς ἀγνοίας σκῆψιν.

9 Λείπεται τοίνυν ὃ πάντες ἂν εἶναι φαύλων ἀνθρώπων ἔργον φήσαιεν, ὅσον ἂν χρῆσθε χρόνον,
τοσοῦτον ἑκάστου φροντίζειν δοκεῖν, μετὰ ταῦτα
δὲ μηδέν' ἔχειν λόγον. εἰς τί γὰρ τῶν ἄλλων χρὴ
προσδοκᾶν τῷ τετελευτηκότι τὴν παρ' ὑμῶν ἔσεσθαι χάριν, ὅταν εἰς τοὺς παῖδας καὶ τὴν εὐδοξίαν
τἀναντί' ὁρᾷ τις γιγνόμενα, ὧν μόνων καὶ τελευ-
10 τῶσι πᾶσιν ὅπως ἕξει καλῶς μέλει; καὶ μὴν οὐδὲ
χρημάτων ποιεῖν εἵνεκα ταῦτα δοκεῖν τῶν καλῶν
κἀγαθῶν[1] ἐστιν· οὔτε γὰρ τῆς μεγαλοψυχίας οὔτε
[1477] τῆς ἄλλης προαιρέσεως τῆς ὑμετέρας ἀκόλουθον ἂν
φανείη. εἰ γὰρ ὑμᾶς λύσασθαι παρ' ἑτέρων ἔδει
δόντας ἐκ τῶν προσιόντων τὰ χρήματα ταῦτα,
πάντας ἂν ἡγοῦμαι προθύμους εἶναι· τίμημα δ'
ὁρῶν ὀκνοῦντας ἀφεῖναι, ὃ λόγῳ καὶ φθόνῳ γέγονεν, οὐκ ἔχω τί καταγνῶ, εἰ μὴ ὅλως πικρῶς καὶ
ταραχωδῶς ἔχειν πρὸς τοὺς δημοτικοὺς ὡρμήκατε.
εἰ δὲ τοῦτ' ἔστιν, οὔτ' ὀρθῶς οὔτε συμφερόντως
βουλεύεσθαι ἐγνώκατε.

11 Θαυμάζω δ' εἰ μηδεὶς ὑμῶν ἐννοεῖ ὅτι τῶν αἰσχρῶν ἐστι τὸν δῆμον τὸν Ἀθηναίων, συνέσει καὶ
παιδείᾳ πάντων προέχειν δοκοῦντα, ὃς καὶ τοῖς
ἀτυχήσασιν ἀεὶ κοινὴν ἔχει καταφυγήν, ἀγνωμο-
νέστερον φαίνεσθαι Φιλίππου, ὃς ἀνουθέτητος ὢν
12 εἰκότως, τραφείς γ' ἐν ἐξουσίᾳ, ὅμως ᾤετο δεῖν,

[1] κἀγαθῶν lacking in papyrus.

indifference to any other action of his naturally eliminate the pretext of ignorance.

So the explanation is left—what all would declare 9 the conduct of vile men—that so long as you have use for each official you seem to be concerned for him but after that feel no obligation ; for where else is one to expect that the gratitude due from you to the dead will be shown, when he observes the opposite treatment meted out to his children and his good name, which are the sole concerns of all men when facing death, that it may continue to be well with them ? And assuredly, to appear to do these 10 things for the sake of money is also unworthy of truly honourable men, for it would be clearly inconsistent either with your magnanimity or with your general principles of conduct. For instance, if it were necessary to ransom the children from foreign captors by giving this sum out of the revenues, I believe you would all be eager to do it ; but when I observe you reluctant to remit a fine which was imposed because of mere talk and envy, I do not know what judgement I can pass unless it be that you have launched upon a course of utterly bitter and truculent hostility toward the members of the popular party. If this be the case, you have made up your minds to deliberate neither righteously nor in the public interest.

I am amazed if none of you thinks that it is a 11 disgraceful thing for the people of Athens, who are supposed to be superior to all men in understanding and culture and have also maintained here for the unfortunate a common refuge in all ages, to show themselves less considerate than Philip, who, although naturally subject to no correction, nursed as he was in licence, still thought that at the moment 12

ἡνίκ' ηὐτύχησε μάλιστα, τότ' ἀνθρωπινώτατα[1] πράττων φαίνεσθαι, καὶ τοὺς παραταξαμένους, πρὸς
οὓς περὶ τῶν ὅλων διεκινδύνευσεν, οὐκ ἐτόλμησε
δῆσαι τὸ τίνων καὶ τίνες εἰσὶν ἐξετάσας· οὐ γὰρ
ὡς ἔοικεν ὁμοίως τῶν παρ' ὑμῖν ῥητόρων ἐνίοις,
οὔτε δίκαι' ἂν εἶναι πρὸς ἅπαντας ταῦτ' οὔτε κάλ'
ἡγεῖτο, ἀλλὰ τὴν τῆς ἀξίας προσθήκην συλλογιζό-
13 μενος τὰ τοιαῦτ' ἐπέκρινεν. ὑμεῖς δ', ὄντες Ἀθηναῖοι καὶ παιδείας μετέχοντες[2] ᾗ καὶ τοὺς ἀν-
αισθήτους ἀνεκτοὺς ποιεῖν δοκεῖ δύνασθαι, πρῶτον
μέν, ὃ πάντων ἀγνωμονέστατόν ἐστι, περὶ ὧν τὸν
πατέρ' αἰτιῶνταί τινες, τοὺς υἱεῖς δεδέκατε, εἶτα
τὸ ταῦτα ποιεῖν ἴσον εἶναί φατε, ὥσπερ ὑπὲρ σταθ-
μῶν ἢ μέτρων τὸ ἴσον σκοπούμενοι, ἀλλ' οὐχ
[1478] ὑπὲρ ἀνδρῶν προαιρέσεως καὶ πολιτείας βουλευό-
14 μενοι· ἐν οἷς ἐξεταζομένοις εἰ μὲν χρηστὰ καὶ
δημοτικὰ καὶ ἐπ' εὐνοίᾳ τὰ Λυκούργῳ πεπραγμένα
φαίνεται, μὴ μόνον[3] μηδενὸς κακοῦ, ἀλλὰ καὶ
πάντων τῶν ἀγαθῶν τοὺς παῖδας αὐτοῦ δίκαιόν
ἐστι τυγχάνειν παρ' ὑμῶν· εἰ δὲ τἀναντία τούτων,
ἐκεῖνον, ὅτ' ἔζη, ἔδει δίκην διδόναι, τούτους δὲ
μηδ' οὕτως, ἐφ' οἷς ἐκείνῳ τις ἐγκαλεῖ, τυγχάνειν
ὀργῆς· πᾶσι γὰρ πάντων τῶν ἁμαρτημάτων ὅρος

---

[1] Reading of papyrus ; ἀνθρώπινα codd., edd.
[2] ἐν παρρησίᾳ ζῶντες papyrus.
[3] μὴ μόνον added by Blass ; papyrus lacks ἀλλὰ following.

---

[a] The battle of Chaeronea, 338 B.C. ; the Greeks magnified
its importance. Their liberty was lost by degrees, not
suddenly.

[b] An Athenian citizen was identified by three items : his
own name, his father's name, and his deme.

of his greatest good fortune [a] he ought to be seen acting with the greatest humanity and did not venture to cast into chains the men who had faced him in the battle-line, against whom he had staked his all, but merely inquired, " Whose sons are they and what are their names ? " [b] For unlike some of your orators, as it appears, he did not consider it would be either just or creditable to take the same action against all, but, taking into his reckoning the additional factor of their deserts,[c] he assorted his verdicts accordingly. You, however, though Athenians 13 and partners in a culture which is thought capable of making even stupid people tolerable, in the first place—and of all your actions this is the most heartless—hold the sons in chains as a penalty for offences which certain parties allege against the father [d] ; in the next place, you claim this action to be equality before the law, just as if you were inspecting equality in the field of weights or measures and not deliberating about men's ethical and political principles. In 14 testing these, if the actions of Lycurgus seem honest and public-spirited and inspired by loyalty, then it is justice that his sons should not only meet with no harm at your hands, but with all the benefits imaginable ; yet if his actions seem quite the opposite, he ought to have been punished while he lived, and these children should not thus incur your anger on the ground of charges someone prefers against the father, because for all men death is an end of responsibility

[c] Antiatticista cites this passage under ἀξία: ἀντὶ τοῦ ἀξίωμα, Bekker, i. p. 77. 17-18. 'Αξία equals Latin dignitas, the degree of distinction possessed by virtue of birth or achievement or both. But that is not the meaning here.

[d] The precise accusation is not known ; it seems to have been concerned with the administration of the treasury.

15 ἐστὶ τελευτή. ἐπεὶ εἴ γ' οὕτως ἔξετε ὥσθ' οἱ μὲν
ἀχθεσθέντες τι τοῖς ὑπὲρ τοῦ δήμου πολιτευο-
μένοις μηδὲ πρὸς τελευτήσαντας διαλλαγήσονται,
ἀλλὰ καὶ τοῖς παισὶ τὴν ἔχθραν διαφυλάξουσιν, ὁ
δὲ δῆμος, ᾧ συναγωνίζεται τῶν δημοτικῶν ἕκαστος, μέχρι τοῦ παρόντι¹ χρῆσθαι μνημονεύσει
τὰς χάριτας μετὰ ταῦτα δὲ μηδὲν φροντιεῖ, οὐδὲν
ἀθλιώτερον ἔσται τοῦ τὴν ὑπὲρ τοῦ δήμου τάξιν
αἱρεῖσθαι.

16 Εἰ δὲ Μοιροκλῆς ἀποκρίνεται ταῦτα μὲν σοφώ-
τερ' ἢ καθ' ἑαυτὸν εἶναι, ἵνα δὲ μὴ ἀποδρῶσιν,
αὐτὸς αὐτοὺς δῆσαι, ἐρωτήσατ' αὐτὸν ἡνίκα Ταυ-
ρέας καὶ Πάταικος καὶ Ἀριστογείτων καὶ αὐτὸς
εἰς τὸ δεσμωτήριον παραδοθέντες, οὐ μόνον οὐκ
ἐδέδεντο, ἀλλὰ κἀδημηγόρουν, τί δήποτ' οὐχ ἑώρα

17 τὰ δίκαια ταῦτα. εἰ δὲ μὴ φήσει τότ' ἄρχειν, οὐδὲ
λέγειν ἔκ γε τῶν νόμων αὐτῷ προσῆκεν.² ὥστε
πῶς ἴσον ἐστὶ τοὺς μὲν ἄρχειν οἷς μηδὲ λέγειν
ἔξεστι, τοὺς δὲ δεδέσθαι ὧν πολλὰ χρήσιμος ἦν

18 ὑμῖν ὁ πατήρ; ἐγὼ μὲν οὐκ ἔχω συλλογίσασθαι, εἰ
μὴ τοῦτο δεῖξαι δημοσίᾳ βούλεσθε, ὅτι βδελυρία

¹ Reading of papyrus ; παρόντος codd., edd.
² Reading of papyrus ; προσήκει codd., edd.

ᵃ Moerocles was archon in 324 B.C. His surrender had
been demanded by Alexander in 335 B.C., which indicates
his importance.

ᵇ Nothing specific is known about these imprisonments,
but it need not be assumed that all four men were under
sentence at a single time. See next note. Taureas and
Pataecus are unknown. For Aristogeiton see the two
speeches against him.

ᶜ If Moerocles ordered the two sons of Lycurgus to be

for all their offences.   Consequently, if you are going 15
to be so minded that those who have conceived some
grudge against those who espouse the cause of the
people will not be reconciled even with dead men, but
will persist in maintaining their enmity against the
children, and if the people, in whose cause every
friend of democracy labours, shall remember their
gratitude only so long as they can use a man in
the flesh and thereafter shall feel no concern, then
nothing will be more miserable than to choose the
post of champion of the people.

If Moerocles [a] replies that this view is too subtle 16
for his understanding, and that, to prevent them from
running away, he put them in chains upon his own
responsibility, demand of him why in the world he
did not see the justice of this proceeding when
Taureas, Pataecus, Aristogeiton and himself, [b] though
they had been committed to prison, were not only
not in chains but would even address the Assembly.
If, on the other hand, he shall say that he was not 17
then archon, he had no right to speak, at any rate
according to the laws. [c]   Accordingly, how can it be
equal justice when some men are in office who have
no right even to speak and others are in fetters whose
father was useful to you in numerous ways ?   I cer- 18
tainly cannot figure it out unless you mean to demonstrate this fact officially—that blackguardism,

imprisoned but left Taureas, Pataecus and Aristogeiton at
liberty, the charge against him is criminal partiality.   If he
denies that he was archon at the time and so lacked the
authority to order these men to be detained in prison, then
the minor charge still stands against him of addressing the
Assembly while technically a prisoner himself.   As a prisoner
he would be subject to partial ἀτιμία or diminution of his
rights as a citizen.

καὶ ἀναίδεια καὶ προαίρεσις πονηρίας ἐν τῇ πόλει
[1479] ἰσχύει καὶ διασωθῆναι πλείω προσδοκίαν ἔχει, κἄν
τι συμβῇ χαλεπὸν τοῖς τοιούτοις, ἀπόλυσις γίγνεται, ἐν δὲ προαιρέσει χρηστῇ καὶ βίῳ σώφρονι καὶ
δημοτικῷ προελέσθαι ζῆν σφαλερόν, κἄν τι γένηται
πταῖσμ', ἄφυκτον ἔσται.

19 Ἔτι τοίνυν τὸ μὲν μὴ δίκαιον εἶναι τὴν ἐναντίαν
δόξαν ἔχειν ἢ ἦν περὶ ζῶντος εἶχετ' ἐκείνου, καὶ τὸ
τῶν τετελευτηκότων ἢ τῶν παρόντων πλείω ποιεῖσθαι λόγον δίκαιον εἶναι, καὶ πάντα τὰ τοιαῦτ'
ἐάσω· παρὰ γὰρ πᾶσιν ὁμολογεῖσθαι ταῦθ' ὑπ-
είληφα· ὅσοις μέντοι πατρικὰς εὐεργεσίας ἀπ-
εμνημονεύσατε τῶν ἄλλων ἡδέως ἂν ἴδοιμ' ὑμᾶς
ἀναμνησθέντας, οἷον τοῖς Ἀριστείδου καὶ Θρασυ-
βούλου καὶ τοῖς Ἀρχίνου καὶ πολλῶν ἑτέρων
ἀπογόνοις. οὐχ ὡς ἐπιτιμῶν δὲ ταῦτα παρήνεγκα.

20 τοσούτου γὰρ δέω τοῦτο ποιεῖν ὥστε συμφέρειν
μάλιστα τῇ πόλει τὰ τοιαῦτα κρίνω· προκαλεῖσθε
γὰρ πάντας ἐκ τούτων δημοτικοὺς εἶναι, ὁρῶντας
ὅτι κἂν ἐν τῷ καθ' ἑαυτοὺς βίῳ ταῖς προσηκού-
σαις αὐτῶν τιμαῖς ὁ φθόνος ἀντιστῇ, τοῖς γε
παισὶν ὑπάρξει τὰ προσήκοντα παρ' ὑμῶν κομί-
σασθαι.

21 Πῶς οὖν οὐκ ἄτοπον, μᾶλλον δὲ καὶ αἰσχρόν,
τῶν μὲν ἄλλων τισί, καὶ παλαιῶν ὄντων τῶν
χρόνων καθ' οὓς ἐγένοντο χρήσιμοι, καὶ δι' ὧν
ἀκούετε τὰς εὐεργεσίας, οὐκ ἐξ ὧν ἑοράκαθ'

ᵃ At times the Athenian Assembly bestowed extravagant
gifts upon the children of famous men, as may be learned
from Plutarch's *Aristeides* xxvii. At other times it acted
heartlessly, if we may believe Demosthenes XIX. 280 ff.

shamelessness and deliberate villainy are strong in the State and enjoy a better prospect of coming off safely, and that, if such men happen to get into a tight place, a way out is discovered, but to elect to live in honesty of principle, sobriety of life and devotion to the people will be hazardous and, if some false step is made, the consequences will be inescapable.

Furthermore, the fact that it is unjust to enter- 19 tain concerning Lycurgus the opposite opinion to the one you held while he lived, and that justice demands that you should have more regard for the dead than for the living, and all such considerations I shall pass over, for I assume them to be universally agreed upon. Of the children of others, however, whom you recompensed for their fathers' good services I would gladly see you reminded ; for instance, the descendants of Aristeides, Thrasybulus, Archinus and many others.[a] Not by way of censure have I cited these examples, for so far am I from censuring as to 20 declare it my belief that such repayments are in the highest degree in the interest of the State, because you challenge all men by such conduct to be champions of the people, when they observe that, even if during their own lives envy shall stand in the way of their receiving merited honours, yet their children, at any rate, will be sure to receive their due rewards at your hands.

Is it not absurd, therefore, or rather even disgrace- 21 ful, toward certain other men to keep alive the good-will justly due them, in spite of the fact that the times of their usefulness are long past and after this interval you learn of their good deeds by hearsay and have not

Archinus was one of the restorers of democracy in 403 B.C., but the greater share of the credit went to Thrasybulus.

DEMOSTHENES

ὑπειληφότας, ὅμως τὴν δικαίαν εὔνοιαν διασώζειν,
Λυκούργῳ δ' οὕτως ὑπογύου καὶ τῆς πολιτείας
22 καὶ τῆς τελευτῆς γεγονυίας, μηδ' εἰς ἃ καὶ τοῖς
ἀγνῶσιν καὶ ὑφ' ὧν ἀδικοῖσθ' ἕτοιμοι τὸν ἄλλον
ἦτε χρόνον, εἰς ἔλεον καὶ φιλανθρωπίαν, μηδ' εἰς
ταῦθ' ὑμᾶς αὐτοὺς ὁμοίους παρέχειν, καὶ ταῦτ'
εἰς τοὺς παῖδας αὐτοῦ γιγνομένης τῆς τιμωρίας,
οὓς κἂν ἐχθρός, εἴπερ μέτριος εἴη καὶ λογισμὸν
ἔχων, ἐλεήσαι;

23
[1480] Θαυμάζω τοίνυν καὶ τοῦτ' εἴ τις ὑμῶν ἀγνοεῖ,
ὡς οὐδὲ τοῦτο συμφέρει τῇ πολιτείᾳ φανερὸν γιγνόμενον, ὅτι τοῖς μὲν ἄλλην τινὰ κτησαμένοις φιλίαν
καὶ κατορθοῦσιν ἐν πᾶσιν πλεονεκτεῖν ὑπάρχει, κἂν
ἀτυχήσωσίν τι, ῥᾳδίους¹ εἶναι τὰς λύσεις, τοῖς δ' εἰς
τὸν δῆμον ἀναρτήσασιν ἑαυτούς, οὐ μόνον κατὰ
τἄλλ' ἔλαττον ἔχειν ὑπάρξει, ἀλλὰ καὶ τὰς συμφορὰς βεβαίους τούτοις μόνοις τῶν ἄλλων μένειν.
ἀλλὰ μὴν ὅτι τοῦθ' οὕτως γίγνεται ῥᾴδιον δεῖξαι.
24 τίς γὰρ οὐκ οἶδεν ὑμῶν Λάχητι τῷ Μελανώπου,
ἁλῶναι μὲν ὁμοίως ἐν δικαστηρίῳ συμβὰν ὡς καὶ
νῦν τοῖς Λυκούργου παισίν, ἀφεθῆναι δὲ πᾶν τὸ
ὄφλημ' ἐπιστείλαντος Ἀλεξάνδρου; καὶ πάλιν Μνη-
σιβούλῳ τῷ Ἀχαρνεῖ, ἁλῶναι μὲν ὁμοίως κατα-
γνόντος αὐτοῦ τοῦ δικαστηρίου ὥσπερ καὶ τῶν
Λυκούργου παίδων, ἀφεῖσθαι δὲ καλῶς ποιοῦντι;
25 ἄξιος γὰρ ἀνήρ. καὶ οὐδεὶς ἐπὶ τούτοις τοὺς νόμους ἔφη καταλύεσθαι τῶν νῦν βοώντων. εἰκότως·

¹ Reading of papyrus : ῥᾳδίας codd., edd.

ᵃ That is, with the Macedonian court.
ᵇ Laches is known from an inscription as a syndic of the deme Aexonê (*I.G.* ii². 1197, p. 560, 13 f.).

240

assumed them from things of which you have been eye-witnesses, but toward Lycurgus, whose political career and death are so recent, you do not show 22 yourselves so ready to display even pity and kindness as you were at all other times toward men whom you never knew and by whom you used to be wronged, and, worse still, your vengeance is visited upon his children, whom even an enemy, if only he were fair-minded and capable of reason, would pity?

Moreover, I am amazed if any one of you is ignorant 23 of this fact also, that it is not to the interest of our political life, either, for this to become public knowledge, that those who have established friendship in a certain other quarter *a* are sure to prosper in all things and fare better and, if some mishap occurs, the ways of escape are easier, but those who have attached themselves to the cause of the people will not only fare worse in other respects but for them alone of all men calamities will remain irremediable. Yet it is easy to demonstrate the truth of this, for who of you does not know the 24 incident of Laches *b* the son of Melanopus, whose lot it was to be convicted in a court of law precisely as the sons of Lycurgus in the present instance, but his entire fine was remitted when Alexander requested it by letter? And again, that it happened to Mnesibulus *c* of Acharnae to be similarly convicted, the court condemning him just as it has the sons of Lycurgus, and to have the fine remitted, and rightly too, for the man was deserving? And none 25 of those who are now making such an outcry declared that by these actions the laws were being nullified.

c Mnesibulus is not otherwise known.

οὐδὲ γὰρ κατελύοντο, εἴπερ ἅπαντες οἱ νόμοι τῶν
δικαίων εἴνεκα καὶ σωτηρίας τῶν χρηστῶν ἀνθρώπων τίθενται, καὶ μήτ' ἀιδίους τοῖς ἀτυχήσασι καθιστάναι τὰς συμφορὰς συμφέρει, μήτ' ἀχαρίστους
26 ὄντας φαίνεσθαι. ἀλλὰ μὴν εἴ γε ταῦθ' οὕτως,
ὥσπερ ἂν φήσαιμεν, ἔχειν συμφέρει, οὐ μόνον τοὺς
νόμους οὐ κατελύεθ' ἡνίκ' ἐκείνους ἀφίετε, ἀλλὰ
καὶ τοὺς βίους ἐσῴζετε τῶν τοὺς νόμους θεμέ-
νων ἀνθρώπων, Λάχητα μὲν πρὸς χάριν δεηθέντος
Ἀλεξάνδρου ἀφέντες, Μνησίβουλον δὲ τῇ τοῦ βίου
σωφροσύνῃ σώσαντες.

27
[1481]

Μὴ τοίνυν τὸ κτήσασθαί τιν' ἔξωθεν φιλίαν λυσι-
τελέστερον δείκνυτε, ἢ τὸ τῷ δήμῳ παρακαταθέ-
σθαι ἑαυτόν, μηδὲ τὸ τῶν ἀγνώτων εἶναι κρεῖττον,
ἢ τοῖς πολλοῖς ὑμῖν τὰ συμφέροντα πολιτευόμενοι
γιγνώσκεσθαι. τὸ μὲν γὰρ πᾶσιν ἀρέσκειν τὸν
συμβουλεύοντα καὶ τὰ κοινὰ πράττοντ' ἀδύνατον·
ἐὰν δ' ἐπ' εὐνοίᾳ ταὐτὰ τῷ δήμῳ τις φρονῇ, δίκαιός
ἐστι σῴζεσθαι. εἰ δὲ μή, καὶ θεραπεύειν ἑτέρους
μᾶλλον ἢ τὸν δῆμον ἅπαντας διδάξετε, καὶ φεύγειν
τὸ τῶν ὑμῖν συμφερόντων ποιοῦντά τι γνωσθῆναι.
28 ὅλως δὲ κοινόν ἐστιν ὄνειδος ἁπάντων, ἄνδρες Ἀθηναῖοι, καὶ ὅλης τῆς πόλεως συμφορά, τὸν φθόνον
δοκεῖν μεῖζον ἰσχύειν παρ' ὑμῖν ἢ τὰς τῶν εὐεργε-
σιῶν χάριτας, καὶ ταῦτα τοῦ μὲν νοσήματος ὄντος,
τῶν δ' ἐν τοῖς θεοῖς ἀποδεδειγμένων.

---

[a] Of the Macedonians.
[b] A verbal play on χάριτες, " feelings of gratitude " or
" Graces."

Quite rightly so, for they were not being nullified, if it be true that all our laws are enacted for the sake of just men and for the preservation of honest men, and that it is expedient neither to render the calamities of the unfortunate perpetual nor for men to show themselves void of gratitude. And furthermore, if it is 26 expedient for these principles to hold true, as we would declare, not only were you not nullifying the laws where you released those men, but you were preserving the lifework of those men who enacted the laws, first, by releasing Laches in compliance with the request of Alexander and, secondly, by restoring Mnesibulus to his rights because of the sobriety of his life.

Beware of demonstrating, therefore, that to acquire 27 some outside friendship [a] is more profitable than to give one's self in trust to the people and that it is better to remain in the ranks of the unknown than to become known as a man who in public life consults the interests of you, the majority. For although it is impossible for one who recommends policies and administers the commonwealth to please everyone, yet if a man, actuated by loyalty, has at heart the same interests as the people, he has a right to security of person. Otherwise you will teach everyone to serve the interests of others rather than those of the people and to shun recognition for doing any of those things that are to your advantage. In short, 28 it is a reproach common to all citizens, men of Athens, and a misfortune of the State as a whole, that envy should be thought to be stronger among you than the grace of gratitude for services performed, and the more so because envy is a disease but the Graces [b] have been assigned a place among the gods.

DEMOSTHENES

29 Καὶ μὴν οὐδὲ τὸν Πυθέαν παραλείψω τὸν μέχρι
τῆς παρόδου δημοτικόν, μετὰ ταῦτα δ' ἕτοιμον εἰς
τὰ καθ' ὑμῶν πάντα. τίς γὰρ οὐκ οἶδε τοῦτον, ὅτε
μὲν τὴν ὑπὲρ ὑμῶν τάξιν ἔχων εἰς τὸ πολιτεύεσθαι
παρῄει, ὡς δοῦλον ἐλαυνόμενον καὶ γραφὴν ξενίας
φεύγοντα καὶ μικροῦ πραθένθ' ὑπὸ τούτων οἷς νῦν
30 ὑπηρετῶν τοὺς κατ' ἐμοῦ λόγους ἔγραφεν, ἐπειδὴ
δ' ἃ κατηγόρει τότε τῶν ἄλλων, νῦν αὐτὸς πράττει,
εὐποροῦντα μὲν οὕτως ὥστε δύ' ἔχειν ἑταίρας, αἳ
μέχρι φθόης καλῶς ποιοῦσαι προπεπόμφασιν αὐτόν, πέντε τάλαντα δ' ὀφλόντα ῥᾷον ἐκτεῖσαι ἢ
πέντε δραχμὰς ἂν ἀνέδειξε[1] πρότερον, πρὸς δὲ τούτοις παρ' ὑμῶν, τοῦ δήμου, οὐ μόνον τῆς πολιτείας
μετειληφότα, ὃ κοινὸν ὄνειδός ἐστιν ἅπασιν, ἀλλὰ
καὶ θύονθ' ὑπὲρ ὑμῶν τὰς πατρίους θυσίας ἐν
Δελφοῖς;

31
[1482] "Οταν οὖν τοιαῦτα καὶ τηλικαῦτα πᾶσιν ἰδεῖν ᾖ
παραδείγματα, ἀφ' ὧν ἀλυσιτελὲς προελέσθαι τὰ
τοῦ δήμου πᾶς τις ἂν κρίναι, φοβοῦμαι μήποτ'
ἔρημοι τῶν ὑπὲρ ὑμῶν ἐρούντων γένησθε, ἄλλως
τε χὥταν τῶν δημοτικῶν τοὺς μὲν ἡ καθήκουσα
μοῖρα καὶ ἡ τύχη χὠ χρόνος παραιρῆται, οἷον
Ναυσικλέα καὶ Χάρητα καὶ Διότιμον καὶ Μενεσθέα

---

[1] Capps : ἔδειξε papyrus, ἀνέξεσθε codd., ἀνέχεσθαι Reiske, Blass.

---

[a] Pytheas was a presumptuous politician of no formal education ; he accused Demosthenes of receiving twenty talents from Harpalus ; after Alexander's death he joined Antipater during the siege of Lamia, 322 B.C.

244

Furthermore, I am not going to omit the case of 29
Pytheas [a] either, who was a friend of the people down
to his entrance into public life but after that was
ready to do anything to injure you. For who does
not know that this man, when, under the obligation
to serve you, he was entering upon public life, was
being hounded as a slave and was under indictment
as an alien usurping the rights of a citizen and came
near being sold by these men whose servant he now
is and for whom he used to write the speeches against
me, but since he is himself now practising what he 30
then accused others of doing, is in such easy circumstances as to keep two mistresses, who have escorted
him—and kind it is of them—on the way to death by
consumption,[b] and to be able to discharge a debt of
five talents more easily than he could have produced
five drachmas previously, and besides all this, with
the permission of you, the people, not only par-
ticipates in the government, which is a common
reproach to all, but also performs on your behalf the
ancestral [c] sacrifices at Delphi ?

So, when it is possible for all to behold object- 31
lessons of such a kind and on such a scale, from which
everyone would conclude that it does not pay to
espouse the cause of the people, I begin to fear that
some day you may become destitute of men who will
speak on your behalf, especially when of the friends
of the people some are being taken away by man's
natural destiny,[d] by accident, and by the lapse of
time, such as Nausicles, Chares, Diotimus, Menes-

[b] The Greek word φθόη was peculiar enough to prick the
interest of Harpocration, who cites this passage.
[c] The point is that Pytheas himself lacked ancestors of
note.
[d] That is, death by disease.

DEMOSTHENES

καὶ Εὔδοξον, ἔτι δ' Εὐθύδικον καὶ Ἐφιάλτην καὶ
Λυκοῦργον, τοὺς δ' ὑμεῖς προῆσθε, ὥσπερ Χαρί-
32 δημον καὶ Φιλοκλέα καὶ ἐμέ, ὧν ἑτέρους εὐνου-
στέρους οὐδ' αὐτοὶ νομίζετε· εἰ δ' ὁμοίους τινάς, οὐ
φθονῶ, βουλοίμην δ' ἄν, εἴπερ ὑμεῖς δικαίως αὐτοῖς
προσοίσεσθε καὶ μὴ ταῦθ' ἅπερ ἡμεῖς πείσονται, ὡς
πλείστους αὐτοὺς γενέσθαι. ἀλλ' ὅταν γε τοιαῦθ', οἷα τὰ νῦν, παραδείγματ' ἐκφέρητε, τίς ἔστιν
ὅστις εἰς ταύτην τὴν τάξιν ἑαυτὸν γνησίως ὑμῖν ἐθε-
33 λήσει δοῦναι; ἀλλὰ μὴν τῶν γε προσποιησομένων
οὐκ ἀπορήσετε· οὐδὲ γὰρ πρότερον. μὴ γένοιτο
δ' ἰδεῖν ἐξελεγχθέντας αὐτοὺς ὁμοίως ἐκείνοις,
οἳ φανερῶς ἃ τότ' ἠρνοῦντο νῦν πολιτευόμενοι,
οὐδέν' ὑμῶν οὔτε δεδοίκασιν οὔτε αἰσχύνονται.
ἃ χρὴ λογιζομένους, ὦ ἄνδρες Ἀθηναῖοι, μήτε
τῶν εὔνων ὀλιγωρεῖν, μήτε τοῖς προάγουσιν εἰς
34 πικρίαν καὶ ὠμότητα τὴν πόλιν πείθεσθαι. πολὺ
γὰρ μᾶλλον εὐνοίας καὶ φιλανθρωπίας τὰ παρόντα
πράγματα δεῖται, ἢ ταραχῆς καὶ δυσμενείας, ὧν
ὑπερβολῇ χρώμενοί τινες, ἐργολαβοῦσιν καθ' ὑμῶν
εἰς ὑποδοχὴν πραγμάτων, ὧν διαψεύσειεν αὐτοὺς ὁ

ᵃ Nausicles and Diotimus are mentioned in the speech
XVIII. 114 ; both are known from inscriptions to have held
important commands. The surrender of Diotimus was
demanded by Alexander in 335 B.C. Chares held important
commands between 367 and 335 B.C. Menestheus was given
command of one hundred galleys in 335 B.C., xvii. 20. Eudoxus seems to be otherwise unknown.

ᵇ Deinarchus i. 33 names Euthydicus as one whom Demosthenes claimed as a friend. Ephialtes was one of the ten
whose surrender was demanded by Alexander in 335 B.C.
He died in 334 while fighting on the side of the Persians
against the Macedonians. For Lycurgus see p. 226, note ᵇ.

ᶜ For Charidemus, leader of mercenaries, see the speech

theus, and Eudoxus,[a] and also Euthydicus, Ephialtes and Lycurgus,[b] and others you citizens have cast forth, such as Charidemus, Philocles [c] and myself, men 32 to whom not even you yourselves believe others to be superior in loyalty, though if you think certain others are equally loyal I feel no jealousy,[d] and it would be my desire, provided only that you will deal fairly with them and that they shall not meet with the treatment accorded us, that their number may be legion. When however, you give the public such object-lessons as the present, who is there who will be willing to give himself to this line of duty with sincere intentions toward you ? Yet surely you will find no dearth of 33 those who will at least pretend to do so, for in the past there has been none. Heaven forbid that I should live to see them unmasked like those men, who, though now openly pursuing policies they then repudiated, feel before none of you either fear or shame ! You should ponder these facts, men of Athens, and not treat loyal men with disdain nor be persuaded by those who are leading the country on the way to bitter hatreds and cruelty. For our 34 present difficulties require goodwill and humanity far more than dissension and malice, qualities of which some people have too great an abundance, pursuing their business [e] to your detriment with the expectation of returns, of which I pray that their

XXIII, Introduction. There is extant a speech of Deinarchus *Against Philocles*. The latter was associated with Demosthenes in admitting Harpalus to Athens with his illicit treasure. His exile was brief.

[d] This is one of several similar colloquialisms signifying " I don't mind."

[e] Antiatticista cites this passage under ἐργολάβος, Bekker's *Anecdota* i. p. 94. 3-4.

DEMOSTHENES

λογισμός. εἰ δέ τις ὑμῶν διασύρει ταῦτα, πολλῆς
ἐστιν εὐηθείας μεστός. εἰ γὰρ ἃ μηδεὶς ἂν ἤλπισ'
[1483] ὁρῶν γεγενημένα ἃ καὶ πρότερον γέγονεν τοῦ
δήμου πρὸς τοὺς ὑπὲρ αὐτοῦ λέγοντας ὑπ' ἀνθρώπων ἐγκαθέτων διαβληθέντος, νῦν μὴ ἂν οἴεται
γενέσθαι, πῶς οὐ τετύφωται;

35 Ταῦτα δ', εἰ μὲν παρῆν, λέγων ἂν ὑμᾶς ἐδίδασκον·
ἐπειδὴ δ' ἐν τοιούτοις εἰμί, ἐν οἷς εἴ τις ἐμοῦ κατ-
έψευσται ἐφ' οἷς ἀπόλωλα, γένοιτο, γράψας ἐπέσταλκα, πρῶτον μὲν καὶ πλεῖστον λόγον ποιούμενος
τοῦ καλοῦ καὶ τοῦ συμφέροντος ὑμῖν, δεύτερον δ'
ὅτι τὴν αὐτὴν εὔνοιαν, ἣν πρὸς ζῶντα Λυκοῦργον
εἶχον, δίκαιον εἶναι νομίζω καὶ πρὸς τοὺς παῖδας
36 αὐτοῦ φαίνεσθαι ἔχων. εἰ δέ τῳ παρέστηκεν ὡς
πολύ μοι περίεστι τῶν ἐμαυτοῦ πραγμάτων, οὐκ
ἂν ὀκνήσαιμι πρὸς τοῦτον εἰπεῖν, ὅτι τῶν συμφερόντων ὑμῖν καὶ τοῦ μηδένα τῶν φίλων ἐγκατα-
λείπειν, ὁμοίως ὥσπερ τῆς ἐμαυτοῦ σωτηρίας
φροντίζω. οὔκουν ἐκ τοῦ περιόντος ταῦτα ποιῶ,
ἀλλ' ἀπὸ τῆς αὐτῆς σπουδῆς καὶ προαιρέσεως καὶ
ταῦτα κἀκεῖνα μιᾷ γνώμῃ πραγματεύομαι. περίεστι
δέ μοι τοιαῦτα, οἷα τοῖς κακόν τι νοοῦσιν ὑμῖν περιγένοιτο. καὶ περὶ μὲν τούτων ἱκανά.

37 Ἡδέως δ' ἂν ὑμῖν τὴν ἐπ' εὐνοίᾳ καὶ φιλίᾳ
μέμψιν ποιησαίμην νῦν μὲν ἐν κεφαλαίῳ, μικρὸν
δ' ὕστερον δι' ἐπιστολῆς μακρᾶς, ἣν ἐάνπερ ἐγὼ

---

^a In this passage there is a running play of words based
upon the common expression ἐκ τῆς περιουσίας, " out of one's
abundance." Note περίεστι . . . ἐκ τοῦ περιόντος . . . περίεστι . . . περιγένοιτο.

calculations may cheat them. If any one of you ridicules these warnings he must be filled with a profound simplicity. For if, observing that things have happened which no one could have expected, he imagines things could not happen now which have happened already before now, when the people were set at variance with those who spoke in their behalf by men suborned for the purpose, has he not taken leave of his senses ?

If I were present in person I should be trying to 35 explain these matters to you by word of mouth, but since I am in such a plight as I pray may be the lot of anyone who has uttered falsehoods against me to my ruin, I have sent my message in the form of a letter, in the first place, having supreme regard for your honour and your advantage and, in the second, because the same goodwill that I felt toward Lycurgus during his lifetime I believe it right to show that I feel also toward his sons. If it has occurred to any- 36 one that I have a great abundance [a] of troubles of my own, I should not hesitate to say to him that I am as much concerned to defend your interests and to forsake none of my friends as I am about my own deliverance. Therefore, it is not out of the abundance of my troubles that I do this, but, actuated by one and the same earnestness and conviction, I devote my efforts to furthering both these interests of mine and those of yours with a single purpose, and the abundance I possess is of such a kind as I pray may abound for those who plot any evil against you. And on these topics I have said enough.

This complaint, inspired by goodwill and affection, 37 though now in outline only, I would gladly enlarge upon a little later in a long letter, which, if only

ζῶ προσδοκᾶτε, ἂν μὴ τὰ δίκαια γένηται[1] μοι
παρ' ὑμῶν πρότερον· οἵτινες, ὦ (τί ἂν εἰπὼν μήθ'
ἁμαρτεῖν δοκοίην μήτε ψευσαίμην;) λίαν ὀλίγωροι,
οὔτε τοὺς ἄλλους οὔθ' ὑμᾶς αὐτοὺς αἰσχύνεσθε, ἐφ'
οἷς Ἀριστογείτον' ἀφείκατε, ἐπὶ τούτοις Δημο-
38 σθένην ἐκβεβληκότες, καὶ ἃ τοῖς τολμῶσι μηδὲν
1484] ὑμῶν φροντίζειν μὴ λαβοῦσι παρ' ὑμῶν ἔξεστιν
ἔχειν, ταῦτ' οὐ διδόντες ἐμοί, ἵν', ἂν οἷός τ' ὦ, τά
τ' ὀφειλόμεν' εἰσπράξας καὶ τοὺς φίλους ἐρανίσας
τὰ πρὸς ὑμᾶς διοικήσω, καὶ μὴ γῆρας καὶ φυγὴν
ἐπίχειρα τῶν ὑπὲρ ὑμῶν πεπονημένων ἔχων, κοινὸν
ὄνειδος τῶν ἀδικησάντων, ἐπὶ ξένης περιιὼν ὁρῶ-
μαι.

39 Βουλομένου δέ μου ἐν μὲν ὑμετέρας χάριτος καὶ
μεγαλοψυχίας τάξει τὴν οἴκαδέ μοι ἄφιξιν γενέσθαι,
ἐμαυτῷ δὲ λύσιν τῆς γεγονυίας οὐ δικαίως βλασφη-
μίας πορίσασθαι, καὶ μόνον αἰτοῦντος ἄδειαν ὅσονπερ χρόνον τὴν ἔκτεισιν δεδώκατε, ταῦτα μὲν οὐ
συγχωρεῖτε, ἐρωτᾶτε δ', ὡς ἀπαγγέλλεται πρὸς
ἐμέ, τίς οὖν αὐτὸν κωλύει παρεῖναι καὶ ταῦτα
40 πράττειν; τὸ ἐπίστασθαι αἰσχύνεσθαι, ὦ ἄνδρες
Ἀθηναῖοι, καὶ τὸ ἀναξίως τῶν ὑπὲρ ὑμῶν πεπολιτευμένων πράττειν, καὶ τὸ τὰ ὄντ' ἀπολωλεκέναι
δι' οὕς, ἵνα μὴ διπλᾶ καταθῶνται ἃ οὐκ ἠδύναθ'
ἁπλᾶ, ἐπείσθην ὑπογράψασθαι τὴν ἀρχὴν τὰς κατα-

---

[1] Reading of papyrus ; γίγνηταί codd.

[a] Harpocration cites this passage under the verb ἐρανίζω.
Photius and the *Etymologicum Magnum* cite the verb only.

I am alive, you may expect, unless justice shall be done me by you before that time, you who, O—what shall I say so as to seem neither to offend nor to fall short of the truth ?—you all too unfeeling men, who neither before the rest of the world nor before yourselves feel shame, who upon the same charges upon which you acquitted Aristogeiton have banished Demosthenes, and the privileges which those who 38 dare to set your authority at naught are permitted to have without your leave you do not grant to me, to enable me, if I can, by calling in the sums owing me and levying contributions *a* upon my friends, to adjust my obligations to you and not, with old age and exile as the guerdon of my past toils in your behalf, be seen wandering from place to place on alien soil, a common reproach to all who have wronged me.

Although it was my wish that my return home 39 might come about by way of an ordinance *b* of gratitude and magnanimity on your part and that for myself I might secure a dismissal of the false charges unjustly lodged against me, asking only for immunity from imprisonment for such time as you have granted for the payment of the fine, yet these requests you do not grant, and you demand, as it is reported to me, " Well, who is preventing him from being here and transacting this business ? " It is knowing how to 40 feel shame, men of Athens, it is faring in a way unworthy of my public services in your behalf, and it is the loss of my property through those men on whose account I was persuaded in the first place to become surety for their payments in order that they might not have to pay double the sum of which

---

b Cf. XVIII. 13 ἐν ἐπηρείας τάξει καὶ φθόνου, " by way of spite and jealousy."   For the meaning cf. § 41 of this letter.

βολάς, παρ' ὧν μετὰ μὲν τῆς ὑμετέρας εὐνοίας
ἀφικόμενος μέρος, εἰ καὶ μὴ πάντ', ἴσως ἂν κο-
μισαίμην, ὥστε μηδὲν ἀσχημονεῖν τὸ λοιπὸν τοῦ
βίου, ἂν δ' ὡς οἱ ταῦτα λέγοντες ἀξιοῦσί μ' ἔλθω,
ἅμ' ἀδοξίᾳ καὶ ἀπορίᾳ καὶ φόβῳ συνέξομαι.

41 Ὧν οὐδὲν ὑμεῖς συλλογίζεσθε, ἀλλὰ ῥημάτων μοι
καὶ φιλανθρωπίας φθονοῦντες, ἂν οὕτω τύχῃ, δι'
ὑμᾶς περιόψεσθ' ἀπολόμενον· οὐ γὰρ ἂν δεηθείην
ἄλλων ἢ ὑμῶν. καὶ τότε φήσετε δεινὰ πεπονθέναι
[1485] μ', ἀκριβῶς οἶδα, ὅτ' οὔτ' ἐμοὶ πλέον οὐδὲν οὔθ'
ὑμῖν ἔσται. οὐ γὰρ δὴ χρήματά γ' εἶναί μοι
προσδοκᾶτ' ἔξω τῶν φανερῶν, ὧν ἀφίσταμαι. καὶ
τὰ λοιπὰ βούλομαι συναγαγεῖν, ἐάν μοι μὴ φιλο-
νίκως, ἀλλ' ἀνθρωπίνως δῶτε τὸ πρὸς τούτοις
42 ἀσφαλῶς εἶναι. οὐ μὴν οὐδὲ παρ' Ἁρπάλου με
λαβόντα δείξετε· οὔτε γὰρ ἠλέγχθην οὔτ' ἔλαβον.
εἰ δὲ τὸ περιφανὲς ἀξίωμα τῆς βουλῆς ἢ τὸν Ἄρειον
πάγον προσβλέπετε, τῆς Ἀριστογείτονος κρίσεως
ἀναμνησθέντες ἐγκαλύψασθε· οὐ γὰρ ἔχω πραό-
43 τερον πρόσταγμα¹ τοῖς ἐξημαρτηκόσιν εἰς ἐμέ. οὐ

¹ πρόσφθεγμα Aristeides, Blass.

ᵃ It was the law at Athens that the amount of a debt owed
to the State should be doubled if not paid when due.   Demosthenes had made a bad loan, which rendered it impossible to
pay his fine of fifty talents.
ᵇ See § 39 " by way of an ordinance of gratitude and
magnanimity on your part."
ᶜ Demosthenes was condemned to be held in prison until
his fine should be paid ; he insists that he must enjoy liberty
if he is to collect the funds necessary for payment.

they were unable to pay the original amount.[a]
From these men, could I but return with your
goodwill, I might possibly recover part, even if
not all, so as not to live sordidly the rest of my
life, but if I come on such terms as those who talk
in this way demand of me, I shall be the victim at
one and the same time of ignominy, destitution and
fear.

None of these considerations do you take into ac- 41
count but, grudging me the paltry words of a decree
and an act of kindness,[b] you will allow me to perish,
if it so happen, through your inaction, for I could
appeal to no others but you. In that day you will say
that I have been shamefully mistreated, I know for a
certainty, when it will do neither you nor myself any
good, for assuredly you do not expect that I have
funds apart from my real and personal property,
from which I am separated ; the rest of my assets I
wish to assemble if in a spirit of humanity instead of
spitefulness you will but give me leave to attend to
this business unmolested.[c] Neither will you ever show 42
that I received money from Harpalus, for neither
was I tried and proved guilty nor did I take money,
and if you are looking for excuse to the notorious
decision of the Council or to the Areopagus,[d] recall
to mind the trial of Aristogeiton[e] and hide your
heads in shame[f] ; because I have no milder injunc-
tion for those who have committed this offence against

---

[d] According to Plutarch, *Demosthenes* xxvi., the orator
himself moved that the charges should be referred to the
Areopagus, which promptly condemned him.

[e] Aristogeiton was acquitted, according to Demosthenes,
upon the same evidence. See § 37.

[f] Eight references to this passage may be found in Walz's
Rhetores Graeci, which has an index.

γὰρ δήπου τοῖς αὐτοῖς γε λόγοις, ὑπὸ τῆς αὐτῆς
βουλῆς ἀποφανθέντα, ἐκεῖνον μὲν ἀφεῖσθαι δίκαιον
εἶναι φήσετε, ἐμὲ δ' ἀπολωλέναι· οὐχ οὕτως ὑμεῖς
ἀλογίστως ἔχετε. οὔτε γὰρ ἄξιος οὔτε ἐπιτήδειος
οὔτε χείρων, ἀτυχὴς μέντοι δι' ὑμᾶς, ὁμολογῶ· πῶς
γὰρ οὐκ ἀτυχής, ᾧ πρὸς τοῖς ἄλλοις κακοῖς καὶ
πρὸς 'Αριστογείτον' ἐμαυτὸν ἐξετάζειν συμβαίνει,
καὶ ταῦτ' ἀπολωλότι πρὸς σωτηρίας τετυχηκότα;

44 Καὶ μή μ' ὑπολαμβάνετ' ὀργίζεσθαι τοῖς λόγοις
τούτοις· οὐ γὰρ ἂν πάθοιμι τοῦτο πρὸς ὑμᾶς ἐγώ·
ἀλλ' ἔχει τινὰ τοῖς ἀδικουμένοις ῥᾳστώνην τὸ λέγειν ἃ πάσχουσιν, ὥσπερ τοῖς ἀλγοῦσι τὸ στένειν,
ἐπεὶ τῇ εὐνοίᾳ γ' οὕτως ἔχω πρὸς ὑμᾶς ὡς ὑμᾶς
ἂν εὐξαίμην πρὸς ἐμέ. καὶ τοῦτ' ἐν πᾶσι πεποίηκα
45 καὶ ποιήσω φανερόν. ἔγνωκα γὰρ ἐξ ἀρχῆς παντὶ
πολιτευομένῳ προσήκειν, ἅπερ ἦ δίκαιος πολίτης,
[1486] ὥσπερ οἱ παῖδες πρὸς τοὺς γονέας, οὕτως πρὸς
ἅπαντας τοὺς πολίτας ἔχειν, εὔχεσθαι μὲν ὡς
εὐγνωμονεστάτων τυγχάνειν, φέρειν δὲ τοὺς ὄντας
εὐμενῶς· ἡ γὰρ ἐν τοῖς τοιούτοις ἧττα καλὴ καὶ
προσήκουσα νίκη παρὰ τοῖς εὖ φρονοῦσι κρίνεται.
εὐτυχεῖτε.

---

[a] This advice for children was possibly a commonplace.
It is voiced by Epicurus, *Vatican Collection* 62.

me. For surely you will not claim it was just, after 43
information was laid in the very same words by
the same Council, for that man to be exonerated
and me to be ruined ; you are not so void of reason.
For I do not deserve it ; I am not that kind of a person
nor worse than he, though I **am** unfortunate, thanks
to you, I admit, for why not unfortunate when on top
of my other calamities I must compare myself with
Aristogeiton, and to make matters worse, a ruined
man with one who has secured acquittal ?

And do not assume from these words that it is 44
anger that moves me, because I could not feel that
way toward you. To those who are wronged, however, it brings a certain relief to tell their sorrows,
just as it relieves those in pain to moan, because
toward you I feel as much goodwill as I would pray
you might have toward me. I have made this plain
in everything and shall continue to do so, for I have 45
been resolved from the beginning that it is the duty
of every man in public life, if only he be a fair-minded
citizen, so to feel toward all his fellow-citizens as
children ought to feel toward their parents, and,
while praying that he may find them perfectly reasonable, yet to bear with them in a spirit of kindliness as
they are[a] ; because defeat under such circumstances is
judged among right-minded men to be an honourable
and befitting victory. Farewell.

DEMOSTHENES

Δ

ΠΕΡΙ ΤΗΣ ΘΗΡΑΜΕΝΟΥΣ ΒΛΑΣΦΗΜΙΑΣ

ΔΗΜΟΣΘΕΝΗΣ ΤΗΙ ΒΟΥΛΗΙ ΚΑΙ ΤΩΙ ΔΗΜΩΙ ΧΑΙΡΕΙΝ

Ἀκούω περὶ ἐμοῦ Θηραμένην ἄλλους τε λόγους
βλασφήμους εἰρηκέναι καὶ δυστυχίαν προφέρειν.
τὸ μὲν οὖν τοῦτον ἀγνοεῖν ὅτι λοιδορίας, ἢ μηδεμίαν
κακίαν καθ' ὅτου λέγεται δείκνυσιν οὐδέν ἐστ'
ὄφελος παρ' εὖ φρονοῦσιν ἀνθρώποις, οὐχὶ θαυμάζω·
τὸν γὰρ θρασὺν μὲν τῷ βίῳ, μὴ πολίτην δὲ τὴν
φύσιν, ἐν ἐργαστηρίῳ δὲ τεθραμμένον ἐκ παιδός,
αἰσθάνεσθαί τι τῶν τοιούτων ἀλογώτερον ἦν ἢ μὴ
2 συνιέναι. τούτῳ μὲν οὖν, ἐὰν ἀφίκωμαί ποτε καὶ
σωθῶ, πειράσομαι διαλεχθῆναι περὶ ὧν εἰς ἐμὲ καὶ
περὶ ὧν εἰς ὑμᾶς παροινεῖ, καὶ νομίζω, καίπερ
οὐδὲν μετέχοντα τοῦ αἰσχύνεσθαι, μετριώτερον αὐτὸν ποιήσειν· ὑμῖν δὲ τοῦ κοινῇ συμφέροντος εἵνεκα
βούλομαι δι' ἐπιστολῆς οὓς περὶ τούτων ἔχω
λόγους δηλῶσαι. οἷς πάνυ τὸν νοῦν προσέχοντες
ἀκούσατε· οἶμαι γὰρ αὐτοὺς οὐκ ἀκοῆς μόνον,
ἀλλὰ καὶ μνήμης ἀξίους εἶναι.
3 Ἐγὼ τὴν πόλιν τὴν ὑμετέραν εὐτυχεστάτην
[1487] πασῶν πόλεων ὑπολαμβάνω καὶ θεοφιλεστάτην, καὶ

---

    ^a This letter is not cited in ancient authorities and there is
less likelihood of its being genuine.
    ^b There is no known connexion between this obscure man
and the Theramenes who played a conspicuous rôle during
the later years of the Peloponnesian War.
    ^c The implication is that Demosthenes was an unlucky
person who brought bad luck to the State. Deinarchus in
his speech *Against Demosthenes* 31-33 asserts that he also in-

IV

ON THE SLANDEROUS ATTACKS
OF THERAMENES [a]

*Demosthenes to the Council and the Assembly
sends greeting.*

I HEAR that Theramenes [b] has uttered various slanderous statements concerning me and in particular that he taunts me with being ill-fated.[c] Now I am not astonished that this man should be ignorant that abusive language, which demonstrates no vice on the part of the one against whom it is spoken, carries no weight with fair-minded people. For if one who in his way of life is insolent, by birth is not a citizen, and was reared from childhood in a brothel, had even a faint perception in such matters, it would be more unintelligible than complete ignorance. As for this man, 2 if some day I return and am restored to my rights, I shall plan to have a talk with him about the drunken abuse he directs at me and at you, and I believe that, even if he is devoid of shame, I shall render him more self-restrained. To you, however, in the interest of the common good, I wish to make known by letter what statements I have to make about these matters. Listen to my words with all attention, for I think they are not only worth hearing but also worth remembering.

As for me, I assume that your city is the most 3 fortunate in the world and the dearest to the gods,

volved his collaborators in his own ill luck. It may be noted that Cicero, *For the Manilian Law* x. 28, places *felicitas* on a par with *scientia rei militaris, virtus* and *auctoritas*.

ταῦτ᾽ οἶδα καὶ τὸν Δία τὸν Δωδωναῖον καὶ τὴν
Διώνην καὶ τὸν Ἀπόλλω τὸν Πύθιον ἀεὶ λέγοντας
ἐν ταῖς μαντείαις, καὶ προσεπισφραγιζομένους τὴν
ἀγαθὴν τύχην ἐν τῇ πόλει εἶναι παρ᾽ ὑμῖν. ὅσα μὲν
τοίνυν περὶ τῶν ἐπιόντων δηλοῦσιν οἱ θεοί, δῆλον
ὡς προλέγουσι· τὰς δ᾽ ἀπὸ τῶν παρεληλυθότων
προσηγορίας ἐπὶ ταῖς γεγονυίαις πράξεσιν τίθενται.
4 ἃ τοίνυν ἐγὼ πεπολίτευμαι παρ᾽ ὑμῖν, τῶν ἤδη
γεγενημένων ἐστίν, ἀφ᾽ ὧν εὐτυχεῖς ὑμᾶς προση-
γορεύκασιν οἱ θεοί. πῶς οὖν δίκαιον τοὺς μὲν
πεισθέντας εὐτυχεῖς ὀνομάζεσθαι τὸν δὲ πείσαντα
τῆς ἐναντίας προσηγορίας τυγχάνειν; πλὴν εἰ
τοῦτό τις εἴποι τὴν μὲν κοινὴν εὐτυχίαν, ἧς ἐγὼ
σύμβουλος, θεοὺς τοὺς λέγοντας εἶναι, οἷς οὐ θέμις
ψεύδεσθαι, τὴν δ᾽ ἰδίαν βλασφημίαν, ἧ κατ᾽ ἐμοῦ
κέχρηται Θηραμένης, θρασὺν καὶ ἀναιδῆ καὶ οὐδὲ
νοῦν ἔχοντ᾽ ἄνθρωπον εἰρηκέναι.

5 Οὐ τοίνυν μόνον ταῖς παρὰ τῶν θεῶν μαντείαις
ἀγαθὴν οὖσαν εὑρήσεθ᾽ ᾗ κέχρησθε τύχῃ, ἀλλὰ καὶ
ἐξ αὐτῶν τῶν ἔργων θεωροῦντες, ἂν ἐξετάζητ᾽
ὀρθῶς. ὑμεῖς γὰρ εἰ μὲν ὡς ἄνθρωποι τὰ πράγματα
βούλεσθε θεωρεῖν, εὐτυχεστάτην εὑρήσετ᾽ ἀφ᾽ ὧν
ἐγὼ συνεβούλευσα τὴν πόλιν γεγονυῖαν· εἰ δ᾽ ἃ
τοῖς θεοῖς ἐξαίρεθ᾽ ὑπάρχει μόνοις, τοῦτον ἀξιώσετε
6 τυγχάνειν, ἀδυνάτων ἐφίεσθε. τί οὖν ἐστι θεοῖς
ἐξαίρετον ἀνθρώποις δ᾽ οὐ δυνατόν; ἁπάντων τῶν
ἀγαθῶν ἐγκρατεῖς ὄντας κυρίους εἶναι καὶ αὐτοὺς
ἔχειν καὶ δοῦναι τοῖς ἄλλοις, φλαῦρον δὲ μηδὲν
[1488] μηδέποτ᾽ ἐν παντὶ τῷ αἰῶνι μήτε παθεῖν μήτε

---

[a] At the shrine of Zeus at Dodona in Epirus it was Dionê,
and not Hera, who was regarded as his consort. Elsewhere
Dionê was identified with Aphroditê or Venus.
258

and I know that Zeus of Dodona and Dionê [a] and the Pythian Apollo are always saying this in their oracles and confirming with the seal of their approval the opinion that good fortune has her abode in the city among you. Note that when the gods reveal something to happen in future, that is obviously prophecy. When, however, their terms reflect past events, they mean them to refer to the past. Now, what I have 4 done as a public man among you belongs in the class of events already past, on the ground of which the gods have bestowed upon you the epithet fortunate. How, then, is it fair for those who followed advice to be denominated fortunate but the adviser to receive the opposite epithet ? Unless someone should give this explanation, that for the common good fortune, of which I was the counsellor, it is the gods who vouch, and to think they lie would be sacrilege, but that the personal slander, which Theramenes has directed against me, it is an insolent, shameless and not even intelligent person who has uttered.

Now, it is not only by the words of the oracles 5 coming from the gods that you will find the fortune you have enjoyed to be good but also by viewing it in the light of the facts themselves, if you will scan them rightly. For if as human beings you are willing to regard our affairs, you will find that our city, as a result of the policy I advised, has been very fortunate, but if you shall demand to receive those blessings which are reserved for the gods alone, you aim at the impossible. What, then, is reserved for gods but for 6 men is impossible ? To be in absolute control of all the blessings there are, both to possess them themselves and to bestow them upon others, and never in all eternity either to suffer anything bad or to look

μελλῆσαι. καὶ μὴν ὑποκειμένων τούτων, ὥσπερ
προσήκει, σκοπεῖτε τὰ ὑμέτερ' αὐτῶν πρὸς τὰ τῶν
7 ἄλλων ἀνθρώπων. οὐδεὶς γὰρ οὕτως ἐστὶν ἀγνώμων ὅστις ἂν ἢ τὰ Λακεδαιμονίοις συμβεβηκότα,
οἷς οὐκ ἐγὼ συνεβούλευον, ἢ τὰ Πέρσαις, πρὸς οὓς
οὐδ' ἀφικόμην πώποτε, αἱρετώτερα φήσειεν εἶναι
τῶν ὑμῖν παρόντων. καὶ ἐῶ Καππαδόκας καὶ
Σύρους καὶ τοὺς τὴν Ἰνδικὴν χώραν κατοικοῦντας
ἀνθρώπους ἐπ' ἔσχατα γῆς, οἷς ἅπασι συμβέβηκε
8 πολλὰ καὶ δεινὰ πεπονθέναι καὶ χαλεπά. ἀλλὰ νὴ
Δία τούτων μὲν ἄμεινον ὑμᾶς πράττειν ἅπαντες
ὁμολογήσουσι, Θετταλῶν δὲ καὶ Ἀργείων καὶ Ἀρ-
κάδων χεῖρον, ἤ τινων ἄλλων, οἷς ἐν συμμαχίᾳ
συνέβη γενέσθαι Φιλίππῳ. ἀλλὰ τούτων καὶ πολὺ
βέλτιον ἀπηλλάχατε, οὐ μόνον τῷ μὴ δεδουλευκέναι
(καίτοι τί τηλικοῦθ' ἕτερον;), ἀλλὰ καὶ τῷ τοὺς μὲν
πάντας αἰτίους εἶναι δοκεῖν τῶν τοῖς Ἕλλησι κακῶν
συμβεβηκότων διὰ Φιλίππου καὶ τῆς δουλείας, ἐξ
9 ὧν εἰκότως μισοῦνται, ὑμᾶς δ' ὁρᾶσθαι ὑπὲρ τῶν
Ἑλλήνων καὶ σώμασι καὶ χρήμασι καὶ πόλει καὶ
χώρᾳ καὶ πᾶσιν ἠγωνισμένους, ἀνθ' ὧν εὔκλειαν
εἰκὸς ὑπάρχειν καὶ χάριν ἀθάνατον παρὰ τῶν τὰ
δίκαια βουλομένων ποιεῖν. οὐκοῦν ἀφ' ὧν ἐγὼ
συνεβούλευσα, τῶν μὲν ἀντιστάντων ἄριστα πράττειν τῇ πόλει συμβέβηκε, τῶν δὲ συνηγωνισμένων
ἐνδοξοτέραν εἶναι περίεστι.
10 Τοιγαροῦν ἐπὶ τούτοις οἱ θεοὶ τὰς μὲν μαντείας
τὰς ἀγαθὰς ὑμῖν διδόασι, τὴν δ' ἄδικον βλασφημίαν
εἰς κεφαλὴν τῷ λέγοντι τρέπουσι. γνοίη δ' ἄν τις,

forward to suffering it. Next, these propositions
having been laid down, as is proper, scan your blessings in comparison with those of the rest of mankind.
No one, for instance, is so foolish as to assert that 7
what has befallen either the Spartans, whom I never
advised, or the Persians, whom I never even visited,
is preferable to your present lot. I pass over the
Cappadocians, the Syrians, and the beings who in-
habit the land of India toward the ends of the earth,
all of whom have had the misfortune to suffer many
terrible and grievous afflictions. O yes, by Zeus, all 8
will agree that you are faring better than these, but
worse, they declare, than the Thessalians, Argives
and Arcadians, or certain others, who had the luck to
be in alliance with Philip. But you have come off far
better than these, not only because you have not been
reduced to slavery—and yet what blessing equals
that ?—but also because, while all those are thought
to be responsible for the evils that have befallen the
Greeks through Philip and their enslavement, in
consequence of which they are hated with good
reason, you are seen to have struggled in defence of 9
the Greeks at the expense of your lives, your property, your city, your territory and all you possess,
in return for which you are entitled to glory and
undying gratitude from all lovers of justice. Therefore, as a result of the counsels I gave, it has been the
city's good fortune to fare best of all the states that
resisted Philip and there is the added gain of standing
in higher repute than those who co-operated with
him.

On these grounds, therefore, the gods, while giving 10
favourable oracles to you, are turning back the unjust
slander upon the head of him who utters it, and any

DEMOSTHENES

[1489] εἰ προέλοιτ᾿ ἐξετάσαι τἀπιτηδεύματ᾿ ἐν οἷς ζῇ. ἃ
γὰρ ἂν καταράσαιτό τις αὑτῷ, ταῦτ᾿ ἐκ προαιρέ-
11 σεως ποιεῖ. ἐχθρὸς μέν ἐστι τοῖς γονεῦσι, φίλος
δὲ Παυσανίᾳ τῷ πόρνῳ· καὶ θρασύνεται μὲν ὡς
ἀνήρ, πάσχει δ᾿ ὡς γυνή· καὶ τοῦ μὲν πατρός ἐστι
κρείττων, τῶν δ᾿ αἰσχρῶν ἥττων· οἷς δ᾿ ὑπὸ πάντων δυσχεραίνεται, τούτοις τὴν διάνοιαν ἀγάλλεται,
αἰσχρορρημοσύνῃ καὶ τῷ διηγεῖσθαι ταῦτ᾿ ἐφ᾿ οἷς
ἀλγοῦσ᾿ οἱ ἀκούοντες· ὁ δ᾿, ὡς ἀφελὴς καὶ παρρη-
12 σίας μεστός, οὐ παύεται. καὶ ταῦτ᾿ οὐκ ἂν ἔγραψα
εἰ μὴ κινῆσαι τὴν ἐν ὑμῖν μνήμην τῶν προσόντων
αὐτῷ κακῶν ἐβουλόμην. ἃ γὰρ εἰπεῖν ἄν τις ὀκνή-
σαι καὶ γράψαι φυλάξαιτ᾿ ἄν, οἶμαι δὲ κἂν ἀκού-
σαντα δυσχερᾶναι, ταῦτ᾿ ἀπὸ τούτων μνησθεὶς οἶδεν
ἕκαστος ὑμῶν πολλὰ καὶ δεινὰ καὶ αἰσχρὰ τούτῳ
προσόντα, ὥστ᾿ ἐμοί τε μηδὲν ἀναιδὲς εἰρῆσθαι, καὶ
τοῦτον ὑπόμνημα τῶν ἑαυτοῦ κακῶν ὀφθέντα πᾶσιν
εἶναι. εὐτυχεῖτε.

Ε

ΠΡΟΣ ΗΡΑΚΛΕΟΔΩΡΟΝ

ΔΗΜΟΣΘΕΝΗΣ ΗΡΑΚΛΕΟΔΩΡΩΙ ΕΥ ΠΡΑΤΤΕΙΝ

Οὔθ᾿ ὅπως χρὴ πιστεύειν οἷς ἀπήγγελλέ μοι
Μενεκράτης, οὔθ᾿ ὅπως ἀπιστεῖν ἔχω. ἔφη γὰρ

---

[a] Blass, who is inclined to reject this letter, calls attention
to the Gorgianic antitheses in the preceding passage.

[b] Schaefer judges the evidence against the genuineness of
these last two letters to be decisive. If this one be genuine,
it must be assumed that Heracleodorus is a citizen of some

man would recognize the facts if he chose to examine the practices in which he spends his life. For instance, he does by preference the very things that one might invoke upon him as a curse. He is an enemy to his 11 own parents but a friend to Pausanias the whore-monger, and though he swaggers like a man he allows himself to be used like a woman. He lords it over his own father but submits to degenerates. He regales his fancy with things by which all are disgusted, with foul language and with stories by which his hearers are pained ; yet he never ceases to talk, as if he were a simple fellow and the soul of frankness.[a] I would 12 not have written this had I not wished to stir in you the recollection of the vices that attach to him. For many terrible and shameful things, which a man would shrink from telling and would guard against mention-ing in writing and, as I think, would be disgusted to hear of, each one of you, reminded by these words, knows to attach to this man, so that nothing indecent has been uttered by me and this man upon sight is a reminder to all of his own vices. Farewell.

V

TO HERACLEODORUS [b]

Demosthenes sends his good wishes to Heracleodorus.

I AM at a loss to know whether I ought to believe or disbelieve the news that Menecrates brings me. For

neighbouring city, such as Corinth, because Demosthenes would have no need to write to a fellow-citizen of Athens.

DEMOSTHENES

Ἐπίτιμον ἐνδεδεῖχθαι μὲν καὶ ἀπῆχθαι ὑπ' Ἀρά-
[1490] του, σὲ δ' ἀγωνίζεσθαι καὶ ἁπάντων αὐτῷ χαλεπώ-
τατον εἶναι. δέομαι δή σου πρὸς Διὸς ξενίου καὶ
πάντων τῶν θεῶν, μή με καταστήσῃς ἀηδεῖ καὶ
2 δεινῷ μηδενὶ περιπετῆ. εὖ γὰρ ἴσθι, χωρὶς τοῦ
μέλειν μοι τῆς Ἐπιτίμου σωτηρίας, καὶ νομίσαι
μεγάλην ἂν συμφορὰν εἴ τι πάθοι καὶ τούτου σὺ
συναίτιος εἴης, αἰσχύνομαι τοὺς συνειδότας μοι τοὺς
λόγους οὓς ἐγὼ περὶ σοῦ πρὸς ἅπαντας ἀνθρώπους ἔλεγον, πεπεικὼς ἐμαυτὸν ἀληθῆ λέγειν, οὐκ
3 ἐκ τοῦ πεπλησιακέναι σοι πεῖραν ἔχων, ἀλλ' ὁρῶν
ὅτι δόξης ἐπιτυγχάνων καὶ παιδείαν ἀπεδέχου, καὶ
ταῦτα τὴν ἀπὸ τῆς Πλάτωνος διατριβῆς, ἥπερ
ἐστὶν ὡς ἀληθῶς τῶν μὲν πλεονεκτημάτων καὶ
τῶν περὶ ταῦτα σοφισμάτων ἔξω, τοῦ βελτίστου
δὲ καὶ τοῦ δικαιοτάτου πάνθ' ἕνεκ' ἐξητασμένη· ἧς
μὰ τοὺς θεοὺς τῷ μετασχόντι μὴ οὐχὶ ἀψευδεῖν
καὶ πρὸς ἅπαντ' ἀγαθῷ εἶναι οὐχ ὅσιον ἡγοῦμαι.
4 γένοιτο δ' ἄν μοι κἀκεῖνο τῶν χαλεπωτάτων εἰ,
παρωρμηκὼς ἐμαυτὸν εὐνοϊκῶς ἔχειν σοι, τὴν ἐναντίαν γνώμην μεταλαβεῖν ἀναγκασθείην, ἂν δ' ὑπολαμβάνω παρεωρᾶσθαι καὶ πεφενακίσθαι, κἂν μὴ
5 φῶ, νόμιζ' οὕτως ἕξειν. εἰ δ' ἡμῶν καταπεφρό-
νηκας, ὅτι τῶν πρώτων οὐκ ἐσμέν πω, λόγισαι ὅτι
καὶ σύ ποτ' ἦσθα νέος καὶ τὴν ἡλικίαν εἶχες ἣν

---

[a] The persons here named are citizens of some neighbouring city and otherwise unknown.

[b] The reference is to the sophists, professional teachers who
undertook to prepare their pupils for worldly success.

[c] If the letter is genuine, this evidence of date would point
approximately to 355 B.C. The *First Philippic* was delivered
in 351.

he said that information had been laid against Epitimus, that Aratus [a] had taken him to prison and that you were supporting the prosecution and were the most uncompromising of all toward him. I do beseech you in the name of Zeus the god of friendship and by all the gods not to get me involved in any disagreeable and embarrassing predicament. For be well assured that, apart from my concern for 2 the safety of Epitimus and my belief that it will be a great misfortune if anything should happen to him and you should be partly responsible for it, I am ashamed to face people who are familiar with the reports I have been making to everybody concerning yourself. I was convinced that I spoke the truth, not because I possessed confirmation from having associated with you, but because I observed 3 that, while gaining some renown, you were also glad to have an education, and that too in the school of Plato, the one that really has nothing to do with getting the better of people and the quackeries [b] that concern themselves with this, but has been demonstrated to aim at the highest excellence and perfect justice in all things. By the gods I swear that it is impious for a man who has shared in this instruction not to be free from all deception and honest in all dealings. It would also be to me one of the 4 most grievous disappointments if, after having started out to feel friendly toward you, I should be compelled to take the opposite decision instead, and if I assume that I have been slighted and deceived, even if I shall deny it, believe me, it will be so. If you have looked 5 down upon us because we are not yet among the foremost men,[c] reflect that you too were once a young man of the same age as we are now, and that you have

ἡμεῖς νῦν, ἐκ δὲ τοῦ συμβουλεύειν καὶ πράττειν
γεγένησαι τηλικοῦτος. κἂν ἡμῖν τοῦτο συμβαίη·
τὸ μὲν γὰρ εὖ βουλεύεσθαι πάρεστι τῆς δὲ τύχης
συλλαμβανούσης καὶ τοὖργον γένοιτ᾽ ἄν.

[1491] ⁶ Καλὸς οὖν ἔρανος χάρις δικαία· ἦν καὶ σὺ ποίησαι
πρὸς ἐμέ. καὶ μηδ᾽ ὑφ᾽ ἑνὸς τῶν σοῦ φρονούντων
χεῖρον ἄγου μηδ᾽ ἡττῶ, ἀλλ᾽ ἐκείνους ἄγ᾽ ἐπὶ τὰ
σοὶ δοκοῦντα· καὶ πρᾶττε οὕτως ὅπως μηδενὸς
τῶν ὁμολογηθέντων στερηθῶμεν, ἀλλ᾽ Ἐπιτίμῳ
γένηται σωτηρία τις καὶ ἀπαλλαγὴ τῶν κινδύνων.
παρέσομαι δ᾽ εἰς τὸν χρόνον κἀγὼ καθ᾽ ὃν ἂν σὺ
φῇς καιρὸν εἶναι. γράψας δέ μοι πέμψον ἢ καὶ ὡς
φίλῳ ἐπίστελλε. εὐτύχει.

ς¹

ΠΡΟΣ ΤΗΝ ΒΟΥΛΗΝ ΚΑΙ ΤΟΝ ΔΗΜΟΝ
ΤΟΝ ΑΘΗΝΑΙΩΝ

ΔΗΜΟΣΘΕΝΗΣ ΤΗΙ ΒΟΥΛΗΙ ΚΑΙ ΤΩΙ ΔΗΜΩΙ ΧΑΙΡΕΙΝ

Ἦλθεν ἐπιστολὴ παρ᾽ Ἀντιφίλου πρὸς τοὺς τῶν
συμμάχων συνέδρους, τοῖς μὲν βουλομένοις ἀγαθὰ

<hr>

¹ Lacking in the best ms.

^a Deinarchus in his speech *Against Demosthenes* 35 may
be making a taunting reference to this boast.

^b This looks like a proverbial expression. The reference
is either to a favour conferred by Demosthenes and not
mentioned here or to the good opinion he claims to have
expressed.

^c Schaefer thinks this letter to be the work of a scribe in
the council of the Greek allies.

reached your present position through speech and action in public life. Such success may attend me also. For deliberative oratory I have mastered already [a] and, with Fortune lending a hand, the practical experience also may follow.

Now a fine tribute, a just return.[b] Please make 6 me this recompense. Neither allow yourself to be led by one of those whose judgement is inferior to your own nor submit to them, but try to bring those men around to your way of thinking, and so conduct yourself that we may not have to give up any of our judgements of you that were assumed to be true, but that for Epitimus some deliverance may be found and release from his perils. I too shall be on hand at whatever time you shall say is the fitting moment. Send me a written message or rather command me as a friend. Farewell.

VI

TO THE COUNCIL AND THE ASSEMBLY OF THE ATHENIANS [c]

Demosthenes to the Council and the Assembly sends greeting.

A LETTER has come from Antiphilus [d] to the councillors of the allies,[e] which, while satisfactorily phrased for

[d] From Plutarch's *Phocion* 24 we learn that Antiphilus was commanding the army of the allies besieging Antipater in Lamia, winter of 323–322 B.C.

[e] The council of the allies is thought to have been meeting at Phylê in northern Attica.

DEMOSTHENES

προσδοκᾶν ἱκανῶς γεγραμμένη, τοῖς δ' ὑπηρετοῦσιν
'Αντιπάτρῳ πολλοὺς καὶ δυσχερεῖς ἀπολείπουσα
λόγους, οἳ παραλαβόντες τὰ παρ' 'Αντιπάτρου
γράμματα πρὸς Δείναρχον εἰς Κόρινθον ἐλθόντα,
ἁπάσας τὰς ἐν Πελοποννήσῳ πόλεις τοιούτων
λόγων ἔπλησαν οἵων εἰς κεφαλὴν αὐτῶν τρέψειαν
2 οἱ θεοί. ἀφικομένου δὲ τοῦ νῦν ἥκοντος μετὰ τοῦ
παρ' ἐμοῦ φέροντος γράμματα παρὰ Πολεμαίστου[1]
[1492] πρὸς τὸν ἀδελφὸν 'Επίνικον, ἄνδρ' ὑμῖν εὔνουν καὶ
ἐμοὶ φίλον, κἀκείνου πρὸς ἔμ' ἀγαγόντος, ἀκού-
σαντί μοι ἃ ἔλεγεν ἐδόκει πρὸς ὑμᾶς αὐτὸν ἀπο-
στεῖλαι, ὅπως πάντα σαφῶς ἀκούσαντες τὰ ἐν τῷ
στρατοπέδῳ γεγονότα τοῦ περὶ τὴν μάχην παρα-
γεγενημένου, τό τ' εἰς τὸ παρὸν θαρρῆτε καὶ τὰ
λοιπὰ τῶν θεῶν θελόντων ὡς βούλεσθ' ἕξειν ὑπο-
λαμβάνητε. εὐτυχεῖτε.

[1] Πολεμαρέτου var. lect.

[a] Deinarchus, youngest of the ten Attic orators, was opposed to Demosthenes and favoured Macedon. His speech
accusing Demosthenes of receiving twenty talents from Har-

those who wish to have good news in prospect, leaves many items unacceptable to those who toady to Antipater. These men, taking along with them the dispatch from Antipater that came to Corinth addressed to Deinarchus,[a] have filled all the cities in the Peloponnesus with such reports as I pray that the gods may turn back upon their own heads. The man who now 2 presents himself to you along with the bearer of this letter from me, having come from Polemaestus to the latter's brother Epinicus,[b] a man well disposed toward you and a friend of mine. was by him in turn brought to me. After I heard his story it seemed to me best to send him to you in order that, having heard a clear account of all that had happened in the camp from one who was present in the battle, you may be of good cheer for the present and assume that, the gods being willing, the final outcome will be as you wish. Farewell.

palus is extant. At the date of this letter he was in exile at Corinth, his birthplace.

[b] It may be assumed that Polemaestus was in the camp of the allies before Lamia and that his brother was attending the council of the allies in Phylê.

GENERAL INDEX

(References are to volume, page, and section.)

271

Cephisophon **5**. 185. 8, 247. 5

Amphictyons, council of Greek states : suit brought against Spartans after Plataea 479 B.C., **6**. 427. 98 ; jurisdiction over temple of Apollo at Delos **2**. 107. 134 ; sacrifices afford sanctuary to slayer of murderer **3**. 237-241. 37-43 ; self-styled Amphictyons not to be provoked **1**. 111. 14 ; met at Delphi **1**. 117. 23 ; meeting at Thermopylae restored to Thessalians by Philip **1**. 137. 22 ; intruded by P. **1**. 321. 4 ; war provoked by Aeschines **2**. 115. 143 ; cause of war **2**. 119. 151 ; resolutions *re* encroachments of Amphissians **2**. 121. 154-155 ; appointed P. general **2**. 123. 155 ; membership sought by P. **2**. 315. 111 ; made war upon Amphissians, charged with having tilled land consecrated to Apollo **2**. 119. 149 f.

Amphilochus, ambassador of Philip, arrested by Diopeithes **1**. 337. 3

Amphiones, heroes : offering prescribed by Delphi as expiation **5**. 105. 66

Amphipolis, Athenian dependency in Thrace, often mentioned in speeches on policy **1**. 7. 5, 9. 8, 21. 27, 25. 6, 75. 12, 163. 23, **2**. 61. 69, 261. 22, 385. 220, 409. 253 f., 461. 326, **3**. 291. 111, 295. 116, 317. 150, 359. 208 ; Athenian claim waived in Peace of 346 B.C., **1**. 117. 25 ; surrendered to Athens by Persia **2**. 333. 137 ; alleged to have been first occupied by Alexander, ancestor of Philip **1**. 347. 21

Amphissa, town near Delphi ; inhabitants alleged to have tilled land consecrated to Apollo, causing Sacred War **2**. 119. 150

Amphissian War, see Amphictyons

ready to serve Athens against Philip **3**. 347. 189

Archedemus, his s., swindled by Stephanus **5**. 227. 70

Archelaüs, f. of Deinomenes **6**. 447. 123

Archeneüs, money-lender, one of three arbitrators for Dem. **4**. 123. 58, **6**. 15. 13, 25. 28

Archenomides, s. of Archedamas, depository of agreements **4**. 285. 14

Archenomides, s. of Strato, deponent **4**. 301. 34

Archepolis of Peiraeus, borrowed money **6**. 117. 20

Archestratus, banker **4**. 353. 43, 355. 45, 357. 48

Archiades, s. of Euthymachus, his estate XLIV : **5**. 123-169

Archiades, s. of Mnesonidas, affidavit of **4**. 291. 20 ; lived in Salamis **5**. 137. 18

Archias, hierophant of Eleusis, convicted of impiety **6**. 441. 116

Archias of Cholargus, member of Council 356 B.C., **3**. 183. 40

Archidamus, king of Sparta, at Plataea **6**. 427. 98

Archidemus of Anaphlystus, money-lender **6**. 17. 17

Archidicê, d. of Euthymachus **5**. 131. 9

Archimachus, g.f. of deponent **5**. 83. 37

Archinus, occupied Phylê **3**. 461. 135 ; descendants honoured **7**. 239. 19

Archippê, widow of Pasion XXXVI : **4**. 319-367 *passim*

Archippus of Myrrhinus, surety for Parmeno **4**. 213. 15, 217. 22

Archippus, s. of Euthymachus, lost life at Methymna **5**. 131. 9

archons, nine : new citizens not eligible **6**. 435. 106 ; wear crown as sign of inviolability **6**. 311. 27 ; scrutiny of **6**. 283. 70 ; initiate procedure in cases of murder **3**. 231. 28 ; have jurisdiction over

GENERAL INDEX

Aristocles of Myrrhinus, member of commission of investigation **3**. 419. 71

Aristocles of Oea, private arbitrator **4**. 211. 14-21, 225. 31-34

Aristocles of Paeania, witness **3**. 115. 168

Aristocrates, boon companion **4**. 439. 27 ; one of the Triballi **6**. 155. 39

Aristocrates of Phalerum, surety for Neaera **6**. 381. 40

Aristocrates, s. of Scelius, fine record in war **6**. 341. 67

Aristodemus, actor, agent of Philip **2**. 309. 97 ; member of first embassy to P. **2**. 455. 315 ; acted in Sophocles' *Antigonê* **2**. 403. 246 ; first to raise question of peace in Amphipolitan War **2**. 31. 21 ; proposed peace with P. **2**. 253. 12, 257. 18

Aristodemus, f. of speaker in XLIV : **5**. 123-124 ; herald at the Peiraeus **5**. 129. 4

Aristogeiton, defendant in XXV-XXVI : **3**. 514-593 ; in pay of Philip's agents **3**. 537. 37 ; in gaol swallows a man's nose **3**. 553. 60-62 ; imprisoned **7**. 237. 16 ; acquitted by Areopagus of same charges as those on which Dem. was exiled **7**. 251. 37 ; the trial shameful **7**. 253. 42

Aristogeiton, tyrannicide **1**. 503. 18, **3**. 117. 170 ; immunity from liturgies granted to descendants **1**. 513. 29

Aristogenes, witness **5**. 9. 8

Aristolaüs of Thasos, enemy of Athens **2**. 151. 197

Aristolochus, s. of Charidemus, banker, lost property **4**. 357. 50, **5**. 221-223. 63-64

Aristomachus, s. of Critodemus, agent of Cersobleptes and Charidemus **3**. 221. 13, 291. 110 ; witness **6**. 317-319. 35, 369. 25 ; thesmothete **6**. 401. 65

GENERAL INDEX

free-lance, formed co-
alition with Thracian
kings Berisades and
Amadocus 3. 219. 10,
333. 170, 347. 189 ;
mention 3. 299. 123

Athens, traditions and
national character (for
criticism see Atheni-
ans) : 1. 203. 49, 327.
16, 367. 21-22, 371. 26,
433. 35, 499. 11-12, 501.
13, 2. 59. 66, 3. 207. 76-
77, 351. 196 f., 357.
206 f., 433. 91 f. ; well-
stocked markets 1. 211.
67, 309. 69 ; freedom
of speech 1. 227. 3 ;
received Corinthian
exiles 1. 527. 54 ; con-
trasted with Thebes 1.
563-565. 109-111 ; con-
trasted with Sparta 1.
563. 106-108 ; supre-
macy of the people 1.
563. 107-108 ; glory of
democracy 3. 207. 76,
491. 184-185 ; wealth
1. 15. 19 ; citizens
more ready of speech
than other Greeks 1.
331. 23 ; Pythian A-
pollo, ancestral divinity
2. 113. 141 ; autoch-

thonous 7. 9. 4 ; saved
the Heracleidae 7. 13.
8 ; superior to Greeks
at Troy 7. 15. 10 ; re-
pulsed the Persians
single-handed 7. 13.
10 ; aided Plataeans 6.
429. 100; deserve glory
from lovers of justice 7.
261. 9 ; their lot pre-
ferable to that of the
Spartans and others 7.
261. 7 ; finances, re-
form suggested by
Dem. 1. 63. 34-36 ;
XIII : 1. 352-377 ; a-
mount of revenue 1.
291. 37-38 ; raising of
deficiency revenues 3.
435. 96 f. ; donations 2.
93-95. 113-116 ; under
the Empire 10,000 tal-
ents 1. 57. 24 ; foreign
policy (general) : hege-
mony in Greece 1. 237.
23-24 ; champion of
Greece and Panhelle-
nism 1. 247-249. 41-46 ;
Athenian tradition of
liberty a menace to
Philip 2. 83. 100 ; bal-
ance of power in Greece
and Thrace 3. 285. 102-
103 ; public works and

119. 25 ; detained Phormio's ships **5**. 223. 64 ; attacked by Philip to shut off Athenian grain **2**. 73. 87, 75. 90 ; interfered with grain-ships bound for the Peiraeus **6**. 9. 6, 17. 17 ; recorder eponymous official **2**. 75. 90 ; to be detested by Athenians **7**. 125. 3

Cabylê, town in Thrace **1**. 199. 44 ; wretched place **1**. 279. 15

Cadmus, f. of Semelê **7**. 29. 30

Calauria, mod. Poros, island off N.E. Peloponnesus, army of Timotheüs in dire straits there **5**. 383. 13 ; refuge of Dem. in exile, temple of Poseidon **7**. 221. 20

Calchedon, see Chalcedon

Callaeschrus, s. of Diotimus, ambassador to Thebes **2**. 145. 187 ; wealthy citizen **3**. 109. 157

Callarus, slave of speaker, suit against **6**. 185. 31-32, 187. 33-34

Callias, hangman, **ban**ished from Athens, welcomed by Philip **1**. 33. 19

Callias of Chalcis, served as Athenian general **1**. 337. 5

Callias of Phrearii, proposed crowns for Charidemus, Diotimus, Nausicles **2**. 95. 115

Callias of Sunium, witness for Dem. **2**. 109. 135

Callias, s. of Hipponicus, negotiated peace of 448 B.C., **2**. 425. 273

Callicles, defendant in LV : **6**. 164-187

Callicles, sailor, s. of Epitrephes **6**. 37. 47-49

Callicrates, b. of Callicles **6**. 167. 2

Callicrates, s. of Eupherus **3**. 195. 60

Callippides, f. of Callicles **6**. 167. 3

Callippus, f. of Phaenippus **5**. 45. 21

Callippus of Aexonê, figured in an incident **6**. 37 ff. 47 ff. ; claimed half the estate of Comon **5**. 351. 29 ; in Sicily **4**. 361. 53

GENERAL INDEX

313

GENERAL INDEX

Eëtioneia, Peiraean fort
6. 341. 67

Egypt, reduced by Pers.
king **1**. 339. 6 ; part of
Pers. Empire **1**. 415. 5 ;
in revolt **1**. 401. 31 ;
successes of Chabrias
in **1**. 543. 76 ; embassy
to **3**. 455. 127 ; in grain-
trade LVI : **6**. 191-227
passim

Eïon, near Amphipolis,
war at **1**. 369. 23, **3**.
353. 199

eisangelia, impeachment :
Hypereides *vs.* Philo-
crates **2**. 319. 116 ;
procedure **5**. 301-303.
42 - 43, **2**. 183 - 185.
250

ejectment (*exoulē*), suit
for XXX-XXXI : **4**.
127-171

Elaeus, member of con-
federacy in Chersonese
2. 77. 92 ; Athenian
stronghold **3**. 323. 158

Elatea, Elean colony in
Cassopia, Epirus **1**. 167.
32

Elatea, in Phocis, seized
by Philip **2**. 121. 152,
133. 169 ; reaction at
Athens **2**. 133-141. 169-
180 ; reported forti-
fied by P. **1**. 133.
15

Eleusinian Mysteries,
celebrated in month
Boëdromion **1**. 45. 5 ;
laws regarding **3**. 121.
175

Eleusis, deme of Hippo-
thontis **3**. 543. 44, **5**.
131. 9, 137. 17, 159. 52 ;
locality : one of 5
strongholds outside
Athens and Peiraeus
2. 43. 38 ; floods **6**. 183.
28 ; mansion of Mei-
dias **3**. 109. 158 ; harvest festival **6**. 443.
116

Eleven, the board re-
sponsible for prisons
and corporal punish-
ments **3**. 189. 49, 425.
80, 441. 105, 467. 146,
477. 162, **4**. 309. 47, **6**.
117. 23, 119. 24 ; bring
impeached persons into
court **3**. 415. 63

Elis, in Pelopon., occu-
pied by Philip **1**. 239-
241. 27 ; massacres in
1. 275. 10 ; Spartans
propose restoration of
territory **1**. 449. 16

317

329

GENERAL INDEX

Isocrates, orator **4**. 287.
15 ; friend of Lysi-
theides **6**. 83. 14 ;
teacher of Timotheüs
7. 73. 46

isonomia, equality before
the law **3**. 51. 67 ;
established by Theseus
7. 27-29. 28 and note *a*

Isthmias, slave girl of
Nicaretê **6**. 365. 19

Ithyphalli, obscene name
adopted by gangsters
6. 139. 14, 141. 16-17,
143. 20

Jason, tyrant of Pherae
in Thessaly **5**. 383. 10

jeopardy, double, forbid-
den by law **1**. 589. 147

judgement granted **6**.
111. 15

judges (see Thesmothe-
tae), in festival con-
tests **4**. 455. 10

jurors, dicasts, selected
by lot **2**. 247. 1 ; sworn
to impartiality **2**. 19. 2,
23. 7, 247. 1 ; fee 4
obols, formerly 3, **7**.
185. 4 ; funds lacking
4. 461. 17 ; vote twice,
on guilt, on penalty **3**.
567. 83 ; assent to de-

cisions of **Areopagus 7**.
211. 1

Justice (Dikê), personi-
fied abstraction **3**. 521.
11, 537. 35

king archon, history of
the office **6**. 407-409.
74-76 ; received infor-
mation concerning im-
piety **3**. 175. 27, **4**. 309.
47 ; in charges of mur-
der **5**. 321. 70 ; his
power to appoint **4**.
455. 9 ; wife is bride
of Dionysus **6**. 407.
73 ; incumbents : Eu-
ctemon **5**. 87. 42 f. ;
Theogenes **6**. 437. 110

King's Portico, Court of
Areopagus in **3**. 529. 23

Lacedaemonians,   see
Spartans

Lacedaemonius, brother
of Satyrus **6**. 385. 45 ;
his sister indicted for
impiety **6**. 237. 8

Laches, f. of Melanopus
3. 455. 127

Laches, s. of Melanopus,
of Aexonê, fine re-
mitted at Alexander's

336

413. 3 ; embassy to **3**. 379. 12

mayhem, action, why instituted **6**. 141. 18

Medeius, f. of Eurydamas **6**. 435. 108

Megacleides of Eleusis **6**. 87. 20

Megalopolis, capital of Arcadia XVI : **1**. 437-459 ; its legislative body of 10,000, **2**. 253. 11, 373. 198 ; counterpoise to Sparta **1**. 457. 30 ; Aeschines made speech at **2**. 253. 11 ; allied with Philip fared better than Athens **7**. 261. 8

Megara, threatened by Philip **1**. 187. 18 ; controlled by P. **1**. 235. 18 ; attacked by P. **2**. 63. 71 ; nearly captured **1**. 275. 9 ; Aphobus emigrated to **4**. 85. 3 ; Neaera at **6**. 377. 35

Megarians, allied with Athens through Dem. **2**. 175. 237 ; obsessed by their own dignity **3**. 361. 212 ; niggardly, favoured Spartans **6**.

377. 36 ; appropriated sacred land **1**. 373. 32

Meidias, friend of Ariston **6**. 135. 10

Meidias of Anagyrus, enemy of Dem., defendant in XXI : **3**. 2-151 ; his silver mines **3**. 115. 167 ; exempt from taxes **5**. 43. 18

Meidylides, s. of Aristoteles **5**. 133. 10

Meidylides, s. of Euthymachus **5**. 131. 9

Melanopus, b. of Thrasymedes **4**. 281. 6

Melanopus, one of three ambassadors to Mausolus, affair of the seized triremes **3**. 379. 12-13, 455. 125

Melantus, his furious attack on Dem. **2**. 183. 249

Melitê, deme of Cecropis **6**. 259. 37, 281. 68, 375. 32, 387-389. 48, 395. 58 ; district of Athens **6**. 133. 7

Melos, harbour of pirates **6**. 333. 56

Memnon, s.-in-law of Artabazus **3**. 323. 157

GENERAL INDEX

GENERAL INDEX

peltasts, light - armed troops **6. 21. 21**

penalty (see debtors, state-, debts, desertion, embassies, law): no penalty for losing suit before archon **4. 407. 46**; for baseless charges **6. 299. 11-12**; false citation **6. 115. 18**; currency debasement **3. 509. 212-214**; double for wilful damage **3. 33. 43**; double penalty illegal in single action **1. 593. 155**; false testimony **3. 457. 131, 4. 95. 16**; no penalty for false testimony before private arbitrator **4. 249. 19**; failure to file inventory **6. 101. 1**; profanation **3. 123. 180**; failure to prosecute **6. 295. 6**; reduction of penalty by jurors **6. 357. 8**; stoning **2. 155. 204**; speaking contrary to laws **6. 61. 12**; theft from Academy, Cynosarges or Lyceum **3. 447. 114**; wrongfully claiming freedom for slave **6. 305. 21**

pentacosiomedimni, laws regarding **5. 97. 54**

Peparethus, island off Thessaly **1. 148-173** *passim*, **341-343. 12-15**; sacked by Philip **2. 61. 70**; loan of Pasion there **5. 199. 28**

Perdiccas I, king of Macedon, attacked Persians after Plataea **1. 369. 24, 3. 353. 200**

Periander, author of law about Navy-Boards **5. 287. 21**

Periander, s. of Polyaratus **4. 485. 6**

Pericles, valued welfare of state above popularity **1. 55. 21**; pupil of Anaxagoras **7. 73. 45**; fined **3. 581. 6**

Perilaüs, or Perillus, Megarian traitor **2. 49. 48, 213. 295**; tried on charge of visiting Philip **2. 439. 295**

Perinthus, Perinthians, friends and kinsmen of Byzantines **2. 75. 89-90**; attack on Athenians **3. 329. 165**; mercenaries at **1. 319. 3, 3. 311. 142**

369

GENERAL INDEX

democracy becomes
suppliant **7**. 125. 3 ;
neutral in war between
Athens and Philip **2**.
175. 234 ; in grain
trade LVI : **6**. 191-227
passim

Rotunda, Tholos, not the
Prytaneum: free meals
for clerks like Aes-
chines **2**. 407. 249 ;
Aeschines once saluted
2. 453. 314

sacred lands, rental of **6**.
279. 63

Sacred Mount, in Thrace,
Cotys gained posses-
sion **3**. 287. 104 ; taken
by Philip **1**. 169. 37,
contrary to peace terms
and armistice **2**. 345.
156, 467. 334 ; Athe-
nian garrison expelled
1. 233. 15

Sacred War **2**. 457. 319

sacrifices, procedure in
6. 411. 78 ; at introduction to clan **5**. 67. 14 ;
upon taking oath in
antidosis **5**. 37. 7 ; at
Eleusis **6**. 443. 116 ; to
various deities **7**. 187.
54

sacrilege, to mention
Olympian gods at tomb
7. 29. 30

Salamis, revolt of **2**. 407.
252 ; recovered by So-
lon **2**. 409. 252 ; battle
of, 480 B.C., **6**. 425. 95-
97 ; victory of the
people, not of Themi-
stocles **1**. 367. 21-22,
3. 351. 198 ; glory of
2. 157. 208, **3**. 165. 13 ;
Plataeans at **6**. 425.
95

Samos, seat of Athenian
democracy in 411 B.C., **3**.
101. 145 ; garrisoned by
Cyprothemis **1**. 417. 9

Sannio, trainer of chorus
3. 45. 58

Satyrus, comedian, friend
of Dem. **2**. 369. 193,
371. 196

Satyrus, freedman of So-
crates, banker **4**. 343. 2

Satyrus of Alopecê, arbi-
trator **6**. 385-387. 45-
47

Satyrus of Melitê **6**. 395.
58

Satyrus, superintendent
of dockyards **3**. 197. 63

Saurias, arbitrator **6**. 385-
387. 45-47

GENERAL INDEX

Scepsis, in Phrygia, seized by Charidemus **3**. 321. 154

Sciathos, Athenian base in north Aegean **1**. 87. 32 ; menaced by Philip's despot **1**. 197. 36-37

Scionê, in Chalcidicê **4**. 283. 10

Scironides, proposed by-law in tribe **6**. 303. 17

Sciton, fined for proposing unconstitutional measure **3**. 125. 182

scrutiny (see audit, auditors) **2**. 379. 211 ; of public officials after election to prove citizenship **4**. 505. 34 ; of nine archons **6**. 283. 70

Scyros, island on grain route to Hellespont, possession risky **1**. 153. 4, **6**. 353. 3

Scythes, s. of Harmateus **5**. 185. 8

Selymbria, in Propontis, allied with Athens **1**. 427. 26 ; besieged by Philip **2**. 67. 77-78

Semelê, d. of Cadmus,

mother of Dionysus **7**. 29. 30

Senate, see Council

Serrium, headland of Thrace, Philip deceived Athens concerning **1**. 209. 64, 307. 65 ; held by Thracian allies **2**. 35. 27 ; occupied by P. **1**. 169. 37, 233. 15, **2**. 61. 70 ; seriousness of Athenian neglect of **1**. 275. 8

Sestus, in the Chersonese confederacy **2**. 77. 92 ; captured by Charidemus **3**. 323. 158 ; Apollodorus at **6**. 17-19. 18-20

Sicily, expedition of 415-413 B.C., **6**. 259. 37 ; Athenian prisoners in **1**. 521. 42 ; ambassador to **6**. 105. 5 ; grain from **6**. 201. 9

Sicyon, exiled trainer restored by Alexander **1**. 475. 16 ; horses from **3**. 109. 158

Sigeum, at entrance to Hellespont, easy plunder for officers and soldiers **1**. 39. 28

silver mines, of Meidias

371

GENERAL INDEX

money **5**. 343. 14-15 ; wrongful assertion of liberty of slave subject to suit **6**. 305. 21 ; capture and sale by pirates of free Athenian as slave **6**. 105. 6 ; capture and sale by enemy **6**. 243. 18

Smicrus, fined for proposing unconstitutional measures **3**. 125. 182

Smicythion, betrayer of Miltocythes **3**. 331. 169

Smicythus, denounced by Eubulus **2**. 367. 191

Socles, banker **4**. 343. 29

Socrates, agent of Philip at Oreus **1**. 255. 59

Socrates, association with Alcibiades **7**. 73. 45

Socrates, banker **4**. 343. 28

Socrates, one of comedy team **2**. 191. 262

Socratidas, eponymous archon 374/3 B.C., **5**. 379. 6, 403. 44, **6**. 375. 33

Solon of Erchia, arbitrator **4**. 493. 16

Solon, one of 7 Sages **7**. 77. 50 ; pursued philosophy **7**. 75. 49-50 ; his laws inscribed on tablets **3**. 231. 28 ; honoured as law-giver **3**. 507. 211 ; author of elegiacs **2**. 409. 254 ; quoted **2**. 411-413. 255 ; recovered Salamis **2**. 409. 252 ; statue at Salamis **2**. 407. 251 ; bronze statue in Market-Place **3**. 591. 23 ; enjoined the spirit of justice **2**. 21. 6 ; safeguards for democracy and public morality **3**. 177. 31-32 ; swift punishment for evil political leaders **3**. 579. 4 ; both parents must be Athenians **6**. 253. 30 ; re-enacted 403 B.C., **6**. 255. 32 ; providing for fair trial **2**. 21. 6-7 ; methods of obtaining redress **3**. 173. 25 f. ; modes of legal procedure **3**. 173-175. 25-27 ; procedure for amending or superseding existing law **1**. 551. 89 ; the laws and currency **3**. 509. 213 ; currency

GENERAL INDEX

Strymodorus of Aegina, banker 4. 343. 29

Styra, in Euboea, return of fleet from 3. 115. 167

succession, law of 5. 77. 27-28 ; in case of intestate decedent 5. 95. 51

summons and counter-summons 5. 305. 45

Sunium, deme 3. 87. 121, 115. 168

Sunium, one of 5 strongholds outside Athens and Peiraeus 2. 43. 38

Susa, winter abode of Persian kings 1. 289. 34

sycophancy, as a profession LVIII : 6. 287-343, 339. 63 ; mention 6. 257. 34, 273. 57, 383. 43 ; in political life 2. 145. 189, 7. 149. 2

symmories, divisions of citizens on basis of wealth 1. 39. 29 and note a, 391. 16

syndicates, for tax collection 1. 39. 29-30, 367. 20, 3. 109. 157 ; for public services 1. 507. 23

Synedrion, board of 6 assessors allowed the

three chief archons 6. 415. 83 ; meeting place of board of overseers of port 6. 295. 8

Syrians less fortunate than Athenians 7. 261. 7

tablets, used in drawing lots 4. 455. 10 ; for testimony 5. 251. 11

talent, value, see table, 5. viii

Tamynae, in Euboea, Ath. troops blockaded at 3. 111. 162, 4. 459. 16

Tanagra, in Boeotia near Attic frontier, occupied by Spartans 2. 79. 96

Taureas, chorus-master, his ears boxed by Alcibiades 3. 103. 147

Taureas, imprisoned 7. 237. 16

taxes, collected by syndicates after 378 b.c., 1. 39. 29 and note a, 367. 20 ; paid in advance 6. 11. 8-10 ; names entered by generals 4. 455. 8 ; procedure for exchange of property if unable to pay 5. 35-37. 5-7 ; collection of

379